MISCELLANIES

LITERARY AND HISTORICAL

MISCELLANIES

LITERARY & HISTORICAL

BY

LORD ROSEBERY

(Archibald Philip Primrose)

IN TWO VOLUMES

VOL. I

Essay Index Reprint Series

 BOOKS FOR LIBRARIES PRESS
FREEPORT, NEW YORK

First Published 1921
Reprinted 1971

INTERNATIONAL STANDARD BOOK NUMBER:
0-8369-2253-0

LIBRARY OF CONGRESS CATALOG CARD NUMBER:
71-152211

PRINTED IN THE UNITED STATES OF AMERICA

NOTE

To Lord Rosebery's friends, and to all lovers of good prose, it has long been a matter for regret that it was difficult to obtain anything like a complete set of his literary and historical addresses and occasional writings, or his consent to their republication. Most were out of print; some had been issued only in small private editions; some had never been rescued from the files of the daily press.

Their author has been so good as to yield to my importunity, and permit me to make a collection of these *opuscula*, he himself standing aside in benevolent neutrality. The responsibility for the selection—and for the original importunity—is therefore mine.

No speeches dealing with controversial politics have been included. A few notes have been added, and now and then a sentence has been omitted which had a purely local and topical application. Otherwise the chapters are reprinted as they were first spoken or written.

JOHN BUCHAN.

CONTENTS

I

APPRECIATIONS

I
APPRECIATIONS

I

ROBERT BURNS

I[1]

I COME here as a loyal burgess of Dumfries to do honour to the greatest burgess of Dumfries. We citizens of Dumfries have a special claim to be considered on this day. We are surrounded by the choicest and the most sacred haunts of the poet. You have in this town the house in which he died, the " Globe " where we could have wished that some phonograph had then existed which could have communicated to us some of his wise and witty and wayward talk. You have the street commemorated in M'Culloch's tragic anecdote when Burns was shunned by his former friends, and you have the paths by the Nith which are associated with some of his greatest work. You have near you the room in which the whistle was contended for, and in which, if mere legend is to be trusted, the immortal Dr. Gregory was summoned to administer his first powders to the survivors of that memor-

I.

[1] An Address delivered at Dumfries on the centenary of the poet's death, July 21, 1896.

3

I.   able debauch. You have the stackyard in which,
——   lying on his back and contemplating

> Thou lingering star, with lessening ray,
> That lov'st to greet the early morn,

he wrote the lines to " Mary in Heaven "—
perhaps the most pathetic of his poems. You
have near you the walk by the river, where, in
his transport, he passed his wife and children
without seeing them, " his brow flushed and his
eyes shining " with the lustre of " Tam o'
Shanter." " I wish you had but seen him," said
his wife ; " he was in such ecstasy that the tears
were happing down his cheeks." That is why
we are in Dumfries to-day. We come to honour
Burns among these immortal haunts of his.

But it is not in Dumfries alone that he is
commemorated to-day ; for all Scotland will
pay her tribute. And this, surely, is but right.
Mankind owes him a general debt. But the
debt of Scotland is special. For Burns exalted
our race ; he hallowed Scotland and the Scottish
tongue. Before his time we had for a long
period been scarcely recognised, we had been
falling out of the recollection of the world.
From the time of the union of the Crowns, and
still more from the time of the legislative union,
Scotland had lapsed into obscurity. Except
for an occasional riot or a Jacobite rising, her
existence was almost forgotten. She had, indeed,
her Robertsons and her Humes writing history
to general admiration, but no trace of Scottish
authorship was discoverable in their works ;
indeed, every flavour of national idiom was

carefully excluded. The Scottish dialect, as Burns called it, was in danger of perishing. Burns seemed at this juncture to start to his feet and reassert Scotland's claim to national existence; his Scottish notes rang through the world, and he thus preserved the Scottish language for ever—for mankind will never allow to die that idiom in which his songs and poems are enshrined. That is a part of Scotland's debt to Burns.

But this is much more than a Scottish demonstration; it is a collection of representatives from all quarters of the globe to own a common allegiance and a common faith. It is not only Scotsmen honouring the greatest of Scotsmen—we stretch far beyond a kingdom or a race—we are rather a sort of poetical Mohammedans gathered at a sort of poetical Mecca.

And yet we are assembled in our high enthusiasm under circumstances which are somewhat paradoxical. For with all the appearance of joy, we celebrate not a festival, but a tragedy. It is not the sunrise but the sunset that we commemorate. It is not the birth of a new power into the world, the subtle germ of a fame that is to survive and inspire the generations of men. But it is perhaps more fitting that we celebrate the end and not the beginning. For the coming of these figures is silent; it is their disappearance that we know. At this instant that I speak there may be born into the world the equal of a Newton or a Caesar, but half of us would be dead before he had revealed himself. Their death is different. It may be gloomy and disastrous; it may come at a moment of shame or neglect; but by that time the man has carved his name somewhere on the Temple of Fame. There are exceptions, of course; cases where the end comes before the slightest, or any but the slightest, recognition—Chatterton choking in his garret, hunger of body and soul all unsatisfied; Millet selling his pictures for a song; nay, Shakespeare himself. But, as a rule, death in the case of genius closes the first act of a public drama; criticism and analysis may then begin their unbiassed work free from jealousy or friendship or personal consideration for the living. Then comes the third act, if third act there be.

No, it is a death, not a birth, that we celebrate. This day a century ago, in poverty, delirium, and distress, there was passing the soul of Robert Burns. To him death comes in clouds and darkness, the end of a long agony of body and soul; he is harassed with debt, his wife is daily expecting her confinement, his bodily constitution is ruined, his spirit is broken. He has lost almost all that rendered his life happy—much of friendship, credit, and esteem. Some score years before, one of the most charming of English writers, as he lay dying, was asked if his mind was at ease, and with his last breath Oliver Goldsmith owned that it was not. So it was with Robert Burns. His delirium dwelt on the horrors of a jail; he uttered curses on the tradesman who was pursuing him for debt. "What business," said he to his physician in a moment of consciousness, "what business has a physician to waste his time upon me ; I am a poor pigeon not worth plucking. Alas ! I have not feathers enough to carry me to my grave." For a year or more his health had been failing. He had a poet's body as well as a poet's mind : nervous, feverish, impressionable ; and his constitution, which, if nursed and regulated, might have carried him to the limit of life, was unequal to the storm and stress of dissipation and a preying mind. In the previous autumn he had been seized with a rheumatic attack ; his digestion had given way ; he was sunk in melancholy and gloom. In his last April he wrote to his friend Thomson : " By Babel's streams I've sate and wept almost ever since I saw you last ; I have only known existence by the pressure of the heavy hand of sickness, and have counted time by the repercussions of pain. Rheumatism, cold, and fever have formed to me a terrible combination. I close my eyes in misery, and open them without hope." It was sought to revive him by sea-bathing, and he went to stay at Brow-well. There he remained three weeks, but was under no delusion as to his state. " Well, madam," he said to Mrs. Riddell on arriving, " have you any commands for the other world ? " He sat that evening with his old friend, and spoke manfully of his approaching death, of the fate of his children, and his fame ; sometimes indulging in bitter-sweet pleasantry, but never losing the consciousness of his condition. In three weeks he wearied of the fruitless hunt for health, and he returned home to die. He was only just in time. When he re-entered his home on the 18th

I.

he could no longer stand ; he was soon delirious ; in three days he was dead. " On the fourth day," we are told, " when his attendant held a cordial to his lips, he swallowed it eagerly, rose almost wholly up, spread out his hands, sprang forward nigh the whole length of the bed, fell on his face, and expired."

I suppose there are many who can read the account of these last months with composure. They are more fortunate than I. There is nothing much more melancholy in all biography. The brilliant poet, the delight of all society from the highest to the lowest, sits brooding in silence over the drama of his spent life : the early innocent home, the plough and the savour of fresh-turned earth, the silent communion with nature and his own heart, the brief hour of splendour, the dark hour of neglect, the mad struggle for forgetfulness, the bitterness of vanished homage, the gnawing doubt of fame, the distressful future of his wife and children,—an endless witch-dance of thought without clue or remedy, all perplexing, all soon to end while he is yet young, as men reckon youth ; though none know so well as he that his youth is gone, his race is run, his message is delivered.

His death revived the flagging interest and pride that had been felt for him. As usual, men began to realise what they had lost when it was too late. When it was known that he was dying, the townspeople had shown anxiety and distress. They recalled his fame and forgot his fall. One man was heard to ask, with a touch of quaint simplicity, " Who do you think will be our poet now ? " The district set itself to prepare a public funeral for the poet who died penniless among them. A vast concourse followed him to his grave. The awkward squad, as he had foreseen and deprecated, fired volleys over his coffin. The streets were lined with soldiers, among them one who, within sixteen years, was to be Prime Minister.[1] And while the procession wended its gloomy way, as if no element of tragedy were to be wanting, his widow's hour of travail arrived, and she gave birth to the hapless child that had caused the father so much misgiving. In this place and on this day it all seems present to us —the house of anguish, the thronged churchyard, the weeping neighbours. We feel ourselves part of the mourning crowd. We hear those dropping volleys and that muffled drum ; we bow our heads as the coffin passes, and acknowledge with tears the inevitable doom. Pass, heavy hearse, with thy weary freight of shattered hopes and exhausted frame ; pass, with thy simple pomp of fatherless bairns and sad moralising friends ; pass, with the sting of death to the victory of the grave ; pass, with the perishable, and leave us the eternal.

It is rare to be fortunate in life ; it is infinitely rarer to be fortunate in death. " Happy in the occasion of his death," as Tacitus said of Agricola, is not a common epitaph. It is comparatively easy to know how to live, but it is beyond all option and choice to compass the more difficult art of knowing when and how to die. We can generally by looking back choose a moment in

[1] See p. 24.

I.   a man's life when he had been fortunate had he dropped down dead. And so the question arises naturally to-day, was Burns fortunate in his death—that death which we commemorate? There can, I fancy, be only one answer ; it was well that he died when he did ; it might even have been better for himself had he died a little earlier. The terrible letters that he wrote two years before to Mrs. Riddell and Mr. Cunningham betoken a spirit mortally wounded. In those last two years the cloud settles, never to be lifted. " My constitution and frame were *ab origine* blasted with a deep incurable taint of hypochondria which poisons my existence." He found perhaps some pleasure in the composition of his songs, some occasional relief in the society of boon companions ; but the world was fading before him.

There is an awful expression in Scotland which one never hears without a pang—" So-and-so is *done*," meaning that he is physically worn out. Burns was " done." He was struggling on like a wounded deer to his death. He had often faced the end, and not unwillingly. " Can it be possible," he once wrote to Mrs. Dunlop, " that when I resign this frail feverish being I shall still find myself in conscious existence? When the last gasp of agony has announced that I am no more to those who know me and the few who loved me, when the cold unconscious corse is resigned to the earth to be the prey of reptiles and become a trodden clod, shall I be yet warm in life, enjoying or enjoyed ? " Surely that reads as if he foresaw

this day and would fain be with us—as indeed he I.
may be.

Twelve years before he had faced death in a less morbid spirit :

Why [he asked] am I loath to leave this earthly scene ?
Have I so found it full of pleasing charms ?
Some days of joy, with draughts of ill between,
Some gleams of sunshine, 'mid renewing storms.

He had, perhaps, never enjoyed life so much as is supposed, though he had turned to it a brave, cheerful, unflinching face, and the last years had been years of misery. " God have mercy on me," he wrote years before the end, " a poor, damned, incautious, duped, unfortunate fool ! The sport, the miserable victim of rebellious pride, hypochondriac imagination, agonising sensibility, and bedlam passions." There was truth in this outburst. At any rate, his most devoted friends—and to be an admirer of Burns is to be his friend—may wish that he had not lived to write the letter to Mr. Clark, piteously pleading that a harmless toast may not be visited hardly upon him ; or that to Mrs. Riddell, beginning, " I write you from the regions of hell and the horrors of the damned " ; or to be harried by his official superiors as a political suspect ; shunned by his fashionable friends for the same reason ; wandering like a neglected ghost in Dumfries, avoided and ignored. " That's all over now, my young friend," he said, speaking of his reign in society, " and werena my heart licht I wad dee." All this was in 1794. Had he died before then, it might have been happier for himself, and we should have lost some parts

I. of his life which we would rather forget ; but
posterity could not have spared him ; we could
not have lost the exquisite songs which we owe
to those years ; but, above all, the supreme
creed and comfort which he bequeathed to the
world—

A man's a man for a' that—

would have remained undelivered.

One may, perhaps, go further and say that
poets—or those whom the gods love—should
die young. This is a hard saying, but it will
not greatly affect the bills of mortality. And
it applies only to poets of the first rank ; while
even here it has its exceptions, and illustrious
exceptions they are. But surely the best poetry
is produced before middle age, before the morning
and its illusions have faded, before the heaviness
of noon and the baleful cool of evening. Few
men, too, can bear the strain of a poet's temperament through many years. At any rate, we may
feel sure of this, that Burns had produced his
best, that he would never again have produced
a " Tam o' Shanter," or a " Cotter's Saturday
Night," or a " Jolly Beggars " ; and that long
before his death, though he could still write lines
affluent with tenderness and grace, " the hand of
pain and sorrow and care," to use his own words,
" had lain heavy upon " him.

And this leads to another point. To-day is
not merely the melancholy anniversary of death,
but the rich and incomparable fulfilment of
prophecy. For this is the moment to which
Burns looked when he said to his wife, " Don't
be afraid ; I'll be more respected a hundred

years after I am dead than I am at present!"
To-day the hundred years are completed, and we
can judge of the prediction. On that point we
must all be unanimous. Burns had honour in
his lifetime, but his fame has rolled like a snow-
ball since his death, and it rolls on. There is,
indeed, no parallel to it in the world; it sets
the calculations of compound interest at defiance.
He is not merely the watchword of a nation
that carries and implants Burns-worship all over
the globe as birds carry seeds, but he has become
the champion and patron-saint of Democracy.
He bears the banner of the essential equality of
man. His birthday is celebrated—one hundred
and thirty-seven years after its occurrence—more
universally than that of any human being. He
reigns over a greater dominion than any empire
that the world has ever seen.

Nor does the ardour of his devotees decrease.
Ayr and Ellisland, Mauchline and Dumfries, are the
shrines of countless pilgrims. Burns statues are
a hardy annual. The production of Burns manuscripts was a lucrative branch of industry until
it was checked by untimely intervention. The
editions of Burns are as the sands of the sea. No
canonised name in the calendar excites so blind
and enthusiastic a worship. Whatever Burns may
have contemplated in his prediction, whatever
dream he may have fondled in the wildest moments
of elation, must have fallen utterly short of the
reality. And it is all spontaneous. There is no
puff, no advertisement, no manipulation. Intellectual cosmetics of that kind are frail and
fugitive; they rarely survive their subject;

I.

they would not have availed here. Nor was there any glamour attached to the poet ; rather the reverse. He has stood by himself ; he has grown by himself. It is himself and no other that we honour.

But what had Burns in his mind when he made this prediction ? It might be whimsically urged that he was conscious that the world had not yet seen his masterpiece, for the " Jolly Beggars " was not published till some time after his death. But that would not be sufficient, for he had probably forgotten its existence. Nor do I think he spoke at haphazard. What were perhaps present to his mind were the fickleness of his contemporaries towards him, his conviction of the essential splendour of his work, the consciousness that the incidents of his later years had unjustly obscured him, and that his true figure would be perceived as these fell away into forgetfulness or were measured at their true value. If so, he was right in his judgement, for his true life began with his death ; with the body passed all that was gross and impure ; the clear spirit stood revealed, and soared at once to its accepted place among the fixed stars, in the firmament of the rare immortals.

II [1]

WHAT the direct connection of Burns with Glasgow may be I am not exactly sure ; but, at any rate, I am confident of this, that in the

---

[1] An Address delivered in the St. Andrew's Hall, Glasgow, on the evening of the same day.

great metropolis of the West there is a clear
claim that we should celebrate the genius of
Robert Burns. I have celebrated it already
elsewhere. I cannot, perhaps, deny that the
day has been a day of labour, but it has been a
labour of love. It is, and it must be, a source of
joy and pride to us to see our champion Scotsman
receive the honour and admiration and affection
of humanity ; to see, as I have seen this morning,
the long processions bringing homage and tribute
to the conquering dead. But these have only
been signs and symptoms of the world-wide
passion of reverence and devotion. That generous and immortal soul pervades the universe
to-day. In the humming city and in the crowd
of men ; in the backwood and in the swamp ;
where the sentinel paces the bleak frontier, and
where the sailor smokes his evening pipe ; and
above all, where the farmer and his men pursue
their summer toil, whether under the Stars and
Stripes or under the Union Jack,—the thought
and sympathy of men are directed to Robert
Burns.

I have sometimes asked myself, if a roll-call
of fame were read over at the beginning of every
century, how many men of eminence would
answer a second time to their names. But of
our poet there is no doubt or question. The
adsum of Burns rings out clear and unchallenged.
There are few before him on the list, and we
cannot now conceive a list without him. He
towers high, and yet he lived in an age when the
average was sublime.

It sometimes seems to me as if the whole

I.

eighteenth century was a constant preparation for, a constant working up to, the great drama of the revolution which closed it. The scenery is all complete when the time arrives—the dark volcanic country; the hungry, desperate people; the firefly nobles; the concentrated splendour of the Court; in the midst, in her place as heroine, the dazzling Queen. And during long previous years brooding nature had been producing not merely the immediate actors, but figures worthy of the scene. What a glittering procession it is! We can only mark some of the principal figures. Burke leads the way; then come Fox and Goethe; Nelson and Mozart; Schiller, Pitt, and Burns; Wellington and Napoleon. And among these Titans, Burns is a conspicuous figure, the figure which appeals most of all to the imagination and affection of mankind. Napoleon looms larger to the imagination, but on the affection he has no hold. It is in the combination of the two powers that Burns is supreme.

What is his secret? We are always discussing him and endeavouring to find it out. Perhaps, like the latent virtue of some medicinal baths, it may never be satisfactorily explained. But, at any rate, let us discuss him again. That is, I presume, our object to-night. What pleasanter or more familiar occupation can there be for Scotsmen? But the Scotsmen who enjoy it have generally, perhaps, more time than I. Pardon, then, the imperfections of my speech, for I speak of a subject which no one can altogether compass, and which a busy man has perhaps no right to attempt.

The clue to Burns's extraordinary hold on mankind is possibly a complicated one; it has, perhaps, many developments. If so, we have not time to consider it to-night. But I personally believe the causes are, like most great causes, simple; though it might take long to point out all the ways in which they operate. The secret, as it seems to me, lies in two words—inspiration and sympathy. But, if I wished to prove my contention, I should go on quoting from his poems all night, and his admirers would still declare that I had omitted the best passages. I know that profuse quotation is a familiar form of a Burns speech; but I am afraid to begin lest I should not end, and I am sure that I should not satisfy. I must proceed, then, in a more summary way.

There seem to me to be two great natural forces in British literature. I use the safe adjective of British, and your applause shows me that I was right to do so. I use it partly because hardly any of Burns's poetry is strictly English; partly because he hated, and was perhaps the first to protest against, the use of the word English as including Scottish. Well, I say, there are in that literature two great forces of which the power seems sheer inspiration and nothing else—I mean Shakespeare and Burns. This is not the place nor the time to speak of that miracle called Shakespeare, but one must say a word of the miracle called Burns.

Try and reconstruct Burns as he was. A peasant, born in a cottage that no sanitary inspector in these days would tolerate for a moment ; struggling with desperate effort against pauperism ; almost in vain snatching at scraps of learning in the intervals of toil, as it were with his teeth ; a heavy silent lad, proud of his ploughing. All of a sudden, without preface or warning, he breaks out into exquisite song, like a nightingale from the brushwood, and continues singing as sweetly—with nightingale pauses—till he dies. A nightingale sings because he cannot help it; he can only sing exquisitely, because he knows no other. So it was with Burns. What is this but inspiration ? One can no more measure or reason about it than measure or reason about Niagara.

Under the limitations which I have imposed on myself to-night, we must take for granted the incomparable excellence of his poetry. But I must ask you to remember that the poetry is only a fragment of Burns. Amazing as it may seem, all contemporary testimony is unanimous that the man was far more wonderful than his works. " It will be the misfortune of Burns's reputation," writes an accomplished lady, who might well have judged him harshly, " in the records of literature, not only to future genera-tions and to foreign countries, but even with his native Scotland and a number of his contem-poraries, that he has been regarded as a poet, and nothing but a poet. . . . Poetry," she continues " (I appeal to all who had the advantage of being personally acquainted with him), was actually not his forte. . . . None, certainly, ever out-shone Burns in the charms—the sorcery, I would almost call it—of fascinating conversation, the

I.

spontaneous eloquence of social argument, or the unstudied poignancy of brilliant repartee." And she goes on to describe the almost super-human fascination of his voice and of his eyes, those balls of black fire which electrified all on whom they rested.

It seems strange to be told that it would be an injustice to judge Burns by his poetry alone ; but as to the magnetism of his presence and conversation there is only one verdict. " No man's conversation ever carried me so completely off my feet," said the Duchess of Gordon—the friend of Pitt and of the London wits, the queen of Scottish society. Dugald Stewart says that " all the faculties of Burns's mind were, so far as I could judge, equally vigorous, and his predilection for poetry was rather the result of his own enthusiastic and impassioned temper than of a genius exclusively adapted to that species of composition. From his conversation I should have pronounced him to be fitted to excel in whatever walk of ambition he had chosen to exert his abilities." And of his prose compositions the same severe judge speaks thus : " Their great and varied excellences render some of them scarcely less objects of wonder than his poetical performances. The late Dr. Robertson used to say that, considering his education, the former seemed to him the more remarkable of the two." " I think Burns," said Principal Robertson to a friend, " was one of the most extraordinary men I ever met with. His poetry surprised me very much, his prose surprised me still more, and his conversation surprised me more than both his poetry and prose." We are told, too, that " he felt a strong call towards oratory, and all who heard him speak—and some of them were excellent judges—admitted his wonderful quickness of apprehension and readiness of eloquence." All this seems to me marvellous. It surely ratifies the claim of inspiration without the necessity of quoting a line of his poetry.

I pass, then, to his sympathy. If his talents were universal, his sympathy was not less so. His tenderness was not a mere selfish tenderness for his own family, for he loved all mankind, except the cruel and the base. Nay, we may go further and say that he placed all creation, especially the suffering and despised part of it, under his protection. The oppressor in every shape, even in the comparatively innocent embodiment of the factor and the sportsman, he regarded with direct and personal hostility. But above all, he saw the charm of the home ; he recognised it as the basis of all society; he honoured it in its humblest form, for he knew, as few know, how unpretentiously, but how sincerely, the family in the cottage is welded by mutual love and esteem. " I recollect once," said Dugald Stewart, speaking of Burns, " he told me, when I was admiring a distant prospect in one of our morning walks, that the sight of so many smoking cottages gave a pleasure to his mind which none could understand who had not witnessed, like himself, the happiness and worth which they contained." He dwells repeatedly on the primary sacredness of the

home and the family, the responsibility of father-
hood and marriage. " Have I not," he once
wrote to Lord Mar, " a more precious stake in
my country's welfare than the richest dukedom
in it ? I have a large family of children, and
the prospect of many more." The lines in which
he tells his faith are not less memorable than
the stately stanzas in which Gray sings the
" short and simple annals of the poor." I must
quote them again, often quoted as they are :

> To mak' a happy fireside clime
>   To weans and wife,
> That's the true pathos and sublime
>   Of human life.

His verses, then, go straight to the heart of
every home ; they appeal to every father and
mother. But that is only the beginning, perhaps
the foundation, of his sympathy. There is something for everybody in Burns. He has a heart
even for vermin ; he has pity even for the arch-
enemy of mankind. And his universality makes
his poems a treasure - house in which all may
find what they want. Every wayfarer in the
journey of life may pluck strength and courage
from it as he passes. The sore, the weary, the
wounded, will all find something to heal and
soothe. For this great master is the universal
Samaritan. Where the priest and the Levite
may have passed by in vain, this eternal heart
will still afford a resource. But he is not only
for the sick in spirit. The friend, the lover, the
patriot, will all find their choicest refreshment
in Burns. His touch is everywhere, and it is
everywhere the touch of genius. Nothing comes

amiss to him. What was said of the debating
power of his eminent contemporary, Dundas,
may be said of his poetry : " He went out in
all weathers." And it may be added that all
weathers suited him ; that he always brought
back something precious, something we cherish,
something that cannot die.

He is, then, I think, the universal friend in
a unique sense. But he was, poetically speaking, the special friend of Scotland, in a sense
which recalls a profound remark of another
eminent Scotsman, I mean Fletcher of Saltoun.
In an account of a conversation between Lord
Cromarty, Sir Edward Seymour, Sir Christopher
Musgrave, and himself, Fletcher writes : " I
said I knew a very wise man, so much of Sir
Christopher's sentiment that he believed if a
man were permitted to make all the ballads, he
need not care who should make the laws of a
nation." This may be rudely paraphrased that
it is more important to make the songs of a
nation than to frame its laws, and this again
may be interpreted to mean that in the days of
Fletcher, at any rate, as in the days of Burns, it
is the familiar songs of a people that mould their
thoughts, their manners, and their morals. If
this be true, can we exaggerate the debt that we
Scotsmen owe to Burns ? He has bequeathed
to his country the most exquisite casket of songs
in the world ; primarily to his country, though
others cannot be denied their share. I will give
only one example, but that is a signal one.
From distant Roumania the Queen of that
country wrote to Dumfries to-day that she has

no copy of Burns with her, but that she knows
his songs by heart.

We must remember, too, that there is more than this to be said. Many of Burns's songs were already in existence in the lips and minds of the people—rough and coarse and obscene. Our benefactor takes them, and with a touch of inspired alchemy transmutes them and leaves them pure gold. He loved the old catches and the old tunes, and into these gracious moulds he poured his exquisite gifts of thought and expression. But for him, those ancient airs, often wedded to words which no decent man could recite, would have perished from that corruption if not from neglect. He rescued them for us by his songs, and in doing so he hallowed the life and sweetened the breath of Scotland.

I have also used the words patriot and lover. These draw me to different lines of thought. The word " patriot " leads me to the political side of Burns. There is no doubt that he was suspected of being a politician ; and he is even said to have sometimes wished to enter Parliament. That was perhaps an excusable aberration, and my old friend Professor Masson has, I think, surmised that had he lived he might have been a great Liberal pressman. My frail thought shall not dally with such surmise, but it conducts us naturally to the subject of Burns's politics. From his sympathy for his own class, from his indignation against nobles like the Duke of Queensberry, and from the toasts that cost him so dear, it might be considered easy to infer his political opinions. But Burns should not be claimed for any party. A poet, be it remembered, is never a politician, and a politician is never a poet—that is to say, a politician is never so fortunate as to be a poet, and a poet is so fortunate as never to be a politician. I do not say that the line of demarcation is never passed—a politician may have risen for a moment, or a poet may have descended; but where there is any confusion between the two callings, it is generally because the poet thinks he discerns, or the politician thinks he needs, something higher than politics. Burns's politics were entirely governed by his imagination. He was at once a Jacobite and a Jacobin. He had the sad sympathy which most of us have felt for the hapless house of Stuart, without the least wish to be governed by it. He had much the same sort of abstract sympathy with the French Revolution, when it was setting all Europe to rights; but he was prepared to lay down his life to prevent its putting this island to rights. And then came his official superiors of the Excise, who, notwithstanding Mr. Pitt's admiration of his poetry, snuffed out his politics without remorse.

The name of Pitt leads me to add that Burns had some sort of relation with three Prime Ministers. Colonel Jenkinson, of the Cinque Ports Fencible Cavalry—afterwards Minister for fifteen years under the title of Liverpool—was on duty at Burns's funeral, though we are told —the good man—that he disapproved of the poet, and declined to make his acquaintance. Pitt, again, passed on Burns one of his rare and competent literary judgements, so eulogistic,

indeed, that one wonders that a powerful Minister
could have allowed one whom he admired so
much to exist on an exciseman's pay when well,
and an exciseman's half-pay when dying. And
from Addington, another Prime Minister, Burns
elicited a sonnet, which, in the Academy of
Lagado, would surely have been held a signal
triumph of the art of extracting sunshine from
cucumbers.

So much for politics in the party sense. " A
man's a man for a' that " is not politics—it is
the assertion of the rights of humanity in a sense
far wider than politics. It erects all mankind ;
it is the charter of its self-respect. It binds, it
heals, it revives, it invigorates ; it sets the bruised
and broken on their legs ; it refreshes the stricken
soul ; it is the salve and tonic of character ; it
cannot be narrowed into politics. Burns's politics
are indeed nothing but the occasional overflow
of his human sympathy into past history and
current events.

And now, having discussed the two trains of
thought suggested by the words " friend " and
" patriot," I come to the more dangerous word
" lover." There is an eternal controversy which,
it appears, no didactic oil will ever assuage, as
to Burns's private life and morality. Some
maintain that these have nothing to do with his
poems ; some maintain that his life must be read
into his works ; and here again some think that
his life damns his poems, while others aver that
his poems cannot be fully appreciated without
his life. Another school thinks that his vices
have been exaggerated, while their opponents

I.

scarcely think such exaggeration possible. It is impossible to avoid taking a side. I walk on the ashes, knowing the fire beneath, and unable to avoid it, for the topic is inevitable. I must confess myself, then, one of those who think that the life of Burns doubles the interest of his poems, and I doubt whether the failings of his life have been much exaggerated, for contemporary testimony on that point is strong ; though a high authority, Mr. Wallace, has recently taken the other side with much power and point.

But the life of Burns, which I love to read with his poems, does not consist in his vices ; they lie outside it. It is a life of work, and truth, and tenderness. And though, like all lives, it has its light and shade, remember that we know it all, the worst as well as the best. His was a soul bathed in crystal; he hurried to avow everything. There was no reticence in him. The only obscure passage in his life is the love passage with Highland Mary, and as to that he was silent not from shame, but because it was a sealed and sacred episode. " What a flattering idea," he once wrote, " is a world to come ! There shall I with speechless agony of rapture again recognise my lost, my ever dear Mary ! whose bosom was fraught with truth, honour, constancy, and love." He had, as the French say, the defects of his qualities. His imagination was a supreme and celestial gift. But his imagination often led him wrong, and never more than with women. The chivalry that made Don Quixote see the heroic in all the common events of life made Burns (as his

I.

brother tells us) see a goddess in every girl that he approached. Hence many love affairs, and some guilty ones ; but even these must be judged with reference to time and circumstance. This much is certain, that had he been devoid of genius, they would not have attracted attention. It is Burns's pedestal that affords a target. And why, one may ask, is not the same measure meted out to Burns as to others ? The bastards of great captains and statesmen and princes are treated as historical and ornamental incidents. They strut the scene of Shakespeare, and ruff it with the best. It is for the unlawful children of Burns, though he and his wife cherished them as if born in wedlock, that the vials of wrath are reserved. Take two brilliant figures, both of royal ancestry, who were alive during Burns's life. We occupy ourselves endlessly and severely with the lapses of Burns. We heave an elegant sigh over the kindred frailties of Charles James Fox and Charles Edward Stuart.

Again, it is quite clear that, though exceptionally sober in his earlier years, he drank too much in later life. But this, it must be remembered, was but an occasional condescendence to the vice and habit of the age. The gentry who pressed him to their houses, and who were all convivial, have much to answer for. His admirers who thronged to see him, and who could only conveniently sit with him in a tavern, are also responsible for this habit, so perilously attractive to men of genius. From the decorous Addison and the brilliant Bolingbroke onward, the eighteenth century records hard drinking as

I.   the common incident of intellectual eminence.
—   To a man who had shone supreme in the most
glowing society, and who was now an exciseman
in a country town, with a home that cannot
have been very exhilarating, and with a nervous
system highly strung, the temptation of the
warm tavern, and the admiring circle there,
may well have been almost irresistible. Some
attempt to say that his intemperance was exaggerated. I neither affirm nor deny. It was
not as a sot he drank ; that no one insinuated ;
if he succumbed it was to good fellowship.

Remember, I do not seek to palliate nor excuse,
and, indeed, none will be turned to dissipation
by Burns's example ; he paid too dearly for it.
But I will say this, that it all seems infinitely
little, infinitely remote. Why do we strain, at
this distance, to discern this dim spot on the
poet's mantle ? Shakespeare and Ben Jonson
took their cool tankard at the "Mermaid"; we
cannot afford, in the strictest view of literary responsibility, to quarrel with them for that. When
we consider Pitt and Goethe we do not concentrate
our vision on Pitt's bottles of port or Goethe's
bottles of Moselle. Then why, we ask, is there
such a chasm between the "Mermaid" and the
"Globe," and why are the vintages of Wimbledon
and Weimar so much more innocent than the
simple punch-bowl of Inveraray marble and its
contents ?

I should like to go a step further and affirm
that we have something to be grateful for even
in the weaknesses of men like Burns. Mankind
is helped in its progress almost as much by the

study of imperfection as by the contemplation of perfection. Had we nothing before us in our futile and halting lives but saints and the ideal, we might well fail altogether. We grope blindly along the catacombs of the world, we climb the dark ladder of life, we feel our way to futurity, but we can scarcely see an inch around or before us. We stumble and falter and fall, our hands and knees are bruised and sore, and we look up for light and guidance. Could we see nothing but distant unapproachable impeccability, we might well sink prostrate in the hopelessness of emulation and the weariness of despair. Is it not then, when all seems blank and lightless and lifeless, when strength and courage flag, and when perfection seems as remote as a star, is it not then that imperfection helps us ? When we see that the greatest and choicest images of God have had their weaknesses like ours, their temptations, their hours of darkness, their bloody sweat, are we not encouraged by their lapses and catastrophes to find energy for one more effort, one more struggle ? Where they failed we feel it a less dishonour to fail ; their errors and sorrows make, as it were, an easier ascent from infinite imperfection to infinite perfection.

Man, after all, is not ripened by virtue alone. Were it so, this world were a paradise of angels. No ! Like the growth of the earth, he is the fruit of all the seasons ; the accident of a thousand accidents, a living mystery, moving through the seen to the unseen. He is sown in dishonour ; he is matured under all the varieties of heat and cold ; in mist and wrath, in snow and vapours,

I.
—

in the melancholy of autumn, in the torpor of winter, as well as in the rapture and fragrance of summer, or the balmy affluence of the spring —its breath, its sunshine, its dew. And at the end he is reaped—the product, not of one climate, but of all; not of good alone, but of evil; not of joy alone, but of sorrow—perhaps mellowed and ripened, perhaps stricken and withered and sour. How, then, shall we judge any one? How, at any rate, shall we judge a giant, great in gifts and great in temptation, great in strength and great in weakness? Let us glory in his strength and be comforted in his weakness. And when we thank heaven for the inestimable gift of Burns, we do not need to remember wherein he was imperfect, we cannot bring ourselves to regret that he was made of the same clay as ourselves.

II

DR. JOHNSON [1]

THREE days hence will occur the two-hundredth anniversary of Johnson's birth in this ancient city of Lichfield. Born poor and scrofulous and half blind, and with an hereditary melancholy not far removed from madness, the advent of the small bookseller's son cannot have caused a ripple among your people. He seemed destined to his father's back shop until in the course of nature he should appear as principal in the front, in the pleasantest and most congenial of all modern trades, but one rarely leading to fame. And yet it is this obscurest of events which we have this week hurried to Lichfield to celebrate.

What is the cause of Johnson's extraordinary hold upon us, of his immortality among us? It does not, I think, mainly rest upon his works. His twelve volumes sleep, I fear, on our shelves; at least they do on mine. He has written two of the noblest poems in the language, yet these, I think, have only once been separately printed, in 1785; though they contain immortal lines, and were the poems that Walter Scott, so remote

[1] An Address delivered at the Johnson bicentenary celebration at Lichfield, September 15, 1909.

II. in style and thought, most admired, much as
Byron admired Pope. His *Lives of the Poets*
are destined, I think, to an enduring reputation.
He cannot always appreciate; he is unjust to
Gray; some of his criticisms remind one of the
poulterer's phoenix of Whitbread; they seem not
infrequently to gauge poetry in the spirit of an
exciseman. His critical faculty indeed did not
always inspire confidence. He could not enjoy
Lycidas; he did not care for Theocritus; his prejudice against Gray was even stronger than it
appears in the *Lives*; he greatly preferred Richard-
son to Fielding. His Shakespearian criticism is,
I believe, held by competent judges not to possess
any special value.

But the *Lives* are terse, vigorous, and delightful
sketches of poets and poetasters, which once one
has taken them in hand one can scarcely lay
down; and one cannot doubt that these are
destined to a long life; for they are the work of a
master of letters dealing with that department of
literature which he loved the best, so that genius
and inclination worked hand in hand. But who
reads the rest? I speak only for myself. The
Ramblers and the *Idlers* are dead for me. I hope
that there are others more fortunate. *Rasselas*, I
read not voluntarily, but assiduously at school,
and, probably for that reason, never wish to
read again. Even the thought of this celebration
could not overcome my repugnance. Of *Irene* it
may be ambiguously said that it is like no other
tragedy in existence, and that it leaves the reader
cold and less than cold. I have read for business
purposes speeches under other names, which

Johnson no doubt composed. But speaking as an II.
individual and illiterate Briton I make this con-
fession ; I make it in dust and ashes, with a sheet
and a candle, under every visible form of penance,
but I cannot honestly withhold it. And, after
all, two poems and some pleasing biographies do
not of themselves as a rule constitute a claim to
lasting fame.

He was, I think, our greatest man of letters in
a large sense of that vague term. The variety of
his writings in what we should now consider as
periodicals, his knowledge of literature, his deal-
ings with literature, his command of literature,
the mass of his writing discovered or untraced
which he could scarcely recall himself, his passionate interest in letters, above all his convers-
ance with literary biography, entitles him to that
position.   It is a reputation which would vaguely
have remained to him even had his works not
survived.   But it would have been a fame widely
different from that concrete and personal base on
which he is now established for ever.

Then, again, there is that which does not
appear in his works, the great *Dictionary.* Here
our consciences are easy, for no one is known
to have read a dictionary through except Lord
Chatham, who boasted that he had read Bailey's
Dictionary twice through. This is an idle vaunt
which none would wish to emulate, though
Boswell tells us, not without truth, that Johnson
" was so attentive in the choice of the passages in
which the words are authorised, that one may
read page after page of his *Dictionary* with
improvement and pleasure." The enterprise of a

II.

dictionary is indeed a vast task, which Johnson like a hero undertook single-handed, and accomplished in less than nine years. That no doubt was what originally gave Johnson his fame. Such a fame of itself would scarcely extend to the fifth or sixth generation, for it is the melancholy fate of dictionaries to be superseded. But the man who frames a dictionary, and a great dictionary, in an age when such collections are few and barren, at once attains a singular, though not necessarily a lasting fame. That reputation Johnson achieved, his work became proverbial, and Johnson's *Dictionary* was the authority to which all appealed. We all remember it as Miss Pinkerton's prize book in the first chapter of *Vanity Fair*, but we do not often handle it in these days.

I come then to this conclusion, speaking always for myself alone, that his literary fame substantially survives in the two supreme poems, the *Lives of the Poets* and the *Dictionary*, but that if these stood alone, remarkable as they are, we should not be assembled here to-day. I pass then to the most solid base, Boswell, and the figure which remains eternally resting on Boswell.

Boswell himself is an enduring problem. He is universally acknowledged as the prince of all biographers, chief in a department of literature which is perhaps the most popular and appreciated of all. And yet until last year, so far as I know, there existed no memorial, no bust, no statue of him anywhere, whereas second-rate poets, third-rate statesmen, fourth-rate soldiers would have their effigies in suitable places. This was not

from want of recognition, but from the complexity
of his character. On one side of him he was the
most preposterous of human beings, of an eccentricity which partook of insanity, but which was
always grotesque. In his youth he aimed only
at notoriety, and was content to exhibit himself
in any capacity so long as he could obtain
attention. In his intimate correspondence with
his bosom friend, Temple, he displays a childish
vanity, a volatile self-sufficiency, a total insensi-
bility to ridicule, which make the collection some
of the most amusing reading on record, till it ends
in piteousness and tragedy. And yet all this
time he must have had the root of the matter in
him. Such a biographer as he is, is born not
made. And so we realise him as a strange compound of incredible vanity, fatuity, and absurdity,
in which, as precious and unexpected as radium,
is amalgamated enough of genius to leaven and
redeem the whole.

He had assuredly the root of the matter in him
from the first. He had primarily the instinct of
hero-worship, but that was not enough ; he had
to know how to turn it to the best advantage.
Here he had an instinct which did not fail him.
To be with his subject by day and by night, on
every possible occasion to absorb him as it were
essentially by the pores of the skin, so as, to use
his own strange expression, " to become strongly
impregnated with the Johnsonian aether," to
disdain no detail as trivial which added to the
completeness and perfection of the portrait, all
this Boswell understood as no other man has
understood. After giving an account of his

II. hero's clucking like a hen, and blowing like a whale, holding his hand on one side and rubbing his left knee in the same direction, and so forth, he says with admirable sense and discrimination : " I am fully aware of how very obvious an occasion I here give for the sneering jocularity of such as have no relish for an exact likeness ; which to render complete, he who draws it must not disdain the slightest strokes." And again : " I cannot allow any fragment whatever that floats in my memory concerning the great subject of this work to be lost. Though a small particular may appear trifling to some, it will be relished by others ; while every little spark adds something to the general blaze ; and to please the true, candid, warm admirers of Johnson, and in any degree increase the splendour of his reputation, I bid defiance to the shafts of ridicule and even of malignity." This is the true Boswellian spirit, content to be a martyr so that he might increase the completeness of his delineation in the slightest degree.

And he immolated himself to his subject. It was not only the bitterness of his critics that he had to encounter. Their shafts of ridicule were blunt compared to those which he had to encounter from the hero himself. For the recorder of Johnson had to be content to bear the heaviest strokes that a random wit could suggest. To portray Johnson in all his moods one had to be out in all weathers, to be tossed and buffeted, with rare consolations of benignant serenity. All this and more Boswell was ready to face provided he could secure what was wanted, the speaking

likeness of his hero ; what he himself called " the
Flemish picture which I give of my friend." And
so we seem to see him like St. Sebastian in the
pictures, bound to Johnson's reputation, and
perforated with arrows from every quarter. His
sufferings, which he did not grudge, have procured to posterity a lasting pleasure, and we here
who all boast ourselves to be " true, candid,
warm admirers of Johnson " tranquilly enjoy the
society that he had enjoyed in full and delightful
measure. Honour and gratitude then to him.
I, speaking from experience, can say that in sickness when all other books have failed, when
Dickens, Thackeray, Walter Scott, and other
magicians have been useless to distract, Boswell's
book is the only one which could engage and
detain the languid attention of an invalid.

By far the most striking feature of their connection to me is how Johnson and Boswell became
connected at all. Let it be at once conceded
that Boswell was determined to make Johnson's
acquaintance, and that when Boswell was determined to make an acquaintance there was no
human possibility of preventing him ; there was
no personage or situation so inaccessible as not
to have to receive him if he desired it. That,
however, might only be a terminable acquaintance. But here is an awkward, rather ridiculous
young Scotsman, with an accent of which the
best that Johnson could say was that it was not
offensive, belonging to a race which Johnson
hated with a hatred which was almost insane, a
youth at once impudent, pushing, and fawning,
in a word, all that was most repellent to Johnson,

II.   attempting to force the acquaintance of the most
formidable and the most dreaded of literary
tyrants. For two years Boswell had hoped and
languished. One year he had expectations from
Derrick, the next he had a prospect through the
elder Sheridan, both rudely marred. At last
Johnson appears suddenly to him as he sits
drinking tea in a bookseller's parlour. The
trembling Boswell is presented, and his nation-
ality is divulged. Johnson at once rends him.
" This stroke," says Boswell, " stunned me a
good deal." But he recovers, attempts another
remark, and receives another mortal snub. " I
now felt myself much mortified . . . and in truth
had my ardour not been uncommonly strong,
and my resolution uncommonly persevering, so
rough a reception might have deterred me for
ever from making any further attempts." But
within eight days he is in Johnson's private room,
sketching, so to speak, on his thumbnail, the little
old shrivelled unpowdered wig striving in vain to
compass the mighty head, the breeches loose at
the knee and so leaving the stockings loose, and
other " slovenly particulars " ; the same costume,
by the by, in which, at a later period, with a
" noise like thunder," Johnson hurried down from
his lodgings into the street to escort Madame de
Boufflers to her carriage in Fleet Street, amid a
wondering and probably scoffing crowd. Before
Boswell leaves the great man he has invited
Johnson to supper and received an acceptance.
And within three months, as he had to pursue his
studies at Utrecht, Johnson volunteers to accompany him to Harwich.

In the meantime they have been supping and drinking and conversing together. Boswell determined to know as much of Johnson as possible, and Johnson not unwilling to be known. And so it culminates in this " raw, uncouth young Scot " (he was only twenty-two) dragging the great man from his moorings, dragging him from London, the place he loved best, and taking him on a frisk to Harwich. It was Johnson, indeed, who volunteered. " I must see thee out of England : I will accompany you to Harwich." That he should use " thee " and " you " in the same sentence shows how deeply the lexicographer was moved. It was the day of their famous jaunt to Greenwich, when they " took a sculler at the Temple Stairs and set out for Greenwich," then " landed at the Old Swan and walked to Billingsgate," where they " took oars and moved smoothly along the silver Thames," a picture which almost consoles us for the present dearth of river steamers. They dined at Greenwich and walked in the Park, which they thought " not equal to Fleet Street," returned in a boat by night, Boswell shivering, for which he was reproved by his illustrious friend, and so returned to genial conviviality at the " Turk's Head," concluding the day " very socially." It was then in the warmth of his heart that Johnson volunteered. The day of their first meeting was May 16 ; in little more than two months Johnson has expressly promised to accompany Boswell to the Hebrides, declaring that " there are few persons whom I take so much to as to you " ; and on August 5 they were

II. setting off in the Harwich stage-coach after a fashion which reminds one irresistibly of Mr. Pickwick setting off with Mr. Winkle. Surely this may be called Love at second sight.

How can one explain this sudden heat of affection, which was to last for the rest of their lives ?

We can only conjecture. There was probably something ingenuous about the young fellow which appealed to Johnson; his open adoration was not displeasing, though it sometimes bored him; he early discerned, I think, that Boswell would be his biographer, though not for years afterwards did Boswell openly talk in that character. Then Boswell probably appealed to his sense of humour, and, above all, the young Scot was an invaluable butt. His pertinacity and tactlessness were sometimes intolerable ; but his pertinacity was a compliment, and his tactlessness would always be open to a rebuff which Johnson did not object to administering. " Sir," he broke out one day, " you have but two topics, yourself and me. I am sick of both ! " But as a rule Boswell's fussiness and grotesqueness did not, to use the modern phrase, get on his nerves. His system, though morbid in some particulars, was in this robust. The family he collected round him would have afflicted a more fastidious benefactor. Add to this that Johnson saw in Boswell a young fellow devoted to himself, a Tory as high-flown as himself, with accesses of melancholy not unlike his own, addicted to various follies, but with a real love of learning and an honest though distracted ambition, whom he could guide and assist as a son. There was much of the paternal in his relation to his biographer.

Lastly, and there is perhaps most in this consideration, Johnson under his rough exterior had a heart of manly tenderness. " No man alive," said Goldsmith, who often suffered under him, " has a more tender heart. He has nothing of the bear but his skin." He realised Boswell's enthusiasm, and his heart went out to the lad. Boswell loved him and so he came to love Boswell. Much more might be said on this point, which is full of interest to students of human nature; but it would occupy too much space in a short address to dwell on it further. What one must remember in this strange partnership is that the canvas was first spread when the artist was twenty-two and the subject fifty-four, and that Johnson was sitting for his portrait for the rest of his life, while Boswell waited pencil in hand and " constantly watched every dawning of communication from that great and illuminated mind."

What then makes this book so extraordinary, so unique, is this, that it is the photographic delineation of a great man by a daily, hourly, and minute observer, who disdained no pains or detail to make his picture perfect, who was willing himself to be a butt, not merely of his patron's cruel pleasantries, but of the world at large, so that he might produce a living speaking portrait. There is nothing like it. The price of success in such a work is more than most men care to pay. For it cannot be denied that as with poverty in Juvenal's famous lines it tends to make those

II. who write it ridiculous ; the recorder has to be a foil to the recorded. And so Boswellian imitations are rare. The books which occur to me as resembling it are all foreign, and, as Boswell's book has never, I believe, been translated into any language, though there is, I am told, an abstract in Russian, they are not strictly imitations. Eckermann's records of Goethe's conversations lack nature and simplicity; we feel that all is transacted in full dress. Another recent journalist was content to endure hard things so that he might collect the crumbs which fell from a great man's table ; but the crumbs had better have gone whither other crumbs go. Gourgaud's Journal at St. Helena comes perhaps nearest to Boswell's life as the faithful constant portraiture of a great man by a resident observer. But Gourgaud had not Boswell's qualities, and there was not sufficient play of life at St. Helena to lighten the record.

Such biographies must be rare, if only because great men are rare, and Boswells still rarer. And great men, even when you find them, are not always various. The conversations of the Duke of Wellington, which have been sedulously recorded, certainly lack this quality. And so if we delight in Boswell for the picturesqueness and fidelity of his representation, we acknowledge that that would be of little value without the greatness and variety of the subject. We may fairly suppose that had Boswell similarly attached himself to Paoli, Oglethorpe, Rousseau, or any other of his idols, he would have produced a remarkable book (though Rousseau, we may be sure, would not long have tolerated his intrusive familiarity), but a book wholly unequal to that on which his fame securely reposes, for in Johnson he had an exceptional model. He would not, it is probable, have added to Rousseau's fame ; he might have prolonged that of Paoli and Ogle-thorpe ; but he has rendered Johnson immortal by the qualities of Johnson himself manifested through his own.

The book then remains and is likely to remain unique because of the peculiar genius of the biographer and the subject. Its rank in litera-ture is unparalleled. It is annotated and com-mentated on as if it were Holy Writ. Except the Greek and Latin Classics and the Scriptures, I know of no book which has been treated with such reverence. Croker began with an edition which Macaulay denounced, but which, whether good or bad, illustrates the elaboration of treat-ment which Boswell's book seems to elicit; and without forgetting the delightful edition of Napier, as well as countless others, we end with Dr. Birk-beck Hill's prodigious and exhaustive collections, a sort of Cornelius à Lapide on Boswell, in which at least ten massive volumes are consecrated to Johnson—all interesting, all worth publishing, an almost unprecedented homage of worship.

From first to last the book is all good, there is not a dull page in it. There is, I think, one unsurpassed episode which is worth recalling as being the gem of the whole book : I mean the story of Dr. Johnson's first meeting with Wilkes. The narrative is told with admirable raciness. We admire the consummate diplomacy of Boswell,

II.

in face of the difficulty of securing Johnson to meet a man he abhorred, luring his elephant to capture with extraordinary skill; then, when they met, Wilkes's material attentions to Johnson: " Pray give me leave, Sir, a little of the brown, some fat, Sir, a little of the stuffing— some gravy, let me have the pleasure of giving you some butter — allow me to recommend a squeeze of this orange," and so forth; so that Johnson, who looks at him at first with " surly virtue," is reconciled through the palate to his bugbear, and they talk together the whole evening with brilliancy and even cordiality. As we read, we realise the whole affair, the crafty crimp Boswell, the wheedling demagogue, and the reluctant moralist.

This is a specimen of the whole book; the best, I think, but there are many scarcely inferior. And so we have for ever before us, living and vigorous, one of the most interesting of our great men, the greatest, I suppose, of our men of letters, certainly our greatest known conversationalist, with his manifold tricks of speech, his eccentricities, his strange, uncouth ways. Of all the men whom we have never seen, Johnson is the man whom we know best, whom we can best imagine, whom we can most easily fancy that we have seen and heard. His appearance in this hall at this moment would no doubt cause a sensation, but in five minutes it would be the sensation of a friend restored to us after a long absence abroad. It is that feeling, common, I think, to all of us, which is the supreme tribute to Boswell's work. We can fancy him approaching now, rumbling and grumbling, " What is this concourse of silly people, Sir ? " " This is strange nonsense, Sir." " To celebrate a man's birthday without his consent is an impertinence, Sir." " What is it to you, Sir, whether I am two hundred years old or not ? Methuselah, of whom we know practically nothing, was undoubtedly my senior, and we do not commemorate him," Boswell at his side obsequiously explaining and anticipating. Dubious grunts follow, possibly an explosion, but Lucy Porter, Molly Aston, Peter Garrick, and the Sewards rally round him ; he beams serenely and calls for tea.

And what manner of man was it whose portrait has been presented with so much unction and fidelity, whose reputation has been thus almost consecrated ?

Well, in the first place he was emphatically a big man, a man who loomed large in his times, whose supremacy was acknowledged by the greatest of his contemporaries, who paid him an unquestioning homage. Gibbon, whose printed work is so much more remarkable and permanent, who was himself a conversational dictator, remained silent before him, and for that reason loved him not. The mighty mind of Burke met his with reverence. He enchained the brilliant intellect of Windham. The delightful genius of Goldsmith worshipped also, though it sometimes chafed. Garrick and Reynolds, in their own arts supreme, acknowledged his supremacy. There is, perhaps, no trustworthy record of so much respect paid by so many remarkable men to one whom they regarded as more remarkable than themselves. Neither of the Pitts nor Mansfield seem to have known him, and they stand out as exceptions from the curious crowd of intellect which came to him. Mansfield's abstinence is strange and unaccountable, except on the hypothesis that he resented or feared Johnson's dislike to Scotsmen, and no doubt Johnson ignorantly disliked him. Otherwise few abstained from the pious pilgrimage, though some did not care to take it more than once. It was the same sort of testimony that was rendered to Bolingbroke, whose character we may not admire and whose works we may not taste, but whose quality we recognise in receiving tribute of admiration from such men as Pope and Swift.

Secondly, we see in him the truest love of his own kind, of humanity at large. If the proper study of mankind be man, Johnson was a supreme student, for it was the dominating interest of his life. He had known and mixed with all classes from the highest to the lowest — all sorts and conditions of men and women, from George III. to Bet Flint. His strangest acquaintance was, perhaps, Santerre, who was destined to drown with his drums the dying words of Louis XVI. Nothing, indeed, is more remarkable in his conversation than the way in which people keep rising up, as it were, whom no one suspected him to have known. In the period of his fame he was brought into contact with almost everybody worth knowing, for every one wanted to know him, and he was readily accessible. But he would readily recur to the years of famine when he prowled about London with Savage, and could

sign his letters " impransus." And when he said
that literary biography was his favourite study,
it was in reality because it was a congenial branch
of the great study of mankind. It presented
itself, however, in its least agreeable form at his
own hearth. Moved by benevolence, by his
intense and compassionate love of his fellow
creatures, he had collected around him a family
of indigent persons, whose only recommendation
was their want, who were querulous to him and
quarrelsome with each other ; Levett, a per-
ambulating apothecary, " obscurely wise and
coarsely kind," whose death he commemorated
in lines of true pathos, but whom he described
in prose as " a brutal fellow, but his brutality is
in his manners, not in his mind " ; then there
were those whom Johnson playfully called his
seraglio, Mrs. Desmoulins, whom Levett hated
with an unbounded hatred ; Mrs. Williams, a
blind and peevish versifier ; and Poll Carmichael,
whom Johnson described as " a dull slut."
" Williams," he once wrote, " hates everybody ;
Levett hates Desmoulins, and does not love
Williams ; Desmoulins hates them both ; Poll
loves none of them." This was the domestic
circle of that great intellect. Surely we may say
that his heart was even greater, and that this is
the part of Johnson's life most beautiful to us.
" If I did not assist them," he said, " no one else
would."

But his charity and generosity were unbounded. It has been truly said by one who
knew him well " that the lame, the blind, and the
sorrowful found in his house a sure retreat."

II.   Once he found a poor woman lying exhausted in
the street—one of the city waifs ; he took her
on his back, carried her to his house, and had her
tenderly taken care of till she was restored to
health, and put in a better way of life. But this
ready and Christian charity was accompanied by
a common sense not less prompt. Of that there
is no more comical instance than his method with
Goldsmith in difficulties. The unfortunate poet
sent word to Johnson that he was in great distress. Johnson at once sent a guinea, promising
to follow it as soon as he was dressed. He went,
and found the guinea had been changed, and that
Goldsmith was sitting before a bottle of Madeira.
Now comes the immortal touch. " I put the
cork into the bottle and desired that he would be
calm." The benefactor then walked off with
The Vicar of Wakefield in his pocket, and sold it
for sixty pounds.

He knew men well, with the exception, perhaps,
of himself, for he was neither a " good-humoured
fellow " nor a polite fellow, as he proclaimed
himself to be : his temper was extremely ex-
plosive, and no one could be so rude. But this
contact with his fellows made him love the
practical side of life. He " loved business, loved
to have his wisdom actually operate on real life."
He liked to advise Boswell on domestic economy
and the management of his estate, to dictate
opinions on legal points, to act as a general
referee. He delighted in bustling about the
brewery as Thrale's executor, with an inkhorn
and pen in his buttonhole. Indeed he did not
altogether escape the fatal fascination which

Parliament exercises over literary men of high
ability. Strahan wrote a letter, to be shown to
Lord North, pointing out the value of the support
which Johnson could give as a member of the
House of Commons; a letter written probably
with the privity of Johnson. And Johnson
himself would sometimes regret that he had not
made an attempt for fame in Parliament : a
regret which has, perhaps, crossed the minds of
most able men, but which is at least compre-
hensible in one who claimed to have composed
many of the speeches attributed to our great
orators. But this was, perhaps, less a matter
of ambition than an aspect of his humanity ; he
wished to have a taste of everything that was
savoury in life.

This essentially human nature of Johnson,
combined with his insular existence, for his trip to
Paris scarcely counts, and his expedition to the
Hebrides strictly speaking was insular too, is
one great secret of his popularity. He was John
Bull himself. He exalted the character, of which
he may be regarded as its sublime type, but he
embodied the spirit. His Toryism was part of
his John Bullism; his love of London was rather
that of the John Bull than the cockney; his
hatred of Scotland was that of the John Bull of
his youth. When Foote threatened to caricature
him, he furnished himself at once with an oaken
cudgel. He asked the price of one, and, being
told sixpence, demanded a shilling one. " I'll
have a double quantity." Could anything be
more John Bullish than this ? Physically and
combatively he embodied the character, not of

II. the ordinary agricultural but of the literary John Bull.

I must not, however, linger on this fancy. For we have to consider him in his most famous character as a conversationalist, and to treat this adequately would require an essay of itself. Talk with him was not a luxury or an amusement, it was an article of prime necessity. He dreaded solitary or vacant moments, for he had then to cope with the terrors of constitutional melancholy, and as nothing but want of money could make him overcome his native indolence sufficiently to compel him to write, he was thrown back on conversation both as a prophylactic and as the intellectual exercise necessary for his mental health.

What is the impression that we derive from the vivid and careful reports of his talk ? Well, the first salient fact is that he sate at the receipt of custom, at the counter of his intellectual bank, ready to honour all drafts. He did not apparently start his own topics, Boswell or some crony had to lure him on. Then he would turn on the powerful mechanism of his mind, twist the subject about, defend, if possible, some glaring paradox, and, warming to his work, might not impossibly gore his opponent. He was " a tremendous companion," as was happily said by one of the Garricks. Then one is struck with his choice of diction. He never seems to pause for a word ; they come to him spontaneously ; but he is never satisfied with the second best, it must always be that which exactly represents his conception. It was not always graceful, it was

often pompous or Latinified, but it was always
exact and expressive. He, again like Bolingbroke, had perfected his conversational style by
a long-standing determination to express himself
as well as possible on every occasion, whether
trivial or not, and so he had acquired without
effort a singular vigour of phrase.

Another signal feature of his conversation is
this, that his little discourses spring forth unpre-
meditated but full-fledged; he gives the number
of his reasons before he utters them, as if what
he were going to say was already complete in
his mind, though the subject has only just been
put before him. And this extraordinary quality
goes far beyond conversation. He is ready at
any moment, so far as one can judge, to dictate
a paper admirable in argument, knowledge, and
form on any topic that may be raised. Boswell
brings him Scottish law cases, the great man bids
him take the pen, pulls out as it were the necessary
organ stop in his mind, and produces a remarkable
essay. Take, for example, that which he dictated
on the liberty of censure from the pulpit, an
apparently mature production put forth on the
spur of the moment, which earned the admiration
of Burke.

What a journalist he would have made!—
not merely from his readiness of ripe composition,
but from the range of his mind and reading, as
well as the ready and inexhaustible stores of his
memory. One example must suffice to-day. At
a dinner at Sir Joshua's, after Johnson has discoursed on the alleged fact that the brook which
Horace describes in his voyage to Brindisi is still

II. flowing, Mr. Cambridge quotes from a Spanish writer as to things fugitive surviving things seemingly permanent. Johnson at once caps this with a quotation from Janus Vitalis, a name which would remain unknown to most of us, did not the invaluable Birkbeck Hill tell us that he was a poet and theologian of Palermo who lived in the sixteenth century. No instance, though scores could be given, so well illustrates his readiness, his range of reading, and his memory. Adam Smith, a high authority, said that Johnson knew more books than any man alive. Dr. Boswell called him " a robust genius born to grapple with whole libraries." He seems indeed to have grappled with them. In his own strange way he tore the heart out of a book without reading it through, but carried away in his memory all that was abiding or material. But though his learning was always at command, it never seems obtrusive : his manliness saved him from pedantry.

Again, and as part of his John Bullism, note his robust common sense. He abounded in common sense, and also in some that was uncommon. But his common sense never failed him. He would break in upon a discussion or sum it up with a sentence sometimes brutal, sometimes coarse, but always tersely expressing the core and common sense of the matter. This quality made him intolerant of anything like sentimentalism or affectation. One of his special irritants was the idea that people composed better at some times and seasons than others, in spite of the case of Milton, whose genius, we are told, flowed most happily "from the autumnal equinox to the vernal." For this he falls foul of Gray, not reluctantly, and of any one else who cherished this "fantastic foppery." He himself sate down, full or fasting, doggedly to work at one time as well as another, though we have to record that a whole year would sometimes pass without his producing anything at all. In the same spirit he would not admit that any one could be affected by the weather. That again was all stuff and fancy. This robustness carried him far. Though he became a water-drinker himself, he uttered many sentiments which teetotalers could not quote. Even in questions of morality he would often fail to satisfy the austere, or even some who are not. He could even on occasion slang a bargee in appropriate language.

Johnson is always called our great moralist, and, indeed, in his writings he earns the title. But when in a mocking mood, or from his love of paradox, or his honest scorn of cant, he often broaches opinions to which he certainly would not have given his deliberate authority. His epigrams should not be quoted as opinions or as anything but epigrams. He knew, indeed, that Boswell was preserving them for publication. But he probably gave posterity credit for discriminating between deliberate judgement and the caprice of easy conversation. In truth, his love of paradox and his delight in the exercise of his dialectic skill would make him sustain or controvert almost any imaginable proposition. This sometimes puzzled the less nimble-witted Boswell, who, however, got to understand him at last, and would lure him or gently goad him. But there were moments when he would not be guided or restrained, when the noble animal broke through all nets and precautions. Woe, then, to his opponent, for he could be truculent and even brutal, and conversation with him was a battlefield. " He fought on every occasion," said Reynolds, " as if his whole reputation depended on the victory of the minute, and he fought with all the weapons. If he was foiled in argument he had recourse to abuse and rudeness." In such a frenzy he could even insult Sir Joshua, the sweetest and most amiable member of his society. As Goldsmith said, who himself had suffered, quoting from a comedy of Cibber's : " If his pistol does not go off, he knocks you down with the butt end."

But that is the way with all, or almost all, who claim predominance in conversation, and no one, when the fit was over, could be more anxious to appease the animosities that he had caused. With old Mr. Sheridan, whom he had hurt by a sarcasm, he sought reconciliation, but in vain. " Great lords and ladies, too," he said once, " I think, give me up . . . they don't like to have their mouths stopped." Others, no doubt, shared the feelings of this sublime class, and after one trial remained away. Some categories of persons he did not seek to conciliate. He hated Whigs with a devout hatred : " the first Whig," he always said, " was the devil." He hated Scotsmen scarcely less, though his hatred came at last to be mainly an opportunity for jests, which now afford only amusement to the most sensitive patriot.

Freethinkers he detested most of all, though he
could not resist Wilkes. And in his conversation
there was this element of harmless and agreeable
gambling. One never knew what side he would
take ; one never could guess his line of argument,
for that was never commonplace ; one never
knew whether he would be warm or cold, irascible
or serene. There was only this certainty, that
he would be human, manly, and profoundly
interesting.

His natural melancholy made him dread solitude ; and he preferred his " seraglio " to a lonely
home. But as visitors were not certain, he sought
mankind where he could find it, haunted taverns
and founded clubs. His own illustrious Club, of
which I have the misfortune to be the father,
was founded in 1764 at the instance of Reynolds,
and still survives in pristine vigour ; successful
candidates are still apprised of their election in
the formula composed by Gibbon. We celebrated
our founder's bicentenary this year, as he would
have wished, by a full dinner. That club he
sedulously cherished so long as it was composed
of a small knot of his most sympathetic friends ;
there he long reigned supreme. But its fame
drew many candidates of a kind impossible to
exclude, but not all congenial. In 1777 it was
proposed to increase the number of its members
from twenty to thirty, which he approved.
" For as we have several in it," he wrote, " with
whom I do not much like to consort with, I am
for reducing it to a mere miscellaneous collection
of conspicuous men without any determinate
character." Thenceforward he attended it but

II. little ; but he dined there on June 22, in the last year of his life. But such was his passion for this form of society that but a twelvemonth before his death he not merely resuscitated a small club of his early days which had met in Ivy Lane ; but, though moribund, and knowing himself to be on the verge of the grave, he founded a new club at the " Essex Head," which he ardently promoted. Reynolds objected to some of the company and refused to belong, but Johnson was less nice. To him, society of some kind was a necessity of life, a refuge from the dark terrors of solitude ; he had known and enjoyed it in all forms ; and so his new club with its dubious element continued, and was prolonged for some years after Johnson's death.

What more remains ? The highest of all, the great Christian soul, the ardent champion and firm bulwark of the faith. It was not always so. For some years, Johnson tells us, he was wholly regardless of religion, indeed a " lax talker " against it. That was in youthful days. But when after meeting Boswell he comes under our close view, all that is changed. This is not to say that he was free from the anguish of doubt, for that is not the impression he gives. But first and last with him stands his religious faith. He was a High Churchman of the old school, sometimes intolerant of Nonconformists, but on the whole of a broad embracing scope. " All Richard Baxter's books are good, read them all," he would say. On other occasions he would speak warmly of the Church of Rome, sometimes defending it so warmly, when it was attacked, that one of

his friends died under the belief that he was of
that communion. Finally, he would declare that
" all denominations of Christians have really little
difference in point of doctrine, though they may
differ widely in external form." He was, it may
be seen, however strict and earnest an Anglican
himself, large and generous in his comprehension.

None the less did his extreme conscientiousness
inspire him with an abnormal fear of death, much
more than men of infinitely less virtue. " Death,
my dear, is very dreadful," he wrote to his step-
daughter ten months before his end. But when
he thought that it was near, he displayed a high
composure, and he wrote the most striking of
his letters: " Dear Sir, It has pleased God this
morning to deprive me of the power of speech;
and as I do not know but that it may be His
farther good pleasure to deprive me soon of my
senses, I request you will on receipt of this note
come to me and act for me as the exigencies of
my case may require." And when the shadow
was finally on him, he was able to recognise that
what was coming was divine, an angel, though
formidable and obscure; and so he passed with
serene composure beyond mankind.

Men like this are the stay of religion in their
time, and for those who come after. Laymen
who hold high and pure the standard of their
faith do more for Christianity, it may safely be
averred, than a multitude of priests. To say
this is not to disparage the clergy; rather the
reverse, for it implies that their course is regular
and habitual. But their championship is felt
to be the natural result of their profession and

II. their vows, while the conspicuous layman, who is also a conspicuous Christian, has all the honours of a volunteer. No one, I think, can doubt that Samuel Johnson and William Ewart Gladstone were priceless champions of their faith, and that their places will not easily be filled.

And now we have lingered long enough, perhaps too long, round this absorbing figure, and must perforce leave him. There is a human majesty about him which commands our reverence, for we recognise in him a great intellect, a large heart, a noble soul. He lived under grievous torments, in dread of doubt, in dread of madness, in terror of death, yet he never flinched; he stood four square to his own generation as he stands to posterity. We leave him more reluctantly than any of the dead, for he is the only one with whom we can hold converse; and so it is with the conviction that it will not be for long, as life is insipid without him. Therefore we do not say good-bye. Rather let us think that we have only paid one more pilgrimage to his shrine; for though his dust rests with a whole Sahara of various kinds in Westminster Abbey, his memory, which lives throughout the Anglo-Saxon world, is especially green in Fleet Street and in Lichfield. We salute once more with reverence to-day the memory of that brave, manly, tender soul, and pass on with the hope that from his abundant store we may draw some measure of faith and courage to sustain our own lives.

III

THACKERAY [1]

I<small>T</small> is not easy from the din and current of a Coronation to bring ourselves back to the cool and quiet of a library, and contemplate the figure and works of a man of letters, even if he be a man of genius. Yet that is our business to-day, to bring back our mind to such a personage, and to wander about a little museum of relics that may refresh our memories.

Celebrations of this kind have become to some extent vulgarised, and they should almost be divided into classes, first, second, third, or the like. For we live in the age of centenaries. As there are only three hundred and sixty-five days in the longest year, and as there are many thousands of excellent and respectable people who deserve commemoration by somebody or other, there is no reason why we should not celebrate such festivals daily or oftener. But as it is, we pick our path through a tropical tangle of centenaries, only pausing by those which detain us whether we will or no.

Two of these overlap this year, the anniversaries

[1] A Speech delivered at the opening of the Exhibition of Thackeray Relics at the Charterhouse on June 30, 1911.

59

III.　of the two great humourists who were among the chief glories of the reign of Victoria, who lived into the times of middle-aged men, and who have been the delight of three generations : I mean Dickens and Thackeray. They are already ranked among the immortals, so that this first century is only an instalment of their lives. They are numbered with the gods, though it is probable that in the course of time their humour may evaporate or lose its savour, and our descendants will examine it with critical curiosity to know what it was that so delighted their ancestors, much as we read Scarron or Rabelais. But their names will survive as representing two mighty influences in the civilised world.

Thackeray is the giant whom we discuss to-day, not without some disadvantage. He left strict injunctions that no authoritative memoir of him should be produced. These it was impossible to obey. He left a daughter and a son-in-law of rare literary endowment, and their filial enthusiasm has to some extent skirted the veto, and has revealed much of Thackeray's inner life. Moreover, there have been two notable biographies by strangers. Thackeray himself no doubt wished that the temple of his home, in which he found his chief happiness, should have a curtain to protect its sanctity. But the tenderness of his children has lifted it with delicate discretion, and perhaps all is known now that need be known. Absolute silence and darkness were impossible, for a genius in these days cannot play the part of an ostrich. Nor

could he foresee the comprehensive net of the III.
Dictionary of National Biography, whose narrow
mesh much lesser men may not escape.

But after all, in the life of a man of letters,
his work is the one notable thing, and there is
rarely much else to record. This is eminently
true of Thackeray. He was born in India, a
circumstance which had some influence on one of
his books, and on his way home saw the distant
form of Napoleon. Then, though with a name
eminently Etonian, he went to Charterhouse,
gathering impressions valuable, but not always
pleasant, and a permanent one of a fist which
broke his nose ; passed fitfully through Trinity
College, Cambridge, led a Bohemian life in Paris
and in Germany, where he saw Goethe in the
flesh, and ended that phase of his life by losing
his patrimony at the gambling table, or in the
not less precarious hazard of a newspaper. This
deplorable incident, which he may well have
viewed with despair, was perhaps his salvation,
as we have always entertained a suspicion that
an opulent Thackeray would have produced no
Vanity Fair. For he was naturally indolent, almost
as indolent as Thomson, and sensitive, almost as
sensitive as Keats — two great hindrances to
successful production. Finally he settled down
and married happily, a brief happiness ; and
became a father—a lifelong joy. For his wife
and children he had to work ; at the age of
thirty-five he produces his masterpiece, claims
his seat on Olympus. Henceforth all is honour
and success. He strays for a moment into
politics, lured by the strange fascination which

III. has beguiled so many men of literary fame and
power. But that is his only aberration. He
enjoys some sixteen years of celebrity, and dies
prematurely at the age of fifty-two.

To judge by the immense number of portraits
which appear to exist of him, he must have
impressed his contemporaries to a singular degree.
His was indeed a commanding figure, for he was
physically as well as intellectually a giant, and
artists have been emulous to portray that tower-
ing form, surmounted by the leonine head and
illuminated by the inseparable spectacles, which
seemed to peer into the very core of the human
heart. As to his personality, one would surmise
that he was rather beloved than popular, enthusi-
astically beloved by his children and his friends,
a little alarming to acquaintances.

The monument of such a man is his work,
and for those who have been soaked in it since
childhood, it is difficult to appreciate, and still
more difficult to criticise. For me to-day it is
out of the question. I have promised to make
a short speech, but that is impossible, for one
cannot sufficiently condense. A long speech is
equally impossible, for if one began to dilate,
one would never end. We must stumble along
as best we may.

Among his books there is one that towers
above the rest, and that we must discuss for a
moment, however severe our limit of time. For
Vanity Fair appears to many of us the most full
and various novel in the English language. Not
the most perfect, that epithet belongs to *Tom
Jones*; not faultless, for the titular hero and

heroine are flavourless and insipid; but the richest, the most interesting, the most piquant.

These judgements are of course mere individual impressions, and carry no weight. A real critic picks the plums with a knife and eats them on the blade. He has rules and a science of his own. He knows the whole business, and perhaps thinks that he could do it better. But the ordinary reader has no such pretension. He comes at last, if not at first, to be guided by the simple fact that he likes what he likes, and dislikes what he dislikes. He does not always know why; he is only conscious of pleasure or the reverse. He knows that he takes one book down a second time or a third, and leaves another to the dust.

And so on that humble but natural footing I disclaim all pretension to discriminate except by an individual palate. To me it seems that Thackeray wrote one great, one immense book, a book which could not be repeated. His previous attempts imperceptibly led up to it, his later books illustrated it. He could live by it had he written nothing else, just as Mrs. Gaskell could have lived by *Cranford*, or Dickens by *Pickwick*. Admirable as is his other work, he could throw it all overboard and face posterity with *Vanity Fair*.

When a genius writes for his livelihood there must be inequality of product. It is the genius that writes for pleasure, as the inspiration comes, as the humour strikes, like the divine Miss Austen, or Gray the poet, who maintains a serene level approaching perfection. Even the gigantic

III. Sir Walter, labouring with a hundred pen power to rear a castle or remove mountains of debt by faith, faith in his good right arm, has to produce volumes, as it were, from hand to mouth, not always with success.

When a man, however, produces a book like *Vanity Fair*, he accomplishes much more than the mere presentation of a supreme work. He gives the world a new standpoint, a new method, new perceptions, a new style. All that he may write afterwards is only the development of this first revelation. He sets his mark on his age by his masterpiece; what he may do afterwards is only to stamp and rub it in.

Vanity Fair, as I have said, is not free from defects. The attraction in it is all to vice, virtue sits gloomily in a garb of whitey-brown. Lord Steyne, Sir Pitt Crawley, the coarse tyrant Osborne, the preposterous poltroon Jos Sedley, the incomparable Becky herself, these are the characters which loom large in the book, and obscure the limp Amelia and the shadowy Dobbin. Lady Jane, indeed, on the virtuous side, seems preferable to either the vapid hero (though a hero is disclaimed in the title) or the impalpable heroine. It is almost pathetic to note the total failure of Amelia, and the elaborate pains that Thackeray takes with her. He sweats blood to make her interesting and attractive, but in vain. And when he at last confesses, as he seems to do in one of the last sentences of the book, that Dobbin himself was bored with her, he throws up the sponge. It is quite easy to imagine that Dobbin was bored

with Amelia or Amelia with Dobbin, but that III.
is not the stuff of which heroes and heroines are
made. The fact is that it is the very earnestness
of elaboration that destroys Amelia. Thackeray
found that he could not strike the right note at
once, so spends pages in vainly trying to catch
it. Genius often fails with great pains to do
what it succeeds in sketching to admiration in
an instant with a piece of charcoal. A portrait
at the first sitting always seems a better likeness
than afterwards. The author himself hoped,
as he wrote to his mother, that Amelia would be
redeemed by Love. But she is not ; she was
beyond redemption ; she remains feeble, plaintive,
mawkish to the last. And yet Thackeray with
a few strokes has drawn one woman in this book
who is virtuous, attractive, delightful—Lady
Jane Sheepshanks, who married the younger
Sir Pitt.

Dobbin is little better than Amelia. He is
always thin and crushed and insipid, except
when he quarrels with Amelia and brings her
to heel. And then, though different, he is worse,
for he speaks unlike himself, and like the hero
of a transpontine drama. " You couldn't reach
up," he says, " to the height of the attachment I
bore you, and which a loftier soul than yours
might have been proud to share." No Dobbin
ever spoke like this, certainly not this one. No,
let us leave this tiresome pair, admirable foils
for the brilliant knaves and vivid fools who
surround them.

Why dwell on these blemishes ? Because
their very heinousness proves the greatness of

III. the book.   No other book could have borne lightly and gallantly such a dead weight. *The Vicar of Wakefield* is a classic in spite of a preposterous story.   That fact makes the success more conspicuous.   *Clarissa* is reputed a classic in spite of its ponderous and endless volumes.   *Sense and Sensibility* holds its ground, though on a lower plane than its sister stories, in spite of the extreme inanity of its hero.   The blemishes of *Vanity Fair* exalt the book ; for what must be the merits of a work which absolutely eclipse such defects ?

And when we turn to the other side, how are we to end in recording its merits ?   The admirable figures, the various play of feature in every page, the dramatic power, the sublime scorn which governs and inspires the book, all are admirable.   How true and stirring are the chapters in Brussels, the city which *Vanity Fair* and *Villette* have combined to illustrate.   How dramatically they close :   " The darkness came down on the field and city, and Amelia was praying for George, who was lying on his face, dead with a bullet through his heart."   How dramatic, again, is the scene with Lord Steyne, where Rawdon knocks him down, and Becky in her shame and terror " admires her husband, strong, brave, and victorious."

It was once my fortune, forty-five years ago, to hear Mr. Disraeli talk about the various representations of Lord Hertford in fiction.   He enumerated Lord Steyne in *Vanity Fair*, Lord Guloseton in *Pelham*, and his own Lord Monmouth in *Coningsby*.   He obviously, as was natural, preferred the last.   Lord Hertford's character,

he said, was more subtle and refined than Lord
Steyne's; Lord Monmouth was the better portrait.
We who did not know Lord Hertford are not
called upon to judge. Both delineations are
excellent in their different ways, but their ways
are so different that both cannot be likenesses.
We may well enjoy and admire, without discriminating as to a resemblance on which we can
pronounce no decision. Probably neither Disraeli
nor Thackeray ever saw Lord Hertford, which
makes the difference which we find in the delineations less difficult to understand.

But if Thackeray in *Vanity Fair* accentuates
the criminal and the vile, and puts virtue at a
discount, how nobly he atones in *The Newcomes*.
Here you have tragedy sublime, the good man
struggling with adversity, overwhelmed by the
black clouds of life and emerging triumphant,
borne to the heavens in an unspeakable glamour
of pathos. He dictated most of this book, but
when he came to the death of the Colonel he had
to take the pen himself. The Colonel had to
die in the livery of poverty, in adversity and
desolation, and Thackeray could not trust his
voice to tell the story.

The story, indeed, told itself, he could not
control it. He wrote, he tells us, by a sort of
instinct : the figures moved beyond his control.
" The characters once created lead me, and I
follow where they direct," he said. " I have
no idea where it all comes from. I have never
seen the persons I describe, nor heard the conversations I put down. I am often astonished
myself to read it after I have got it on paper."

III.

III. He would receive appeals, such as I suppose all great novelists receive, to give a pleasant turn to his story or happiness to some favourite character. But he could not yield, for he could not guide. People wished Clive Newcome to marry Ethel, and Thackeray conceded a shadowy hope. But one sees that this was not his real conviction, and that as the figures moved in his mind the real fifth act was something different. That is by the way, only an illustration of the writer's methods. The great fact is that just as he had depicted in *Vanity Fair* vice clever, brilliant, and on the whole sympathetic, so in *The Newcomes* he displayed an heroic, simple, almost apostolic character of chivalrous honour which attracts the affection of every reader and remains supreme through all the pains and tribulations of life. In the great country dance of fiction, when the characters cross hands in the Elysian Fields, let us hope that Colonel Newcome will have Becky Sharp as a partner to represent Thackeray's most consummate creations.

Even under stress of time I must say a word of *Esmond*. For *Esmond* is a great effort, a wonderful revival, a triumphant masquerade. So marvellous is the skill of the master in reproducing the words, the thoughts, and the manners of a past age that some have placed this remarkable book as high as *Vanity Fair*. I must frankly own myself a dissentient. The plot to me is simply repulsive. The transformation of Lady Castlewood from a mother to a wife is unnatural and distasteful to the highest degree. Thackeray himself declared that he could not help it. This,

I think, only means that he saw no other than III.
this desperate means of extricating the story.
I cannot help it, too. One likes what one likes,
and one dislikes what one dislikes, and so I must
face the just indignation of Thackeray idolaters
by declaring that, much as I admire this masterpiece in one respect, it is to me a story with a
painful blot. I must reluctantly pass *Pendennis*,
a delightful story, in which the most striking
characters are a fogey major and his volcanic
valet, but marred again, I think, by an unsympathetic heroine. That, however, does not
affect the charm. The book is full of light and
full of character. I must pass by *The Virginians*,
a bright story on a new scene, not sufficiently
appreciated ; *The Great Hoggarty Diamond*, a
special favourite of some of us as a simple story
full of fun and sprightliness, not overlaid with
discussions and moralising, containing one of
the most touching passages that Thackeray ever
wrote, wrung out of his own sorrows. I must
pass by *Barry Lyndon*, which many good judges
esteem a masterpiece, and which is at any rate
an admirable eighteenth - century panorama. I
must pass by the terrible and sardonic tragedy of
Deuceace. These omissions and others only prove
the hopelessness of the task of dealing with this
prodigious and multifarious genius in a short
speech. Only the other day I was reading *Philip*
again, and felt that, though it was not one of
his great books, no one else could have written
it, and one paused now and then at a passage to
exclaim, " How marvellously good this is ! "

It may also fairly be maintained that *Vanity*

III. *Fair* and its kindred fictions of the first class do not represent the only department of letters in which Thackeray left a masterpiece. There are at least two others to which he contributed original works of the highest merit : I mean the collection of essays called *The Book of Snobs* and *The Rose and the Ring*. This last, as a mere expression of genius, seems to me to come next to *Vanity Fair*. The exquisite irony and extravagance of this unique piece would, perhaps, not have attracted adequate notice had it not had an illustrious name upon its title-page. But with that name we realise that this is another facet of the big diamond, and then we can give ourselves up to pure enjoyment. That enjoyment is the same whether the reader be seven or seventy, and grows from the one age to the other. How often in reading the most solemn and dreary histories does some analogy to *The Rose and the Ring* flash out, and one sees a corner of the portentous tapestry lifted and the queer face of Titmarsh peep out with a wink and a leer of irresistible drollery. Nor are the rhymed headings or the drawings inferior. It is a perfect whole, harmonious through and through.

As with *The Rose and the Ring*, so it is with *The Book of Snobs*. There is seldom a week spent with the human race in which one does not, so to speak, rub up against *The Book of Snobs*. This is not to imply that one's sweet converse is with snobs, but it is to indicate that the universal touches of nature constantly remind one of that shrewd little volume. The fact is that *The Book of Snobs* is ill-named. It is not

a book of snobs, but a book of impostors. The III.
characters, for the most part, are not snobs at
all, and the snobs are chiefly female. Ponto,
whose germ we find, by the bye, in *Vanity Fair*
(for Dobbin, when he married, hired the " Ever-
greens " of the gallant major), Ponto was not a
snob, though Mrs. Ponto was one without doubt.
So was Miss Wirt, who also makes her début
as a " raw-boned vestal " in *Vanity Fair*. But
as a rule the characters are impostors and hum-
bugs, and Thackeray had a keen nose and de-
testation for humbug. Still, they are not, strictly
speaking, snobs. The word has a curious history,
and I am not sure that Thackeray himself understood it. Originally meaning a shoemaker, and
then a townsman as against a gownsman at
the Universities, it is now superseded by the
modern synonym of bounder, a better word. But
Thackeray interpreted it as one who meanly
admires mean things. That is far too capacious
a definition. A snob is one who basely aims at
or apes social superiority. He would only furnish
out a lean treatise. But the theme of imposture
is illimitable and eternal.

However we may differ as to the category,
this at least cannot be denied, that Thackeray
as an essayist, whether on snobs or on other
topics, ranks among our greatest. There is
perhaps no Englishman who can weave wit, and
allusion, and sarcasm, and knowledge of human
nature into a poignant but delightful whole so
deftly as he. That is another aspect of his
various and powerful genius, another art in which
he may claim the highest rank.

III. There are also two other aspects of Thackeray's genius which are apt to be overlooked in the general splendour of his other work—I mean his poetry and his drawings. Now these have both a quality in common : they lack form, but what is wanting in grace is made up in character. Thackeray is not reckoned among the poets, and yet his verse has the inexplicable knack of leaving a strong impression ; it is terse, vigorous, and original. I will only give two specimens. Take the first stanza of the ode on the Crystal Palace :

But yesterday a naked sod
The dandies sneered from Rotten Row
And cantered o'er it to and fro :
    And see 'tis done.

As though 'twere by a wizard's rod
A blazing arch of lucent glass
Leaps like a fountain from the grass
    To meet the sun.

That may not be high poetry, but it pleases ; it is brisk and vivid, it dwells. Where, again, will you find a stanza more exquisite in its pathos than the one on Charles Buller ?

Who knows the inscrutable design ?
    Blessed be He who took and gave !
Why should your mother, Charles, not mine,
    Be weeping at her darling's grave ?

It rings in the memory where poems of greater reputation leave us cold.

So much for his verse. There is the same quality in his sketches. I suppose that as drawings they are not very good. But that makes their success all the more remarkable, for he contrives to give a life and character to his illustrations such as few artists but Hogarth have been able to impart. Some of them I admit are incredibly bad. At no time could he delineate beauty and charm in a woman. His Becky Sharp, who should have been fascinating, is repulsive. His Dobbin, too, who should be a hero, looks like one of Mr. Squeers's ushers after six months at Dotheboys Hall. His Rawdon Crawley is never a dandy dragoon, and is sometimes squalid. Thackeray in these cases is always trying to force his conception through a medium which will not respond. But, when he succeeds, how well he succeeds. How admirable are Lord Steyne and both the Crawley baronets, how inimitable the drawing of Lady Southdown taking medicine to Becky. The drawings in *The Virginians* seem to me even better. Then there comes the matchless series in *The Rose and the Ring*. Where can one find greater fun or more delight ? I must not omit the illustrations to " Mrs. Perkins's Ball," or the striking sketch of O'Connell as Lord Mayor of Dublin. And yet I am only taking those that occur to me at the moment. The list could be indefinitely prolonged. His real ambition was to be an artist, but his literary genius was too strong for his art, it could only adequately express itself in literature, and his pencil has to be satisfied with rude, untutored, but unmistakable force. So strong is the inspiration that it overrides art.

Let us sum up these hasty and inadequate remarks. In the first place, no one will deny to Thackeray the rare and priceless gift of genius.

III.

III. He produced what many would call the greatest
novel in our language, certainly, one would say,
the first or second. He produced several others
which must be ranked high in any list. His
penetration, his humour, his imagination formed
an immense combination of qualities, and when
he chose to touch the note, his pathos rings true.
He had imbibed the spirit of the eighteenth
century, and knew well what he had seen of
the nineteenth, though it was unhappily very
incomplete when he died. His strength lay in
dealing with the middle class, their foibles and
ambitions ; he loved, too, to dwell on Bohemia
and its inhabitants, boasting that he had lived
in Bohemia all his life ; but the idea of titular
rank drove him off his balance, the sight of a
coronet made him run amuck with a scourge,
and the specimens which received the lash well
deserved punishment if they ever existed. He
himself, secretly sensitive as a new-born child,
could pick out all the tenderest places for the
whip.

And so with all these priceless gifts he has
bequeathed a range of works all brilliant and
all interesting. It is difficult to name any writer
of fiction who has produced so much on so high
a level of interest and power, though he appealed,
no doubt, to a much smaller audience than
Dickens. " Saul has slain his thousands and
David his tens of thousands." But that was
natural and inherent in the work of the two men ;
it is no disparagement to Thackeray. If one
must criticise, one would say that his point of
view was a little monotonous, that one sometimes

feels that one knows what he is going to say, or
that what he is saying he has said more than
once before. And one has perhaps the same
feeling about his characters that he expressed
himself. " All I can do now," he said towards
the end, " is to bring out my old puppets and
put new bits of ribbon upon them. I have told
my tale in the novel department. I only repeat
things in a pleasant way, but I have nothing
fresh to say." One may also regret that he lacks
the realism say of Defoe, that he delights too
much in being the showman and the moralist,
in by-discourses on life and morals and in handing
out his puppets for inspection by his audience,
lest they should be mistaken for real figures—
all this to the disparagement of the story itself.

There are other points more minute : in so
much production there must be flaws. Every
author who is worth his salt must be conscious
of his own shortcomings, he must always be
aware of inadequacy, he must sometimes feel
that if he wrote all the book over again it would
be better done ; and even then he may be wrong.
But who are we that we should criticise ? Let
us be grateful and enjoy. Let us be grateful
for the imagination which inspires, and for the
labour which completes and embodies imagination ; let us unreservedly enjoy the wit, the
romance, and the pungent perception ; let us
remember with thankfulness the writer who has
given us so many happy hours, constantly renewed, and who, if he has not achieved an
impossible perfection or produced a mass of
virgin gold without dross, has left supreme

III.

III. and precious work. Let us remember, too, the simplicity and purity of his gospel. Let us never forget that in his sincerest moods he always inculcated charity in its largest sense, that that was his deepest, innermost note; and that he was the mortal enemy of imposture and hypocrisy in every form. *Écrasez l'infâme* was as much his motto as it was Voltaire's, but with him the infamous reptile to be crushed was humbug. Those were his two messages : hatred of all that was false, charity human and divine; and though the first may sometimes have clouded over the second, the last was strong, penetrating, and profound. " I think, please God, my books are written by a God-loving man, and the morality —the vanity of success and so forth, of all but love and goodness—is not that the teaching of Domini Nostri ? " he wrote towards the end of his life, and we join with him in thinking that the better his teaching is known the loftier it will appear. He faces posterity as a great figure of rich genius and honest purpose, a purpose occasionally obscured by the force of imagination and the irresistible promptings of humour ; weighing mankind in a gloomy balance, but not without hope; and bequeathing to us rich and various treasures of literature, which may well survive, if anything survives.

IV

CROMWELL[1]

I AM very glad to be here to-night. We are all, I imagine, glad to be here to-night, even if we are not proud to be here. For, after all, this is no great occasion for pride, as we are commemorating the erection of the first statue to Cromwell in London—a statue which ought to have been erected long ago, and which has even now met with some not unimportant difficulties.

I do not know whether you remember the history of the inception of this statue. It was promised by Mr. Herbert Gladstone, as First Commissioner of Works under the late Government; then under pressure in the House of Commons that promise was withdrawn, and immediately on that promise being withdrawn an individual, who, I understand, felt that Cromwell's immortal memory should not be made a football for contending factions in the House of Commons, wrote to offer to bear the cost of the memorial. The Government of the day accepted that offer, and it was ratified by the Government now in power. Since that time a new opposition

[1] A Speech delivered at the Cromwell Tercentenary celebration, 1899.

IV.   has sprung up. It is slender in numbers, but I
‾‾   do not pretend to say that it is not representative
of a considerable volume of prejudice and even
of passion; but as far as it has gone it has not
assumed a very serious complexion. It has,
indeed, carried in the House of Lords, when the
House of Lords was not very crowded, a resolution
denouncing the present position of the statue;
and though the Government loyally stood to
their pledges, they were unfortunately defeated
by a majority of six to four.

I for one do not complain of that opposition;
but there are two features in connection with it to
which I would call attention for a moment. The
first is that it is not very logical, because in the
very heart of the House of Commons—that sacred
shrine of the Constitution, to which the presence, I
presume, of Oliver Cromwell was supposed by the
majority in the House of Lords to be deleterious—
there has been placed by the present Government,
not by arrangement with the late Government
and not under any pressure whatever, a bust
of Oliver Cromwell. I do not, therefore, quite
understand that tenderness of conscience which
protests against a statue in the open air and outside Parliament, but which raises no objection to
a bust in the very heart and centre of Parliament
itself. Secondly, I would urge this—that if this
opposition were to be raised, it would have been
more graceful and fair had it been urged some
four years ago. A statue was promised, and the
sculptor was commissioned somewhere about June
1895, for I remember it preceded almost immediately the fall of the late Government—not that

I associate the two facts in the slightest degree.
Some four years ago the commission was given,
and it is not till the pedestal has been actually
erected, and the statue itself is rumbling on its
way to occupy that pedestal, that the opposition
lifts up its voice, and in the House of Lords even
goes to a division. I think that that was, to
speak in the vernacular, hardly playing the game,
and I hope that we shall hear no more on this
subject.

But there is an evil fate which attends
statues of Cromwell, and Manchester, I believe,
had the honourable distinction of being the only
city that possessed one. Scotland was prepared
to erect a statue to Oliver, although he had
inflicted a considerable defeat upon her forces ;
yet so great was her gratitude for the good
government that came from this unwelcome
source that a statue was ordered to be erected
to Cromwell on the site now occupied by a statue
of his successor, Charles II. Unfortunately, the
statue was not more than rough-hewn at the time
of the Protector's death, and therefore it lay an
almost shapeless mass, a figure in a shroud, at
Leith, until it was put up in some obscurer part of
Edinburgh, and ultimately went no man knows
whither. We, at any rate, are more fortunate,
for we have a statue which, so far as I can judge
from seeing it in the Academy, is worthy of the
subject and worthy of the genius of the sculptor
—I am glad that the sculptor is here to listen to
your applause.

Sir, you have insinuated that I am going to
give to-night an exhaustive description of Oliver

IV. Cromwell. That is exactly what I shall not attempt to do ; for to do so in a speech would be inevitably to fall short of my object, and also altogether to mistake the character of a speech. Were I going to write you an essay it might be possible to make some such attempt ; but the character of a speech must be of necessity comparatively shallow, and must not attempt more than it can well achieve. Moreover, so as to make my survey in its very inception imperfect, there are two great acts in the Protector's career on which I propose to offer none but the very fewest and sparsest observations. The first is his policy towards Ireland. With regard to that I am bound to say that it admits of explanation, but it hardly admits of excuse. I am one of those who feel that were I an Irishman I, at any rate, should not be a contributor to a statue to Oliver Cromwell. I am not sure that even as a Scotsman I may not have to bear some little censure for being present on this occasion. But to our Irish friends I may say that as we do not interfere with the statues which they choose to put up in Dublin, they might refrain from interfering with the statues which we choose to put up in London. It is true that the policy of Cromwell towards Ireland was ruthless and cruel in the extreme, but two things should be remembered, not by way of palliation, but of explanation. In the first place there was great provocation ; and in the second place the Puritans, of whom he was the leader, were deeply imbued, for reasons which it would take too long to explain, with the lessons of the Old Testament. They

believed that they were the chosen people of God
and had the right to deal with their enemies as
the Israelites dealt with the Amalekites. The
Amalekites, it should be noted, were not the Irish,
but the Roman Catholics. It is indeed stated
on high authority that the majority of the
garrison of Drogheda, which was put to the
sword, consisted of English people. However
that may be, this Old Testament view is the
explanation, but not the palliation, of Cromwell's
conduct towards Ireland.

Nor will I say anything about the execution
of Charles I. That was an act which I think was
barely justified by the circumstances. But it
was an act as to which one or two facts are
generally forgotten, if they were ever known, by
the critics of the memory of Cromwell. The
first is that it was not a willing act on the part of
Cromwell. He endeavoured as far as he could
to work with the king; and it was not until he
found that the king would accept no position
short of the absolute ideal of kingship which he
had formed for himself that Cromwell was forced
to desist from the attempt. You must remember
also that he had found from painful experience
that Charles held no measure with his opponents;
that he was in no respect to be trusted; and you
must also recollect what is now better known—
that it is not possible for a feudal monarch to be
his own constitutional successor. The two things
cannot combine in one man. That was made
clear nearly a century and a half later in the case
of Louis XVI. of France, who was willing to be
a constitutional sovereign, to be his own con-

IV.

stitutional successor, which Charles I. was not. But it was not possible. If, then, you were to have a constitutional sovereign, you were bound in one way or another to get rid of Charles I. ; though it seems to me that as a stroke of policy means much more gentle might have been adopted, which would have prevented the act being, as in essence it was, not merely a crime, if crime you call it, but a political blunder as well. There is only one further remark that I will make on this subject. Happy is the dynasty which can permit without offence or without fear the memory of a regicide to be honoured in its capital. Happy the sovereign and happy the dynasty that, secure in their constitutional guarantees and in the world - wide love of their subjects, can allow such a ceremonial as this to take place without a shadow of annoyance or distrust.

What manner of man was this Cromwell whom we seek to honour to-night ? Probably we shall get as many answers as there are people in this hall. Every one has his own theory of Cromwell, and they are apt to be jarring theories. There is, of course, the popular but perhaps illiterate view which you sometimes hear expressed, that he was " a damned psalm-singing old humbug, who cut off the head of his king." To a considerable number of those who talk about Cromwell, the knowledge of him is limited to that simple assertion. I do not know whether that is the opinion of the majority of the House of Lords. At any rate let me quote two or three testimonies on the other side. Lord Macaulay said of him that he was " the greatest prince that ever ruled England." The greatest living authority on that period—Samuel Rawson Gardiner, who by no means is a favourable critic of all the policy of Cromwell, sums him up in these words : " It is time for us to regard him as he really was, with all his physical and moral audacity, with all his tenderness and spiritual yearnings—in the world of action what Shakespeare was in the world of thought ; the greatest because the most typical Englishman of all time." But there is one testimony which I regard as more valuable because—I cannot say it is more unbiassed—it is more naturally biassed in the other direction : it is the testimony of Southey, the great Tory man of letters in his day—not Conservative, remember, but the Tory historian of his day. He speaks of Cromwell thus : " Lord of these three kingdoms and indisputably the most powerful potentate in Europe, and certainly the greatest man of an age in which the race of great men was not extinct in any country, no man was so worthy of the station which he filled." I balance these testimonies against the majority in the House of Lords.

But if I am asked on what grounds I personally admire him, I could not give them all to-night ; but I should say that in the first place he was a great soldier ; that in the second place he was a great ruler ; and that in the third place he was a great raiser and maintainer of British influence and power abroad.

Let me take him as a soldier. I am not, of course, competent to give any technical opinion

IV.   upon his merits as a soldier ; but I believe that the experts of the day do now pronounce the opinion that Cromwell was one of the great soldiers of his day and of all days. But, at any rate, whether we can judge of him as a strategist or not, we laymen who are not soldiers can, at any rate, understand certain broad features of Cromwell's military career which appeal to us all. In the first place, it was so marvellously short. It was begun at so late a period of life. I think he was forty-three when he entered the Army, and fifty-two when he finally sheathed his sword. His military career lasted only nine years. That seems to me to be a most remarkable feature. I think that no man ever entered the Army so late who rose to so great a position, except, perhaps, that still more singular and startling instance, considering the time in which he lived, of Lord Lynedoch, who entered the Army at about forty-six and who lived to be a Field Marshal. Another peculiarity about Cromwell was that he won every battle that he fought. And we also know the fervour of enthusiasm which he managed to inspire in his soldiers ; the coolness and judgement with which, even on the battlefield, he managed to guide and restrain that enthusiasm ; the extraordinary instinct by which he was able to detect the weakest point of the enemy's battle array and to direct his full force on that weak point. In a word, it was his eye for battle. No one who has read the account of the battles of Cromwell can doubt that he was a born soldier ; that he had military capacity in its truest sense and in the highest degree.

Let me take him now as a ruler. I have
deliberately not called him a statesman, because
Cromwell had no opportunity of showing what
were his qualities as a statesman. His reign was
too short ; his life was too short. He died at an
age at which a man would be thought almost
young for a Prime Minister in these days. But
there is also this to be recollected of him—he
was always ruling on behalf of a minority. It is
perfectly true that he was fighting the battle of
freedom. It is perfectly true that he was fighting
the battle of toleration. But I think it is equally
and indisputably true that the majority of the
nation were not favourable to his policy, and
that if he were fighting for their rights he had to
fight against their instincts and prejudices. That
I believe to be the explanation of his parliamentary difficulties—the Parliaments that he
had to dissolve, the Parliaments that he had to
watch, the Parliaments that he had to sift, the
Parliaments in which he had to guard the doors,
so that no member of the Opposition could
possibly gain entrance. If we consider what
Cromwell's position really was—how in truth
he was a destructive agent, appointed as it were
to put an end to the feudal monarchy, and to be
the introducer of a new state of things—and
consider also that he had to do all this not resting
upon the will of the people, but upon the will of
the army, I think we shall feel that Cromwell
achieved extraordinary results. Even in Scotland, where he was no welcome intruder, he
governed the country as Scotland—and I am
sorry to say that it was no great compliment—

IV. had never been governed before, and was not governed for a long time afterwards. He effected the union between Scotland and England, and he effected what was practically far more important to Scotland—freedom of trade between Scotland and England : a measure which was regarded with so much prejudice that it was one of the causes of the opposition to him in England. These alone are great achievements in any reign, especially so short a one as Oliver's.

There is one more feature which has been already alluded to in his policy as a ruler, and on which we cannot lay too great an emphasis. He was the first ruler who really understood and practised toleration. It is quite true that it was by no means universal. For example, it did not extend, generally speaking, to Episcopalians. It is quite true that some Episcopalians were not allowed to practise their faith so freely as they might have desired ; but I believe that in that case the reasons were political, and that it was the Royalist and not the Episcopalian who was forbidden to influence the people. But we do know that he was capable of an act of toleration almost incredible in those days, and not even in these days by any means universal. He was the first prince who reigned in England who welcomed and admitted the Jews. I am glad to see that the heads of that community, such as Lord Rothschild, Sir Samuel Montagu, and Mr. Benjamin Cohen, are here to-night to show their appreciation of that act of beneficence.

It is a peculiarity of great men that they have a tendency to wreck the throne on which they

sit. Take Frederick the Great : he led the life
of a drill sergeant, of an estate steward, of a
bureaucrat, of a minister and a general, all in
one, making the details of every department
of government centre in himself. He indeed
absorbed everything, and nothing could be done
without his sanction and knowledge. Such a
man makes himself the mainspring of the machine,
and when he withdraws the machine collapses and
has to be constructed afresh. Take Napoleon :
he differed from Frederick in that he did not
find a throne, and had to construct one, but,
being on it, one of his objects would appear to
have been to make it impossible for any one else
to occupy it. Combining the activity of a score
of men with a mind embracing the largest questions and the smallest details, directing everything, making everything derive light and guidance from him, so completely did he centralise
all in himself, that, had he died as Emperor,
his disappearance would have caused not a
vacancy, but a gulf in which the whole apparatus
of government must have disappeared. And so
of Cromwell, but in a different sense. He, too, has
a throne resting on the support of 60,000 armed
men, so that if it loses their support it falls, because
it is antagonistic to the nation at large. Cromwell
soon sees his throne is held on a personal tenure.
So fully does he realise that he could not bequeath
to any one the power on which his rule rested,
that it is by no means certain that he ever thought
it worth while to name a successor. He dies,
and the fabric disappears. The real founder of
a dynasty is one who produces not merely a

throne, but institutions, and if the institutions are sound the throne remains part of the fabric. That is why so few lasting dynasties are founded ; the founder is ordinarily the only potent institution, and he is essentially mortal.

Then I take Cromwell as the raiser and maintainer of the power and empire of England. I do not propose to-night to trace the method by which he made his name and the name of his country honoured and respected ; it would take me too long, and, indeed, it is not particularly easy to define. But there is one ground, one clear ground, upon which he fixed the attention of Europe. He was not born to the title as were his predecessors and successors, but he was essentially the Defender of the Faith. You know what he did with regard to the Waldenses, those persecuted Protestants, the massacres and horrors perpetrated upon whom remain so black a page in European history. Cromwell spoke —he did not interfere by arms, though I have seen his action on this subject cited as a precedent for religious interference by arms—he did not interfere by arms, but he wrote despatches, and by the force of diplomacy, backed by a great army and his supreme reputation, he achieved his object, and what remained of the Waldenses were saved. When Europe saw that Cromwell was in earnest, Europe had no hesitation as to the course it had to adopt. Indeed it is very remarkable—it is not, as I have said, wholly explicable—the extraordinary deference, I had almost said the adoration, that Europe paid to him. Spain and France contended for his

alliance. Two great Roman Catholic countries
strove for the honour of the alliance with the
Defender of the Protestant Faith. The great
Roman Catholic monarch, Louis XIV., put on
mourning for him. Cardinal Mazarin, a Prince
of the Roman Church, earnestly, almost humbly,
sought his alliance ; and, as showing the position
of power and honour Cromwell held, I may
quote a letter from the great Condé, the greatest
general on the continent of Europe at a time when
the continent of Europe produced many great
generals : " I am exceedingly delighted," he
says, " with the justice which has been paid to
your Highness's merit and virtue. I consider
that the people of the three kingdoms are in the
height of their glory in seeing their goods and
their lives entrusted at last to the management
of so great a man." That is no republican
sentiment, that is no Protestant testimony ; it
is that of a great Roman Catholic French Prince.

Well, I would ask, What is the secret of this
extraordinary power ? As I said before, you
will all of you probably give one answer or
another, many of them likely to conflict. There
is one answer I suppose everybody here would
give—that the secret of Cromwell's strength
rested in his religious faith. I discard that
answer, because it would be begging the question.
No, my answer is this—that he was a practical
mystic, the most formidable and terrible of all
combinations. A man who combines inspiration
apparently derived — in my judgement really
derived—from close communion with the super-
natural and the celestial, a man who has that

IV.

inspiration and adds to it the energy of a mighty man of action, such a man as that lives in communion on a Sinai of his own, and when he pleases to come down to this world below seems armed with no less than the terrors and decrees of the Almighty Himself.

Let me take him first as a man of action. I present to you the portrait of Cromwell as he has come down to us depicted by contemporary writers such as Sir Philip Warwick, and, having given you his portrait as the man of action, then we will get glimpses of him from the other side. How does he appear to us ? He comes tramping down to us through the ages in his great wide boots, a countenance swollen and reddish, a voice harsh, sharp, and untunable, with a country-made suit, a hat with no band, doubtful linen with a speck of blood upon it. He tramps over England, he tramps over Scotland, he tramps over Ireland, his sword in one hand, his Bible in the other. Then he tramps back to London, from whence he puts forth that heavy foot of his into Europe, and all Europe bows before him. When he is not scattering enemies and battering castles he is scattering Parliaments and battering general assemblies. He seems to be the very spirit of destruction, an angel of vengeance permitted to reign for a season to efface what he had to efface and then to disappear. Then there comes the end. The prophetic Quaker sees the " waft of death " go out against that man, there is a terrible storm, and he lies dying in Whitehall, groaning out that his work is done, that he will not drink or sleep, that he wishes

to " make what haste he can to be gone," and
the sun as it rises on his great day, the 3rd of
September, the day of Dunbar and of Worcester,
finds Cromwell speechless, and, as it sets, leaves
him dead. That is practically the view that we
get from contemporary portraits.

Yet there is another side ; for with all his
vigorous characteristic personality there is something impersonal about Cromwell. Outside the
battlefield he never seems a free agent, but
rather the instrument of forces outside and about
him. The crises of nations, like the crises of
nature, have their thunderbolts, and Cromwell
was one of these ; he seems to be propelled, to
be ejected into the world in the agony of a great
catastrophe, and to disappear with it. On the
field of battle he is a great captain, ready,
resourceful, and overwhelming ; off the field he
seems to be a creature of invisible influences, a
strange mixture of a strong practical nature with
a sort of unearthly fatalism, with a sort of spiritual
mission. It is this combination, in my judgement, which makes the strength of Cromwell.
This mysterious symbolism appears to have
struck the Eastern Jews so much that they sent
a deputation to England to inquire if he was the
Messiah indeed. That is not exactly a combination that can be produced in bronze or any
known metal, but Mr. Thornycroft has given us
in his statue the nearest equivalent to it. He
has given us Cromwell with sword in one hand
and Bible in the other. Well, I suppose our
critics will say there is no question whatever
about the appropriateness of the sword, but there

is a great deal of doubt about the genuineness of the Bible ; indeed, the whole controversy as to Cromwell really hinges on the question, Was he a hypocrite or not ? That is why I told you the answer resting his success on his religious faith would be begging the question, and that is why I discarded it. It is a question that must stand unanswered until the secrets of all hearts are revealed ; for it is a secret between Cromwell and his God.

Those who hate his memory for other reasons are determined to believe that he was a hypocrite, but, at any rate, we who are here to-night do not believe that he was a hypocrite, or we should not be here. I think those who call Cromwell a hypocrite can never have read his letters to his children. Those are not state documents. Those were not meant to be published in blue-books—it was a happy age when there were no blue-books—they were not meant to put the Governor and Protector in a favourable light. They were the genuine outpourings of a sincere soul. Let me take a further incident of Cromwell's life not familiar perhaps to those who have called him hypocrite. The pious Quaker, George Fox, not then in the position that Quakers occupy now in this country—for they were harried, imprisoned, and persecuted—he, an outcast among men, was brought in bonds to see the great Protector. He did not beg compassion for his people or ask for any particular favour. He came to testify to the great man, to preach to the great man, and in his leathern jerkin he did preach to him. I think the account of this little interview, which I will not read at length but only summarise, is one of the most interesting and touching episodes in the whole of Cromwell's career. George Fox, when he came in, said nothing apologetic. He uttered a prayer : " Peace be in this house." Some Sovereigns might have been annoyed at this condescension from a man continually within the grasp of the law, one who was still a prisoner. But Cromwell receives it with humility.

" I exhorted him," says Fox, " to keep in the fear of God that he might be directed, and order all things under his hand to God's glory. 1 spoke much to him of truth, and much discourse I had with him about religion, wherein he carried himself very moderately." Then Fox and Cromwell held a discussion on " priests, whom he (Cromwell) called ministers. . . . As I spoke he several times said it was very good, and it was truth. . . . Many more words I had with him, but people coming in I drew a little back ; and, as I was turning, he caught me by the hand, and, with tears in his eyes, said, ' Come again to my house, for if thou and I were but an hour a day together, we should be nearer one to the other ; ' adding that he wished me no more ill than he did to his own soul."

What had Cromwell to gain by being civil to this man and by listening to what many people would have thought rodomontade ? Most people would have thought it a duty to hand him back to justice ; but Cromwell saw the sincerity of the man, welcomed him, released him, and took him to his heart.

IV.   Let me tell you another little story you may
not have heard before—not much in itself, but
curious for the directness with which it comes.
It was told me by a friend of mine, a Bishop of
the Established Church — by no means one of
the oldest of the Bishops, because he is of my
own age—and he was told it by a gentleman who
had it from a doctor—that makes three people—
and the doctor heard it from the Sir Charles
Slingsby of his day, who had it from a nurse.
That is but five people, and covers a long period.
Sir Charles Slingsby heard it from the nurse, who
as a girl was the heroine of the story.   The day
before Marston Moor, Cromwell arrived at Knares-
borough, and while there he disappeared from
among his troops.   Search was made for him for
two hours, but he could not be found ; but this
girl, who afterwards became a nurse, remembered
an old disused room at the top of the tower ; it
was the only possible place where Cromwell could
be, and the girl, peeping through the keyhole of
the locked door, saw the Protector on his knees
with his Bible before him, wrestling, as he would
have said, in prayer, as he had been wrestling for
the two hours he had been missing.   Was there
anything to be gained by this ?   Was there any
effect to be made by his locking himself in the
neglected, ruined chamber, and imploring the
blessing of the God of battles in the contest of
the following day ?   I at any rate see nothing to
be gained, and if those who read the story still think
him a hypocrite, why then he must have become a
hypocrite so consummate that hypocrisy became
as much part of his being as the air he breathed.

But I will give a more practical reason for IV.
my belief that Cromwell was not a hypocrite.
Had he been, he could not have achieved such
enormous success ; he could not have wielded
the prodigious force that he did. A religious
force which is based on hypocrisy is no force at
all. It may stand inspection for a moment, like a
house built upon the sands, but when the storms
come, when the rain descends, and when the
winds blow, under the stress of adverse circumstances, the house and the fabric disappear.
I believe, then, that had Cromwell been a
hypocrite he would have been found out ; I
believe that if he had been a hypocrite he would
not have been able to maintain himself in the
dazzling position which he attained ; and had
he been a hypocrite he could not have formed
that army which he commanded, and which was
indubitably the greatest army in Europe at the
time of his death.

Let me take the point of the army. He early
became aware of the overwhelming force which
religious fervour would give to his army, but he
did not utilise this conviction by making hypocrites of his army. He utilised it by selecting
those men who he knew were of good repute
among their neighbours ; steady, earnest, God-
fearing men who would be equal to sustaining
the onset of the brilliant army commanded by
the King and his cousin. Cromwell told his
friend and kinsman, the illustrious Hampden—
and I think that we have the pleasure of seeing
a descendant of Hampden and the possessor
of Hampden's house here to-night—he told

IV.　　Hampden that the men whom he was leading were no match for the chivalry of the King's army. Let me give Cromwell's account. " I told him . . . ' You must get men of a spirit ; and take it not ill what I say—I know you will not—of a spirit that is likely to go on as far as gentlemen will go ; or else you will be beaten still ? ' I told him so ; I did truly. He was a wise and worthy person ; and he did think that I talked a good notion, but an impracticable one. Truly I told him I could do somewhat in it. I did so, and the result was—impute it to what you please—I raised such men as had the fear of God before them, as made some conscience of what they did. And from that day forward, I must say to you, they were never beaten, and wherever they were engaged against the enemy they beat continually." With these men he won his battles and beat down the chivalry of England. Are we to believe, then, that these Ironsides were merely canting hypocrites, that they rode to death with a lie on their lips and a lie in their hearts ? Surely not. To believe that would be to misunderstand the nature of the forces that sway mankind. Nor did the lives of these men belie them. As a contemporary chronicler says : " The countries where they come leap for joy of them "—which I believe is not always the welcome given to an army by the peaceful inhabitants of the country they traverse—" and come in and join with them." And so by his selection, and by influence, he welded that impregnable force, that iron band which he himself at the last could hardly sway to his will. Had

they been hypocrites this could not have been; IV.
and as they could not have been hypocrites, their
exemplar, their prophet, their commander could
scarcely have been a hypocrite either.

It is quite true that Cromwell's action not
unfrequently jars with Christianity as we in this
nineteenth century understand it. But, as I
have said, his religion and that of the Puritans
was based largely on constant, literal, daily
reading of the Old Testament. The newer criticism would have found no patron in Cromwell.
Indeed, I believe that its professors would have
fared but ill at his hands. He himself lived with
an absolutely childlike faith in the atmosphere
and with the persons of the Old Testament.
Joshua and Samuel and Elijah were as real and
living beings to him as any people in history, or
any of the persons by whom he was surrounded.
His favourite psalm, we are told, was the 68th
—the psalm that, even in the tumult of the
victory of Dunbar, he shouted on the field of
battle before he ordered the pursuit of the re-
treating army. But it always seemed to me that
another psalm, the 149th, much more closely
reproduces the character, the ideas, and the
practice of Cromwell: " Let the saints be joyful
in glory. . . . Let the high praises of God be in
their mouth, and a two-edged sword in their
hand; To execute vengeance upon the heathen,
and punishments upon the people; To bind their
kings with chains, and their nobles with fetters
of iron; To execute upon them the judgement
written: This honour have all his saints." It
is not a comfortable or patient or long-suffering

creed, it is true ; but, remember, it is the creed that first convulsed and then governed England —the faith of men who carried their iron gospel into their iron lives, who could not have done what they did had they been hypocrites, and who would not have received their incomparable inspiration from a hypocrite.

To the end of time the contest will rage as to the merits and the sincerity of Cromwell. Cowley, in a noble piece of prose, such prose as was only produced in the seventeenth century, pictures himself as returning from the funeral of the Protector. He records the pomp of the obsequies, and continues thus : " But yet, I know not how, the whole was so managed that, methought, it somewhat expressed the life of him for whom it was made—much noise, much tumult, much expense, much magnificence, much vainglory, briefly a great show, and yet, after all this, but an ill sight." Cowley was a Royalist, and he wrote when no unbiassed opinion was possible. But his words are striking enough, and I make a present of them to the opponents of the Cromwell statue. But was it indeed a splendid administration, a masculine and honest career, or, as Cowley says, an ill sight ? On that point, at any rate, my mind is clear. I will go so far as to say that great and opulent and powerful as we are, so far from banishing his memory, we could find employment for a few Cromwells now. The Cromwell of the nineteenth or the Cromwell of the twentieth century would not be the Cromwell of the seventeenth century, for great men are coloured by the age in which they live. He

would, at any rate, not be Cromwell in his
externals. He would not decapitate; he would
not rise in rebellion; he would not speak the
Puritan language. But he would retain his
essential qualities as a general, as a ruler, as a
statesman. He would be strenuous. He would
be sincere. He would not compromise with
principles. His faith would be in God and in
freedom, and in the influence of Great Britain
as promoting, as asserting, both. In that faith
he lived, by those lines he governed, imperfectly,
no doubt, as mortals must be imperfect, but
honestly. In that faith, by those principles,
he lived, and governed, and died.

I hope that we, too, as a nation are animated
in our patriotism by no lower an ideal. I speak
of the nation as a whole, for I know that there
are some individuals to whom this theory is
cant, and the worst of cant. I know it, and I
am sorry for them. But, on the other hand, I
believe that the vast majority of our people are
inspired by a nobler creed; that their Imperial-
ism, as it is called, is not the lust of dominion or
the pride of power, but rather the ideal of Oliver.
If that be so he is influencing us yet, and a
statue more or less matters little. So long as
his tradition pervades the nation the memory of
Cromwell is not likely to suffer disparagement
for the want of an effigy. And, even were it
otherwise, he has a surer memorial still. Every
man, I think—every man, at any rate, who is
worth anything—has in his heart of hearts a
Pantheon of historical demigods, a shrine of
those who are demigods for him; not even

IV.   demigods, for they would then be too far and too
        aloof from mankind, but the best and noblest
        of born men. In that Pantheon, in many
        English hearts, and those not the worst—whether
        the effigy of Cromwell be outside or inside Parlia-
        ment, cr altogether invisible—will be found eter-
        nally engraved the monument and the memory
        of the Great Protector.

V

FREDERICK THE GREAT [1]

CATT's book on his relations with King Frederick
II. is a book of human interest. It has, too,
the unexpected advantage of being written in
French, for Catt was a French-speaking Swiss,
and Frederick disdained to speak German.
Indeed, on Thiébault's expressing a wish to learn
that language, the King forbade him almost
with violence, and made him give his word of
honour not to acquire it, as he was fortunate in
being ignorant of such a tongue.

Catt's narrative is one of the most faithful
portraits of that monarch that we possess. It
covers, indeed, only two years of the long period
during which Catt served him, but they are
tremendous years of trial and stress, and there
could not be a better test period. Zorndorf,
Hochkirch, and Kunersdorf are all comprised :
doubtful and bloody victory, crushing defeat,
annihilation or little less, and we can see how
Frederick comported himself under all. Prussian
critics with all the elaborate minuteness of
German editorship have picked holes in Catt,
which are not serious. They think, for example,

---

[1] An Introduction to the *Memoirs of Henri de Catt*, 1916.

v.   that Catt wrote or rewrote much of his memoirs
at a later date than the professed one.   That is
highly probable ; of few memoirs can it not be
said.   Memory amplifies the rude notes of the
time, and imagination perhaps is kindled.   We
certainly would not wish to swear to every word
of Catt's record.   Nevertheless we believe it
to be a generally veracious account of Frederick
as seen through the medium of highly-coloured
glasses.

Catt was a Swiss student at the University of
Utrecht.   He was, we are told, well acquainted
with French literature, and had besides the
manners and usages of good society, having
frequented the best houses in Holland.   Moreover, he possessed a still more precious treasure
in a disposition the cheerfulness of which must
have been invaluable to him in his official life.
An element less congenial to his master was
a strict adherence to the doctrines of Calvin.
Still, so pleasing was he to Frederick that the
King bestowed on him the customary compliment
of an epistle in verse, and the affectionate nickname of Gresset, after the graceful French poet.
Moreover, not satisfied with an epistle to Catt,
he also composed love poems for Catt addressed
to his betrothed : so close were their relations for
a long period of years.

The meeting of Catt and Frederick was almost
a romance.   It was on a canal boat in Holland.
Catt, a Swiss teacher twenty-seven years old,
out on a holiday, sees a gentleman in a black
wig and cinnamon-coloured coat who describes
himself as first musician to the King of Poland,

and who, after staring at him some time, asks him abruptly who he is. Catt, nettled at his summary manners, refuses to reply. But presently the musician becomes more polite, and draws Catt into amiable converse. They discuss government, religion, literature, and such high topics. Finally Frederick, for he is the strange gentleman, parts with the young man as from a friend, and soon sends for him, keeps him for some score of years under the title of " reader," which should rather be " listener," and which veils the duties of a Literary Crony, Catt's real employment. To listen reverentially to Frederick declaiming tragedies or funeral orations or any pieces that he happens to know by heart, or, worst of all, his own intolerable verses, to profess enjoyment of these recitations, and to place adroitly sympathy or compliment, —these are Catt's functions. Great men, and even men not great, often have need of such retainers. Johnson had Boswell, Goethe had Eckermann, Byron had Moore, Southey had Grosvenor Bedford, and so forth. It is something to possess a blind and devoted admirer in whose presence one can, so to speak, unbutton oneself and discourse about one's emotions, recite one's works, and explain their subtle meaning or sublime intention—a friendly conduit of egotism.

Catt joined Frederick at Breslau in March 1758, and boasts of having retained his entire confidence for twenty-four years—a unique boast if true—till their relations chilled in the last five years of the King's life.

As to this breach there is an allegation, true

v. or false, which would serve to explain it. A gentleman, it is said, wished to obtain a Prussian Order and gave Catt a hundred louis-d'or to procure it for him. Catt failed, but bought the insignia of the " Order of Generosity," which he sent to his friend, who wore it with pride. We are not surprised to learn that the " Order of Generosity " had come to an end at the accession of Frederick, at least as regards his own subjects ; so the reappearance of the Order brought about an inquiry damaging to Catt. Then there was a suspicion that Catt was in the pay of the French Government, and also that he had levied a share of the profits on the books supplied to the King's library. Truly or falsely, Frederick suspected or discovered some such circumstance, and rid himself of Catt. It may only have been a pretext. " You may serve the King faithfully and always," said the hapless Colonel Balbi, when writhing under Frederick's " infernal " sarcasms, " but if you fail once, all the rest goes for nothing." And Marwitz, one of the King's aides-de-camp, confirmed this. " For the least thing, and even for nothing, he will send you about your business after thirty years' service." Bielfeld, too, just before he bids a final farewell to Berlin, makes a not less significant remark : " A small fault is sufficient to obliterate the memory of twenty years' faithful service."

Catt was, of course, a devoted admirer, but his incense was not of that gross kind, burned by others, which obscures the idol and defiles the worshipper. He was, indeed, a Court official, librarian or secretary, and might by the ill-natured be considered a sycophant. That he was not. He was an innocent young student, overawed and enchanted by contact with a great monarch, but capable of speaking out frankly, and even boldly. At an early period of their intercourse he gave Frederick clearly to understand that he would not submit to the brutal practical jokes in which that monarch indulged. And his candour was constantly tested, for Frederick was perpetually asking what was said about him. Catt was, moreover, used as a channel to convey to the King the criticisms and alarms of the camp. These Frederick would dismiss, intent on reading aloud his newest stanzas, which the most loyal of secretaries cannot follow with relish when full of the dismal forebodings of the army. On one occasion these were amply realised, while Frederick occupied himself with a parody on Ecclesiastes.

It is clear, of course, that Frederick knew and intended that Catt should keep a journal. At such close quarters Catt could not have kept such a record without the knowledge and therefore connivance of the King, who indeed bids him write. It is obvious, too, that when Frederick discoursed about his plans and battles to the young man, it was with the intention that they should be recorded; otherwise it would not have been worth his while. This, however, by no means lessens the value of the journal. It is well to know what Frederick said and wished to be thought. Moreover, in certain supreme junctures the poignancy of his position deprived

v. him of his mask, and he displayed the natural
man, so far as there was a natural man to display.

This last phrase is not intended by way of
disparagement. A great general inured to tremendous hazards and vicissitudes has to curb
and disguise his emotions until he almost loses
the sensations of nature. He has to appear calm
when uneasy, imperturbable in the face of
calamity, confident when least confident, so as to
inspire his officers and his troops ; he is, in fine,
ground by fortune into temper harder than steel.
Little or nothing of nature survives, or is possible.
And this is pre-eminently true of Frederick.

If tears be a test, however, this is subject to
modification; though tears vary in kind. But
whatever their quality, the quantity of Frederick's
tears is undeniable. Catt reveals him as the
most lachrymose of monarchs. He bursts into
tears when reading Racine's *Britannicus* aloud,
and is unable to continue. He weeps, and no
wonder, on hearing that the brother whose heart
he had broken was dead. He weeps, and no
wonder, when he hears of the illness and death
of his sister, the Margravine of Baireuth. She
was his favourite in early years, but the Margravine's account of their latest relations hardly
makes one expect any violent explosion of
sorrow. However, any allusion unlocks new
fountains. When he returns from Kunersdorf,
tears. When he hears that the disaster of
Maxen has only enhanced the zeal of his troops,
tears. Catt, indeed, represents him as constantly
weeping. There is nothing discreditable in these
emotions, but they comport little with the con-

ception of the grim sardonic sovereign; they
remind one rather of the "iron tears down
Pluto's cheek."

It is, of course, true that we have frequent
records of Frederick's lachrymatory powers. But
these tears were public and theatrical tears,
tears of ceremony, tears of etiquette. The flow
recorded by Catt on various occasions was for
Catt alone, and is perhaps less open to suspicion.
This aspect of Frederick is alien to Englishmen.
But it should be remembered that the habits of
continental nations are more emotional than our
own. Men here do not embrace each other, and
they weep with difficulty. On the mainland it
is different, and we must make this allowance
when we record the constant sobs of this re-
doubtable warrior.

But the King has a stranger and even more
copious relief than tears. Each calamity has a
welcome aspect for him in that it provides an
occasion for verse. When he hears of the critical
condition of his sister he announces the news to
Catt, and also the fact that he has already drafted
an epistle on the melancholy topic, and at once
reads it aloud to Catt, till interrupted by his
emotion. " Vous me voyez tout triste, mon
ami, et dans de grandes angoisses sur l'état de
ma sœur, *je m'occupe d'elle dans cet instant, j'ai
fait un croquis d'une épître pour elle,* je veux la
travailler avec soin pendant le temps de notre
séjour dans ce quartier-ci." Presently he is
anxious to read this sketch, but is again silenced
by tears. He read it aloud constantly next day,
and again the day afterwards. The third day

he again read it to Catt, who remained with him two hours. He was engrossed with it. It was the eve of Hochkirch. Next day he seemed to be ruined.

The evening of the defeat he summoned Catt, and declaimed a passage from Racine's *Mithridate*. When Catt mentions the anxiety of the soldiers for the preservation of his life, the ready tears stream down his cheeks. Catt is dismissed and recalled. The King has heard of the death of Marshal Keith. He laments his loss in a sentence, then asks what the Earl Marischal will feel under such a bereavement. A method of consolation at once occurs to him : " Je célébrerai en vers notre perte commune."

Here there is a tragic interlude. He laments his fate and the odious trade to which the chance of his birth has condemned him. A strange self-deception. But he adds that he has that about him which will end the drama when it becomes insupportable ; and he produces from below his shirt a little oval gold box containing eighteen opium pills. " There are enough here," he says, " to take one to those gloomy shores whence there is no return."

His other and less drastic consolation is Lucretius. " That is my breviary."

His compositions, however, are by no means confined to the elegiac epistles we have mentioned. Once, for example, we catch a glimpse of a " Plan of Education " for those destined to the ecclesiastical profession. To this, too, the hapless Catt has to listen, and he alone seems to have been cognisant of it, as it was burned—

unfortunately, as every school of theology would
welcome such a treatise from such a hand.

What are we to make of this portrait, of this
strange figure thus represented ?

We must acknowledge at once that we are not
in a position at this time to be confident of the
impartiality of our judgement. Waves of blood
are washing over the world at this moment,
and the source of much of this is Frederick.
For his policy of rapacity without scruple and
without conscience has inspired or tainted
Prussian policy ever since. The House of
Brandenburg has, it is true, both before and
after him, pursued its elevation with a single
mind and energy, without any tenderness as to
the means. Even Frederick William II. could
distract his mind from his mistresses sufficiently
first to guarantee and then plunder Poland.
Even the conscientious and molluscous Frederick
William III. filched Hanover from his ally when
he got the chance, and attempted to swallow
Saxony, though with only partial success. Sometimes by money-lending, sometimes by pawn-
broking, sometimes by grabbing, the burgraves
of Nuremberg pursued their undeviating purpose.
But Frederick as their greatest sovereign con-
densed this practice into avowed and definite
policy. It had been a tradition ; it was new an
heirloom from a national hero, as sacred as such
an unsanctified heirloom could be. Frederick
stamped himself ineffaceably on Prussia.

The greatest success of the family was perhaps
the appropriation of East Prussia, the territory
of the Teutonic Knights, of which one of their

princes was the Grand Master and Trustee for life. This Hohenzollern, by deftly converting his life interest in trust property into a freehold for himself, secured this great province for his future realm. Acquisition by any means was the object of the successive Hohenzollerns, until at last they fashioned a long, lean kingdom which was said from its shape and aggressiveness to be all sting. Then there came the King of preparation, Frederick William I., a half-crazy boor with a shrewd zest for accumulation of money and men, giants if possible, which he had the wit not to attempt to use, but to prepare for the son whom he had wished to kill. Then came the man who was to use them for the further aggrandisement of his house. Frederick lost no time. His father had been one of the guarantors of the Austrian dominions, and almost at the moment of his own accession the guarantee came into force when there succeeded to the Austrian throne a young woman whose interests that guarantee was framed to protect and whose father was thought to have saved his life. That solemn bond and that claim of gratitude did not cause Frederick a moment's hesitation. While exchanging cordial assurances with the young Queen he poured a great army into her territories and seized Silesia. Not otherwise did his Prussians in the twentieth century deal with guaranteed Belgium.

To his plunder or acquisition, call it what you will, Frederick clung with superb and indomitable tenacity. That is the one sublime strain in his character. And he rounds off his reign by parti-

tioning Poland. In this nefarious scheme, of v.
which he was the prime instigator, he was also
the greatest gainer, for he obtained West Prussia,
which linked the two portions of his kingdom
together, and entitled him to declare himself
King *of* instead of *in* Prussia. Again, in the
affair of the Bavarian succession, when he took
up arms, he declared, for the purest and highest
motives in the interests of Germany alone, it
transpired at the peace that the reversion of
Anspach and Baireuth had, as it were by accident,
accrued to him as the reward of his altruism.

Rich slices of Austria and Poland, these satisfy
the Hohenzollern for the time. But the reign
of Frederick means much more than these
provinces. For, as has already been set forth,
he stamped and moulded Prussian policy into
the shape which it wears this day. Get what
you can when occasion offers, reputably if
possible, if not, unscrupulously; keep up huge
armaments as a menace to the world and a means
of taking advantage of opportunity,—this, stated
crudely, is the policy that Frederick bequeathed
to his country. Prussia has been ever since like
a pike in a pond, armed with sharp teeth and
endless voracity, poised for a dart when the
proper prey shall appear. But this policy, brutal
as it is, requires genius, and Prussia has not
been richly endowed in that way. There was
one such, but he was discarded, and Phaeton
mounted the chariot of the sun in his stead,
with the results that we know.

This is a digression only intended to show
that Frederick, and so Catt's book, is well worthy

v. of study at this time. Let us then renew our examination of the portrait presented by our faithful Swiss. We have seen Frederick's tears and his verses. His only other pleasure, except those of the table, was the flute, in which he was no mean proficient. The flute was to Frederick what smoking is to the men of to-day. It filled up gaps in his time, soothed him, assisted meditation and digestion. Tears, verses, flute, there is something in this Meliboean aspect of a great Captain fighting for desperate life in a welter of war which is not without its fascination.

Is all this natural? Were these tears, shed in conjunction with the composition of unreadable odes, a theatrical posture intended to impress Catt, or the irrepressible ebullitions of a stern and repressed nature? It is hard to say, for human nature has strange labyrinths, but it is scarcely possible to think that they were not the result of dramatic art. They seem to us the necessary screen of the passionate emotions of ill-fortune and disaster. So considerable is the imposture, indeed, that did one only know Frederick through Catt one might regard him as a man mainly of literary tastes. But it was his duty to wear a mask.

Both as a general and as a sovereign he was bound to dissimulate; in both it is often not a vice but a virtue. Moreover, we must remember that the King was well aware that his officers cross-questioned Catt as a sort of royal confidant with regard to the King's demeanour and intentions, while Frederick would constantly ask Catt as to what was being said in the camp.

On the whole, we may say that Frederick knew   v.
his business, that he regarded Catt as a channel,
but that frequently he forgot that character
and enjoyed a debauch of odes and recitations
without any afterthought.

But the young scribe gives at least some
lamentations of Frederick which indicate, if
not an attempt to deceive others, at least an
effort to deceive himself. One of the reasons,
he says, which must make him always regret the
death of his beloved brother was that it put an
end to a favourite plan of his own, which was
to hand over the government to this prince and
retire to a chosen society of enlightened friends
with whom to pass the rest of his existence.
Whether Frederick ever seriously entertained
such an idea seems much more than doubtful
when we remember that he devoted the peaceful
remainder of his life to the work of administration, a toil in which he delighted and which he
carried on till the very moment of death. If he
did, no man ever deceived himself so completely.
If he did not, Catt would seem to have recorded
either a passing mood or an attempt to impose
on his hearer. More than once did he expatiate
to the secretary on his passion for a quiet life
had not the gods disposed of him otherwise,
and dilate on the repose which he loved above
all things, except it may be presumed in the
autumn of 1740. But he did not impose on our
innocent Swiss, for at last Catt blurted out, " It
is an admirable plan, Sire, but it will never be
realised." And when Frederick asks, " Why
not ? " Catt points out that when the King

v. has concluded an advantageous peace, he will not be willing to descend from a throne which will have been assured by so many sacrifices. And the clear-sighted secretary does not hesitate to indicate an opinion, though not to Frederick, that the whole is a little comedy. In which we are disposed to agree with him.

We must remember, and this is a vital consideration, that Frederick had passed a terrible youth under the tutelage of a mad, intemperate father, who had caned and degraded him, and taunted him with his degradation. By the same paternal monarch he had been imprisoned and condemned to death, and rescued with difficulty from execution. He had had, moreover, the supreme horror of witnessing the execution of a friend who died for being his confidant. His experience had been that of those wooden effigies of their heroes which the Prussians of to-day delight to honour by driving nails into them; but in his case the nails had been driven into his living body by his own father. When love might have afforded a consolation he was driven into a marriage which he ostentatiously abhorred. Hence when he came to the throne he came with a shrivelled heart and a sardonic scorn for all mankind, its morals, its conventions, its cant; there was little human left. That, it seems to us, is the secret of Frederick's character. It is revealed in his wish to be buried with his dogs. Friends he had none, with the possible exception of the Earl Marischal, who had almost made him believe in virtue.

The dual nature of his famous intimacy with

Voltaire is notable as throwing light on Frederick's character. It was proclaimed to the world as a sublime friendship, but it was strongly modified by shrewd and cynical penetration. Frederick never ceases talking with Catt about the great Frenchman. An idolater of Voltaire's vast and active intellect, he never flags in his admiration, submits his compositions to him as to a schoolmaster with diffidence and apprehension, but never fails to speak of his character as the vilest and most contemptible that can be conceived. He regards him, in fact, with the rigid discrimination which makes a Russian official ask a pope's blessing as a priest after having been compelled to flog him as a man. He was always ready to adore Voltaire as a poet and repudiate him as a friend. So definite a distinction was a hindrance to genuine affection. Another symptom of his cynicism was that though there were some in his circle like the Earl Marischal who would not tolerate liberties, he had enough of his father in him to delight in coarse practical jokes, and even more in cruel sarcasms on those who were his boon companions at Sans-Souci. One of these practical jokes he narrated with glee to Catt. Pollnitz and d'Argens could have reported many others. Men in private life who are guilty of such outrages soon find themselves alone, or alone with dishonest sycophants; and kings against whom no reprisals are possible are apt to discover that, though they may still be surrounded by an abject and mercenary court, they have forfeited all possibility of friendship. It is not too much to say that Frederick died

v.   as friendless as his father, though with his spaniels
pigging around him, and that his isolation was
the deliberate and not unwelcome result of his
scorn and distrust of mankind.

Indeed, in spite of the tears and epistles, we
see no proof of real sensibility recorded by Catt,
with the exception of his apparent emotion on
hearing of the anxiety of his soldiers for his
safety. His sorrow for his brother and sister
and Marshal Keith falls in the category of his
tears and epistles, and need not be analysed
here. We are not offering blame. We have
already explained that in our judgement great
generals must be composed of beaten steel.
When to that composition is added the hardness
produced by Frederick's training in childhood
and youth, enough has been said. One cannot
make puddings out of a grindstone.

Again, his cynicism reveals itself in his method
of recruiting his forces from deserters, prisoners,
and crimped men. On one occasion the whole
Saxon army, some fifteen thousand men, after
surrendering to him, was incorporated without
its officers in his own, though they never ceased
to show their abhorrence of his service, and
deserted in numbers at every opportunity. " They
make as good cannon fodder as any others; what
does it matter to these wretches on which side they
fight." So, we can fancy, the King reasoned.

Was, too, his vaunted tolerance more than the
expression of a cynical contempt for all creeds ?
A " conscientious objector " who crossed him
would, we apprehend, have speedily found the
limit of Frederick's toleration.

Frederick, then, if entitled at all to the epithet   v.
of Great, by which it is indeed convenient to
distinguish him from the crowd of Fredericks,
deserves it only as a general, an administrator,
and as a man of heroic persistency.   Apart from
these it would be a daring advocate who would
claim anything in his character that entitled
him to such a title.   It is one which requires the
assent of mankind ; it cannot be conferred, as such
epithets were wont to be by the Roman Senate
in its degradation.   The present German Emperor,
William II., has constantly endeavoured to affix
it to his grandfather, the Emperor William I.
But the label will not stick ; it falls off as often
as it is placed, and history will not recognise it.

As to his generalship, only experts can decide,
and they, it would seem, have pronounced a
high and final judgement in his favour.   When
Napoleon has pronounced at least one of his
battles to be a masterpiece, there is nothing
more to be said.   But it may be alleged, though
we are not competent to decide the question,
that Frederick does not seem to have been a
born general like his eulogist, but to have learned
his business on the battlefield, not without painful and sometimes disastrous experience.   Even
our author, a humble but candid idolater, did
not shrink from criticism.   Before the disaster
of Hochkirch, he tells Frederick that his officers
said that his camp was commanded by the
enemy and was exposed to imminent danger.
But as Marshal Keith had told the King the
same with emphasis and vigour, it was not likely
that Catt would be successful.   " If the Austrian

v.

generals let us stay quiet in this position," the
Field Marshal had remarked, " they deserve to
be hanged." After Kunersdorf, Catt tells the
King that many people think he was too eager
to engage in that battle, and that if he had been
satisfied with the great advantages he gained at
first the enemy would have retreated, but that
in pushing things too far he had given Loudon
the opportunity to fall on him with fresh cavalry.
Frederick thanks him for his frankness and
answers the criticism at length.

A few months later Catt tells his master that
he has observed that when Frederick was too
confident he was usually unsuccessful, and successful when he was despondent; hinting at rash-
ness and lack of foresight. The King challenges
instances. "Olmütz," cites Catt. "Vero," is the
reply. "Then Zorndorf, where you expected to
smash the Russians without much loss. Then
at Hochkirch you said you would drive the
Austrians into Bohemia." If this conversation be
not an afterthought of Catt's, it required no slight
courage in him to remind an irascible monarch,
smarting under disaster, of former faults.

But we have not the competence nor the
courage, as we have said, to follow Catt's example
and criticise in the slightest degree the generalship of this great soldier. Still, thus much must
at least be admitted, that it was the death of
the Empress Elizabeth that saved Frederick
from ruin, rather than his own splendid achievements.[1] When the odds against which he fought

[1] Catt and Frederick had a bet on this event which Catt won.
But he cannot conceal his disappointment. The wager was to be a

are considered this is not remarkable, but it shows how precarious was the triumph on which his fame rests.

V.

We must, however, under present circumstances call attention to his views of " frightfulness " as now practised by his countrymen. " Le premier qui pillera ou détruira une maison doit être pendu sur l'heure," he said, speaking of his own soldiers. Speaking of the enemy and of the havoc they had wrought in the house where he lodged, and of a dead woman in the garden, he asks, " Tout cela ne fait-il pas dresser les cheveux de la tête, est-ce là faire la guerre ? *Les princes qui se servent de telles troupes, ne devraient-ils pas rougir de honte ? Ils sont coupables et responsables devant Dieu de toutes les horreurs qu'elles commettent.*" And again, " Les nouvelles que je reçois de ces cosaques barbares font dresser les cheveux à la tête, ils mettant tout à feu et à sang dans mon pauvre pays, leur marche est sans cesse ensanglantée par toutes les horreurs imaginables ; *j'espère que la justice divine me vengera un jour ou l'autre de ces chefs qui ordonnent ou qui permettent de pareilles abominations.*" Admirable and memorable as are these sentiments, it is strange to hear this professed infidel appealing to the Almighty for redress.

And again, speaking of atrocities alleged to have been committed by the troops of Loudon :

" discretion." " I shall make you a present if I lose, and you what you please if I win," said the King. The supreme news arrives, and Frederick with low bows hands poor Catt an epitaph on the Empress ; priceless, no doubt, in its way, but still something less than the young Swiss had expected.

v.
" Je vous l'ai dit, mon cher, la guerre qui ne se fait qu'en barbare perd toutes les mœurs et fait de l'homme un être sauvage, elle les rend brutaux, féroces et barbares ; je ne saurais vous dire, mon cher, jusqu'où va mon indignation et ma colère."

It would have been well, we think, if the Prussians of to-day had assimilated this part of the heritage they received from Frederick as devoutly as they have adopted his other methods.

We pass from his generalship to his civil administration. Here there is something to admire and much to criticise. His devotion to his duty is beyond praise. He fagged like a clerk under the eye of a stern master, and his master was duty. In summer he generally rose at three, in winter an hour later, and worked at his correspondence till eight. Then till ten he received his Cabinet secretaries, unhappy slaves condemned to unremitting toil; then till noon he gave audiences, rode or walked or reviewed. At noon he dined, and digestion was facilitated by the flute. Then came the secretaries with his letters. After this task he might walk. But the hours four to six he rigidly and unfortunately reserved for literary composition. Later he supped or received his intimate associates, and at nine went to bed.

This was his day at Potsdam. But this represents but a small part of the labours of this indefatigable man. He was always pervading his kingdom, reviewing, inspecting, planning, or surveying improvements. Nothing was above or below his notice. His finger, to use an expressive

vulgarism, was in every pie. He scrutinised
every penny that was spent. In his own household he knew the proper price of every dish,
the place of every bottle of wine. And the
same system was applied everywhere. Uneasy
were the heads of those who had to render to
him an account of their stewardship.

Frederick, like his father, administered the
whole kingdom as a vigilant and frugal proprietor
manages his estate. The father would hang a
man whose accounts showed a defalcation, and
he no doubt got his pennyworth. But Frederick,
with far greater application and immeasurably
more ability, proceeded on the same principles.

Now a virtuous and able despotism, when it
can be secured, is held by many to be the best
form of government. But a meddling and minute
despotism, however beneficently it may sometimes operate, whether exercised by a man or a
community, is, we take it, one of the most intolerable ; and Frederick's can hardly be characterised
otherwise. He cut, no doubt, some Gordian
knots in a way which provokes our envy. No
lawsuit, for example, was to last more than a
year. But even this summary jurisdiction did
not always secure justice. Still worse was it
when Frederick personally intervened. The case
of the miller Arnold is memorable, in which he
arbitrarily punished the innocent and rewarded
the guilty. Nor, when convinced of his error,
would he atone for it ; that was left for the
tardy equity of his successor's reign. A mistaken
sense of royal dignity, we are told, prevented
Frederick from revoking his decision. But the

maintenance of the royal dignity does not solace defrauded parties or imprisoned judges, nor does it reassure a nation as to the administration of justice. A county court judge would have been a greater blessing to Prussian justice than Frederick's meddlesome interference.

One reads of the hundreds of schools and villages built by the King, of the advances in money and kind made to communities and individuals, of the areas of waste land reclaimed. For all this part of his administration we cannot award praise too high, more especially when we consider the exiguity of his means. Here also he no doubt made mistakes, as who would not who insisted on so minute a supervision as he exercised. But it cannot be doubted that in his agricultural and colonising policy he must have done much good.

In another direction, however, what he did was extremely injurious and derogatory to his subjects. On the advice of Helvetius he inaugurated a new system of customs and excise, with a multitude of Frenchmen to work it. Why he should have insisted on importing a financial executive from a country whose finances, to say the least, were in a most questionable condition, does not appear. Prussians might well resent the tutelage of the French, but they resented more than the reproach to their honesty and capacity the intolerable vexations which they experienced at the hand of these foreigners. The increase in the revenue was small, but as Sir Andrew Mitchell remarked, " The French were beaten once in the field of Rossbach by the

Prussians, but they are every day taking their revenge in the towns." It cannot be doubted that this strange attempt at drastic but alien reform profoundly affected the popularity of the monarch. But it was eminently characteristic of Frederick, for it displayed his cynical indifference to the resentment and the proper pride of his people. To be tickled by a plausible project, and to introduce it at once without for a moment balancing the effect on the feelings of his subjects, was part of his universal scorn. These poor tax-payers were pawns, to be moved at will. It is in this way that great legislators meet with great catastrophes.

Indeed, one feels inclined to ask what were the feelings of Frederick's own Prussians under the oppression of his blessings. In every one of these there was the fatal taint of despotism : paternal if you like, benevolent if you will, but interfering and oppressive. Free initiative was guided, controlled, or suppressed. Everything proceeded from the King. The same despotism which enabled Frederick to drench Europe with blood without a word of consent or authority from a single subject, enabled him to hedge and ditch and drain. To people in other countries these gifts of Frederick would have been unwelcome under such conditions. It does not seem to have been so in Prussia. The severe discipline of the army pervaded the nation.

In one curious instance there were signs of recalcitrancy. Frederick, following his father's example, abolished villeinage and serfdom in his dominions. But it was proved to the King

v. this emancipation, so far from being welcome, would cause every able-bodied man to leave the country. Another local experiment of the kind actually caused the peasants to sell their stocks and emigrate, hiring themselves out as labourers elsewhere. They were afraid, it would seem, to cultivate for themselves without the customary assistance of their lords. Frederick appears to have learned this lesson so thoroughly that he afterwards decreed that all disbanded soldiers should return as serfs to their former lords, and that their wives, widows, and children, though born free, should be bound in the same way. And with the same pen he was writing declamatory letters in a tone of exalted philosophy.

This is all part of the man. He was the last person in the world to deceive himself or be deceived by phrases. No doubt, on the other hand, he thought that he could so deceive other men. That Voltaire and he when interchanging compliments were never each other's dupe is, we think, certain. But Voltaire was a genius from whom Frederick could not bear to be altogether separated, while Frederick was a king whose assiduities flattered Voltaire. This is, however, an exceptional case, for they were exceptional men. But Frederick's phrases were, we think, the outcome of his general contempt for mankind. The phrases might be accepted at their face value, or they might not, what did it matter ? They had a good appearance and might succeed. If they did not succeed, nothing was lost but a little paper and ink. In this system

of florid but transparent professions he had only
one rival, his great contemporary, Catherine II.

But, to return to his domestic administration,
it may be said, except on the intellectual side,
the encouragement of universities, academies,
and the arts, to have been an intelligent development of his father's, tainted perhaps with an
even greater predominance of paternal interference and oppression. Of its kind there was
nothing better to be seen. But his system,
like that of Napoleon, had one mortal defect, it
was personal and suited only to his own powers.
It was a fatal inheritance, for the qualities
necessary to its efficient working could not be
bequeathed with it. Fredericks and Napoleons
are exceptional products. The ordinary man
cannot wield the weapon of the giant ; Excalibur
passed with Arthur. Frederick was succeeded
by a voluptuous mystic who could only emulate
his uncle in perfidy. The Napoleonic Empire
must have crumbled on the accession of the
King of Rome. Neither Frederick nor Napoleon
could have imagined that his administration
could be successfully continued by any beings
much inferior to himself.

There is perhaps this difference in the case of
Frederick. He could not follow the advice of
Dr. Pangloss, as he had no garden to cultivate ;
he had to plough sands. And he may well
have felt that his first duty was to make the
very best of his barren estate and bequeath
it, fertilised as much as possible and developed,
to his successor, who must do the best he could
to administer it by any available means. But

v. it would have been more reasonable, one would
think, to have framed a less centralised system
which would not depend for success on the single
supervision of one exceptional man.

What, in fine, did Frederick bequeath to
Prussia ? Well, he bequeathed his name and
fame as a great conqueror. He became in a
secular sense the Patron Saint of Germany. To
him they looked up, to him they could always
appeal when they contemplated some peculiarly
flagrant act. His immediate successor, warmed
by his example, pocketed British subsidies without an effort to perform the service for which
they were bestowed, and employed them in the
dismemberment of Poland which he had just
sworn to guarantee. In truth, except under
the tepid personalities of Frederick William
the Third and Fourth, we find Frederick in all
Prussian history. Why not ? He had succeeded
to scattered territories and left a compact, homo-
geneous, Prussian kingdom, doubling its population, nearly doubling its territory, and trebling
its revenue. And how had he done this ? By
seizing the guaranteed province of Silesia, and
the convenient provinces of Poland. That, it
was felt henceforth, was obviously the proper
policy : take what you can and how you can
without regard to the means. He bequeathed
territory, power, and comparative prosperity,
but he also bequeathed the terrible heritage of
systematic perfidy. He bequeathed too, what
is not so easily transmissible, an heroic and indomitable tenacity. With a heterogeneous army
of Prussians, deserters and prisoners of war, he

bade defiance to Europe. Whatever storms might
rage round him, although every great military
power was arrayed against him, himself often
racked with disabling illness, he survived, with
poison next his heart, composing and reciting
to Catt with death and destruction on either
side.   How splendid a figure had his cause been
just.

He also bequeathed, it is fair to say, abhorrence
by anticipation of the nameless deeds of infamy
which the Prussians of our day have perpetrated,
though his own hands were by no means clean in
this respect !

Finally, he bequeathed the doctrine that all
was right for Prussia, which had a code of public
morality that did not apply elsewhere.   The
end, the aggrandisement of Prussia, justified
any means.   But no such extenuation was valid
for any other country.   Prussia, to apply a
common proverb, might steal a horse when
another Power might not look over a hedge.
When Joseph II. attempted to annex Bavaria,
not by spoliation but by agreement with the
Elector, the stern Prussian moralist was up in
arms at once to prevent so obvious an iniquity.
And now, when we hear Prussia which starved
Paris denouncing to God and man a blockade
which affects her supply of food, we plainly
discern once more the voice and heritage of
Frederick.

Again, all through the Seven Years' War we
hear the King complaining of the wanton malice
of his enemies who will not leave him alone,
the wail of oppressed innocence, with Silesia in

v.   the background. So now we hear his kingdom, after preparing for a generation a vast conspiracy against the freedom of mankind, protesting against the iniquitous attack of her neighbours, the wolf attempting to bleat. This too is part of the heritage of Frederick.

Again, when Bute withdrew the British subsidy, the pure indignation of Frederick, who shifted his alliances as he shifted his shirt, was little less than sublime.

Systematic perfidy, rapacity, and hypocrisy, these would seem to be the sinister inheritance that Frederick bequeathed to his people. If in the Elysian Fields he should meet with one who charged him with this, he would, we think, shrug his shoulders and admit it, for denial would no longer be useful.

The contemplation of this repulsive and formidable personage has led us far from Catt and Catt's book, and for this we must apologise. We must also repeat that under present circumstances it is scarcely possible to judge Frederick impartially, for we regard him as not remotely the cause of the holocausts of to-day. But we further contend that it is well worth while, for that very reason, to investigate and analyse his sinister character, for if his spirit and example be allowed to permeate the world there is little hope for the future of mankind. Nations will become mere herds of wild beasts, preying on each other when occasion offers, and planning with bestial cunning a favourable opportunity for treacherous attack.

What is greatness ? What is glory ? These

V.

are the questions which arise on a contemplation of Frederick's life. He indeed had his full measure of glory and is usually designated as " Great." But his death was preceded by scores of thousands of others for which he was solely responsible, a gloomy and sorrowful procession of plain folk slaughtered because " ambition, interest, the desire to make people talk about me " had let him seize without provocation or justification a province from a young woman unable at the moment to defend it. These souls surely await him at the gates of the future.

And at this time Howard, in obscurity, was lightening prisons and succouring hopeless prisoners. Jenner was ridding mankind of the loathsome scourge of smallpox. An obscure group of pious enthusiasts were striving to free the world from the curse of slavery. Wesley was bringing a new joy of hope and faith into the dark places of his country. No one called these men great and glorious for their poor achievements ; they were merely preserving and solacing humanity, while the great and glorious were earning laurels by destroying it.

But history, when it is written in just proportion and with regard to the eternal truths which ultimately govern the world, may distribute its honours in a different spirit. Then these humble benefactors may rank higher than the wanton conqueror who, possessing consummate qualities of brain and fortitude, was a curse to his age and to his kind.

VI

BURKE

I [1]

WE meet to-day to fulfil a tardy act of expiation. It is about 114 years since Bristol dismissed Edmund Burke from her service. She has long since repented that dismissal. She repents it to-day, not in sheet and with candle, not in dust and ashes, but in the nobler and more significant form of that effigy which has been unveiled outside. It is well to be a great city. It is well to have your port filled with the commerce of the seas. But it is better to be able to own that you have been in the wrong and to put up a signal monument of acknowledgment. But there is this to be remembered on the other side. Bristol gave Burke the greatest honour that Burke had ever received, for in what we call honours, contemporary honours, the career of Burke was singularly deficient. A subordinate office in the Government, a pension or two, the Rectorship of a Scottish University about represent all that Burke received of official honour in his lifetime.

[1] A Speech delivered at Bristol on the occasion of the unveiling of a statue of Burke on October 30, 1904.

But Bristol returned Burke unsolicited, as York-shire returned Brougham; and when we re-member that the representation of Yorkshire was more to Brougham than the woolsack, we may measure without difficulty what Bristol was to Burke. Brougham, in a moment of unwisdom, left Yorkshire for the woolsack. But Burke would never have left Bristol of his own accord, for he well knew the strength and power that is given to a public man when he stands forward, not on his own merits, but as the representative of a great public constituency. And in those days great popular constituencies were infinitely rarer than they are now, and Bristol was then the second city of the Empire.

Well, then, why did Bristol dismiss Burke? We know the ostensible reasons, because he has given them himself. One was because he voted for the relaxation of the penal laws against Roman Catholics and for the relaxation of the hide-bound commercial policy that separated England and Ireland. But I am inclined to think that the real reasons were more practical and less magnificent; I am inclined to think that the first reason why Bristol rejected Burke was that he was too negligent of his constituents, did not pay visits enough, was too long absent from them, and that through his absence his opponents were always on the spot, were constantly em-ployed in sowing tares among his wheat. And the other reason I shall give is this, that he had no money to fight Bristol in those days, and that in those days a contest for Bristol was enormously expensive; and that while he had no money, his supporters at the first election had become impoverished owing to the unjust and foolish American War and were unable to come to his assistance. Those, at least, are the deductions I arrived at after reading the most interesting and exhaustive book on the connection of Burke with Bristol published by Mr. Weare. I confess I could hardly lay down that book until I had finished it. I have only one fault to find with it. It went to disprove a historic story of Cruger, Burke's colleague, who, when Burke sat down at the end of his great oration to the electors of Bristol, said, " Gentlemen, I say ditto to Mr. Burke." I am happy to think that time-worn anecdote is beyond reach of Mr. Weare or any other seeker after historical truth, because so good a story, when it has been current for a century, is certain to be immortal whether it be true or false.

You must remember that, as I have said, you were then the second city of the Empire and your seat was not an easy seat to win. You now get through the poll in a day. The poll then lasted from three weeks to five. All that time new electors were being admitted under the guise of freemen, and as often as they were admitted they voted. Two thousand of these freemen and more were admitted during the course of the three weeks' poll when Mr. Burke was elected, and the certificates of these freemen, " copies " as they were called, were begged, borrowed, and stolen with the greatest readiness in the world. And when it was impossible to beg, borrow, steal, or manufacture any more of these certificates, one desperate course was at last resorted to, which was this—the widow or the daughter of a freeman of Bristol could confer on her second husband or on her husband the privilege of the franchise by marriage, and so these interesting ladies were dug out and discovered wherever they might exist, even in the recesses of the workhouse, and were taken to church to be married to some enterprising and ambitious politician who wished to exercise for that occasion the privilege of the franchise. It is recorded that these conscientious couples were invariably separated at the church door ; the husband hurried to fulfil the new duties that had been enforced upon him by his union, and when he had done that the ceremony of divorce was gone through with equal expedition. Proceeding to the churchyard, the couple stood, each on one side of a grave, and, in allusion to the solemn words of the marriage service, they said to each other what was true in a sense, " Death does us part." Both parties went their way rejoicing. That was considered sufficient divorce of such a marriage, and I am not sure that the opinion was ill founded.

Well, for one reason or another, Burke and Bristol parted ; but, after all, whether they parted or not, it is a noble episode in both their histories. That was a great period for Bristol. Four years before Burke came to this city, a lonely, starving, desperate Bristol lad of seventeen burned his manuscripts in a London garret, took poison, and made an end of himself—one of the two great poetical prodigies of the eighteenth century, Thomas Chatterton, perhaps the greatest instance on record of lonely, self-relying, self-

VI. sufficing, precocious poetical genius. Well, the short space of twenty-eight years from 1752 to 1780 covers the whole life of Chatterton and the whole connection of Burke with Bristol. But think how those names decorate Bristol for all time ! They are, after all, the two foremost names of their time in their several departments —Chatterton, to whom Wordsworth, who was not prone to external admiration, bent in reverent homage, and Burke. Surely we may say that Bristol was then in every sense the second city of the Empire, if not the first.

Now, let me say one word to you of Burke as apart from Bristol. It is too vast a subject for me to enter upon in any detail or as approaching any but a corner of the subject, for so wide and various are the genius and career of Burke that you might as well attempt to exhaust the character of Shakespeare in a speech of this kind as attempt to deal adequately with the genius of Burke. But what is the key to Burke's character ? There is, on the face of it, some apparent complexity. Burke was an ardent reformer all his life, but ended in a frenzy of Toryism so violent that it transcended the ministerial Toryism of that day. That appears inconsistent on the face of it, but it seems to me to bear no real inconsistency. The secret of Burke's character is this in my judgement—that he loved reform and hated revolution. He loved reform because he hated revolution. He hated revolution because he loved reform. He regarded revolution as the greatest possible enemy of that large, steady, persistent, moderate reform that he loved,

and because by its indiscriminating violence it
provoked indiscriminate reaction. And, on the
other hand, he regarded reform not merely as
good in itself, but as tending by its action to
prevent and anticipate the horrors of revolution.

Now, you know his horror of anything like
parliamentary reform. He would not touch the
smallest rotten borough; he would move no hand
in doing away with the slightest of those abuses
which all Englishmen have long agreed to see in
the parliamentary history of his time. In my
opinion that is no real exception to the rule I
have laid down, because in his judgement the
balances and safeguards of the Constitution hung
so nicely and by so delicate an adjustment that
he had the greatest fear that if you touched
them at all they would all come tumbling down
together; and so when at last he did see the
violence, the massacre, and the bloodshed of the
French Revolution, transcending all that he had
feared in a cataclysm of that kind, he burst out
in a sublime frenzy of passion and denunciation.

I think to this day we feel the thrill of what
he wrote then. If you remember, Sir Philip
Francis wrote to complain that his description
—his famous description—of Marie Antoinette
and the contrast with her fallen fortunes was too
florid for the exact canons of good taste. What
was Burke's reply? He said, " I tell you again "
that it " *did* draw tears from me and wetted my
paper. These tears came again into my eyes
almost as often as I looked at the description—
they may again." And I think that when a
genius such as this puts tears into prose, posterity

VI.

VI.

may still continue to shed them. Where he failed with regard to the French Revolution was in being blinded, by his disgust at what was passing, to any appreciation of the other side of the question. He saw the horrors as we see them and as we read of them. What he did not see was that they were the outcome of a century of misgovernment, and of misrule and debauchery such as had caused a long continuance of terrible calamity. The palaces and the campaigns and the mistresses of the last two Louis had ground down the faces of the poor in France, and had made life not merely intolerable, but almost impossible to them. There is no doubt that those who suffered on the scaffold in the French Revolution were not the real causes of the Revolution, but they expiated a long series of intolerable crimes against the nation itself. And the result is that Burke passes out of history with the appearance of a reactionary to whom the reaction of his day was totally insufficient, while he passed his life as a reformer, daring and grasping enough to frighten the very souls of his admirers.

I would ask you to remember two other points in the career of Burke, two admirable points to my mind. The first was his superiority to everything in the nature of private friendship and party ties when the call of duty summoned him. There was no stronger party man than Burke. He was a Whig of the Whigs. He glorified Whigs. He inspired the Whigs. He was, if I may so express myself, the prose Poet Laureate of Whiggery. And yet, without hesitation or murmur, he forsook all and followed what he believed to be the truth. He loved Charles Fox and all his other political associates. His eulogy on Charles Fox in his speech on his India Bill is perhaps the noblest tribute ever paid in eloquence by one politician to another. But he forsook them all, Charles Fox and all, to follow what he believed to be the truth. The wrench was terrible. It brought tears to the eyes of all who witnessed it. But Burke never flinched and never blenched. He went home to his lonely country home. He went home to see his son die, and all his hopes and future die with that son, and then to die in solitude and sorrow himself.

There is another point to which I would call your attention in regard to Burke which, as I have said, seems to me eminently creditable to him. When, in 1784, he saw himself out of office for life he did not contentedly settle down to the functions of a barren and windy opposition. He seized and grappled with the huge problems of Indian administration, a topic which then in Great Britain was imperfectly understood and imperfectly appreciated, and, with a courage which may almost seem heroic, he brought the great pro-consul of those days, Warren Hastings, to an impeachment, which was indeed unsuccessful, but which will remain always one of the most enduring monuments of his fame. I have no personal application to draw from that lesson, but I think that every earnest man must have felt in opposition the want of sincere and serious and patriotic work which may enable him to fulfil his duty to his country even when he is not able to do it in office, and that the lesson of

VI. Burke is one that has not been lost and will not be lost on our statesmen.

The last point I would call your attention to in the character of Burke is this, for there is much of practical consolation to be derived by the politicians of to-day from a contemplation of the life-work of Burke. Burke, though his reputation is so prodigious and is perhaps still on the rise, did not during his career perceive many of the contemporaneous symptoms of success. His speeches when they were delivered fell on deaf or heedless ears. There are two famous instances. He made a speech on Indian administration which was so wearisome and so ineffective that Dundas, who was the Minister to answer it, turned round to Pitt and they both agreed that it was not worth answering. When it came to be printed it was that famous speech on the Nabob of Arcot's debts, which Pitt and Dundas both read with a stupor of admiration and wondered how they could have so mistaken it when it was delivered. Another was a speech—I do not recollect at this moment which it was—but it was one which Sir Thomas Erskine, surely no mean judge of eloquence, found absolutely intolerable to listen to. I forget whether he fell asleep or went out. When it came to be published he wore out one or two copies in reading and re-reading it in a frenzy of admiration. So we see that Burke's speeches were unsuccessful as speeches but not as treatises. In the next place, he rose to no high office in the State. For a few months he held one subordinate office which used to be held by men of great eminence because it had been

so extremely lucrative, the office of Paymaster-
General. But Burke, as the first-fruits of his
economic reform, practised it, which is rare, upon
his own office. He cut down the emoluments
and held the office with a salary which in those
days was considered comparatively insignificant.

Well, then, his speeches were ineffective. He
held no high office. What is the last point in
which his life as regards temporary success was
a failure ? The last point, in my mind, is this.
In none of the great objects of his earlier days
did this sublime genius see any real success while
he was alive. His success has followed after
death, but he never lived to see it. What were
his great objects ? Roman Catholic emancipation.
He never lived to see Roman Catholic emancipation, though it has come after his death. Conciliation with America. That never came about;
Ministers would not listen to it. Economical
reform, the India Bill, the impeachment of
Hastings, the control of the French Revolution.
Is it not a consolation for us pigmies of this time,
with our halting tongues and feeble weapons, to
reflect that this great master of eloquence and
political genius saw so little of success in his
lifetime ? It only exemplifies the truth of almost
the last exclamation that arose from his lips in
this city of Bristol, those words of which I would
remind you—" What shadows we are and what
shadows we pursue ! " Those memorable and
pathetic words which he uttered, and which sum
up the life of every politician and perhaps of
every man, are not less applicable to the career
of Burke than to many lesser men. It is not yet

a century since he passed away. We are able to realise him as he was, but in life the objects that he pursued must have seemed to him to be shadows, and they have only petrified into monuments since his death. After a long struggle between the forces of Europe and the forces of France, the French Revolution was at length controlled and subdued for a time. Roman Catholic emancipation was carried. His great policy of conciliation both towards India and towards Ireland was largely carried into effect, and his prospects of economical reform have been much more than realised.

And what of him? Is he a shadow? No, he is, in my opinion, the one figure of the time which is likely never to be a shadow. He brightens on the historic canvas—as the other figures fade— by virtue of those speeches, which, as I have said, were read and not listened to. He will be remembered as long as there are readers to read, when those orators on whose lips Parliaments and people hung enthralled are forgotten with the tongues that spoke and the ears that listened to them. Day by day the powerful Ministers whom he could not persuade, the great nobles whom he had to inspire and to prompt, the sublime states-men who, forsooth, could not admit him to their Cabinets, wax dimmer and dimmer, and he looms larger and stronger ; for their fame rests on Bills and speeches — ephemeral Bills and ephemeral speeches—but his is built on a broader and stronger foundation, built on a high political wisdom ; like some noble old castle or abbey which while it stands is a monument and beacon

to man, but which even in its decay furnishes   VI.
a landmark, remarkable to posterity.

II [1]

LORD CURZON has alluded to the part—the very
small part—that I have played in to-day's
ceremony. Small as that part was, it was
distinguished by, I believe, a crucial error on a
critical point. As I have been reminded by my
friend the rector, I spoke of Beaconsfield, not
" Beconsfield." I well knew what I was doing,
and I think my friend Lord Curzon, who so ably
represents this part of the world on the Conservative side of politics, will agree with me in
thinking I was right. I was brought up to believe
the pronunciation was " Beconsfield " until on
the creation of the title of Lady Beaconsfield,
and still more of Lord Beaconsfield, I was impressed by those distinguished persons with a
creed, which will only leave me with my life, that
the proper pronunciation was Beaconsfield, and
not " Beconsfield." I can assure you it would
have required more courage than I possess to
address Lady Beaconsfield as Lady " Beconsfield," or Lord Beaconsfield as Lord "Beconsfield." I do not know how it will be fought out
in this district, that conflict of pronunciation ; I
only give you the historical authority on one side,
and I do not know whether it will countervail
local tradition on the other.

[1] A Speech at a luncheon given by Sir Edward Lawson (Lord
Burnham) at Hall Barn on July 7, 1898, after a memorial to Burke had
been unveiled in the Church of St. Mary and All Saints, Beaconsfield.

VI.
—

I think we have had a most interesting
ceremony to-day. It has been interesting in
part because of its simplicity, not because of
the grandeur or of the celebrity of those who
attended it, though I confess I was very glad
to see a detachment of Irishmen present to
do honour to the greatest of Irishmen. But I
think some of us who stood in the church to-day
must have felt their thought revert for a moment
to the sublime ceremony a few weeks ago in
which all that was mortal of one of the greatest
of Englishmen [1] was enshrined in Westminster
Abbey. There is a great contrast between that
noble and signal procession and our little ceremony of to-day. But the little ceremony of
to-day is not incongruous. It would not have
taken place had Burke been buried among the
great of the earth in Westminster Abbey ; and,
indeed, Charles Fox proposed it, but by his will
Burke absolutely forbade it. It would not have
been out of place had Burke been buried in
Westminster Abbey, but it seems to me to be
more strictly appropriate that a man whose life
was distinguished in the higher walks of thought
—but not by many of the outer rewards of this
world, for he was never a Cabinet Minister—
should be buried, not in Westminster Abbey
among those who have achieved those distinctions,
but in that quiet home of his where he was seen
at his best, and in the church where he worshipped
among the poorer neighbours whom he loved.

There was, of course, more than one Burke.
There was the Burke who has left works which

[1] Mr. Gladstone.

will only perish with the English language; but to-day we are thinking more of the Burke as he was seen at Gregories, the farmer, the unsuccessful farmer—as all gentlemen farmers are—the man who strolled about his place, who showed with pride his pigs and his cattle and his horses and his sheep, the man for whom nothing was too small or too simple in the midst of this home. There have been published in a Scottish paper quite recently extracts from the diary of a Miss Shackleton, belonging to that family of Shackletons to whom Burke had been attached all his life, which, I think, give almost the most perfect picture of Burke at Gregories I have ever read. She describes with the greatest reverence how she came to see Burke, and how he presented her to Crabbe the poet, and how Burke took her into the grounds and made his dog jump into the pond after a stick to show her how well it swam, how he showed her his stables, his granaries, and his domestic animals. And then, how does Burke end the day? There is no light more instructive on this extraordinary man than that he ended by compounding pills for his poorer neighbours who were ill. Talk of cutting blocks with a razor! The man whose eloquence was the delight of his country, whose writings created an impulse over the world such as no political writings perhaps have ever exceeded, sat down to waste his time, as some might have thought it, in compounding rhubarb with other disagreeable adjuncts into remedies for his poorer neighbours. And as he did so he told a story which I think is worthy to be told on such an occasion as this.

VI.
He said, " I am like an Irish peer whom I used to know, who was also fond of dealing out remedies to his neighbours. One day that nobleman met a funeral, and asked a·poorer neighbour whose funeral it was. ' Oh, my lord,' was the reply, ' that's Tady So-and-So, the man whom your lordship cured three days ago.' "

Well, that is the side of Burke we are thinking of to-day. There has been no pompous procession to hallow this centenary, nothing in the nature of ceremony, nothing that would attract the outer eye. But I think we who have been present in the little church to-day have felt that we have taken a moment out of the world and its cares and its businesses for a higher and more sublime process of thought, that we have been enabled to enshrine in our lives a memory in thought and in prayer to-day—a memory which the world will never let die.

VII

WILLIAM WINDHAM [1]

WILLIAM WINDHAM, though by no means flawless, was one of the great gentlemen of our history. Had he lived in the great days of Elizabeth, he would have been one of the heroes of her reign; indeed he almost seemed out of place in the times of George III. As a country gentleman no doubt he was not the equal of his friend and neighbour Coke, whom genius and fortune made the greatest of benefactors to agriculture; but Coke as a politician was narrow and fanatical. And with devotion to rural life and manly sport Windham combined much more. He was a statesman, an orator, a mathematician, a scholar, and the most fascinating talker of his day. He was brilliant in that galaxy which comprised Johnson and Burke, Pitt, Fox, and Sheridan, though their memory will survive his. For, by the irony of events, he is now best remembered as the successful advocate of bull-baiting. So that it is worth while to revive his real character and repute.

As a statesman he was proud of his inde-

[1] An Introduction contributed to the *Windham Papers*, London, 1913.

VII.   pendence, a rare and intrepid quality in political
—   life.   It was indeed reproached against him that
he was so enamoured with this virtue that he
sought out occasions of being on the unpopular
side.   This, indeed, if it were true of him, is not
likely to be a contagious quality.   It could only
exist, so far as parliamentary life is concerned, in
the House of Lords or in close boroughs, and
Windham was at last driven to this latter refuge.
He was more than once invited to join the House
of Lords, but he greatly preferred Higham
Ferrers or St. Mawes.

This aloofness, mainly due to the paramount
influence of Burke, is shown by the fact that
Windham in domestic politics could be found
arrayed with both the great political parties.
He was the enthusiastic advocate of Roman
Catholic emancipation, and the unflinching opponent of parliamentary reform.   He had a foot,
therefore, firmly planted in each of the two
camps.   He was, however, in reality by temperament a Tory.   No disciple of Burke could be
other than a supporter of Catholic emancipation.
But where Windham was left to himself his
attitude to politics was strongly conservative.
He was not, indeed, often left to himself.   For
it is strange to find of a man who piqued himself
on independence that no one was so susceptible
to personal influence.   It is this circumstance
which gives a strange and fickle appearance to
his political career.   He was called by turns a
Foxite, a Pittite, a Grenvillite, and a Greyite,
but was always and supremely a Burkite.   Burke
influenced many minds, but none so much as

Windham's. It was his essential fidelity to the creed of Burke which made him apparently variable. No man, indeed, under an appearance of change was so truly faithful to his principles and himself. But as Burke was charged with inconsistency, so, as a necessary consequence, was Windham. He seemed to wish always to know what Burke thought or would have thought on any subject, and when he knew, to feel no doubt or misgiving. In the great agony of the Whig party, when every Whig felt the anguish of a separation from Fox, Windham hesitated for a moment. He was under the charm of Fox, whose tastes he shared ; but as soon as the voice of the master was heard, clear and imperative, Windham came to his side, without further question or doubt.

When the storm of the French Revolution broke, it swept all minor issues away ; you were either a " Jacobin " or an " anti-Jacobin " ; you either thought that good might come out of the convulsion while deploring its excesses, or you saw in it the root of all evil, you descried its poison in all sorts of unexpected forms and developments, and you proclaimed that the Revolution was the monster to be destroyed at all costs. The reader, indeed, becomes a little weary of the monotonous denunciation of " Jacobinism " and " Jacobins " in the speeches of Windham and the writings of Burke. No consideration of means or proportion weighed with either for one moment. The dragon must be utterly exterminated, even should it devour all the available St. Georges in the process. Then

VII.   and then only should we have done our duty.
——   Then and then only would the world know peace.

This violence of conviction kept Windham
both uncompromising and independent. Though
he joined Pitt he regarded Pitt as little less than
a necessary evil, as a minister who had parliamentary power and so was able to carry on the
war with France, but who fell sadly short of
grace. They were only colleagues in a war, as
to the methods and objects of which they funda-
mentally differed.

To Pitt the war was a disagreeable necessity
forced on him by circumstance, but from which
he hoped that circumstance would relieve him
and his country. To Windham it was a high
and holy crusade to be carried on to extermina-
tion. The object with him was to replace on the
throne of France the sacred race of Bourbon.
Pitt cared less than nothing for the Bourbons;
his object was the preservation of his country,
and of some sort of balance of power. Windham
looked on him, therefore, as a Peter the Hermit
may have looked on a soldier of fortune. When
Pitt retired Windham felt relief; he was no longer
linked to an uncongenial colleague, and was free
to pummel the luckless Addington and Addington's peace. He thundered against this truce
with the evil one, but some years afterwards
acknowledged his error manfully enough to
Addington. For he saw in 1809, what Pitt had
seen in 1801, that a pause was necessary to
recruit the exhausted energies of Great Britain.
When Pitt returned to office, Windham thundered
against Pitt; Pitt was inadequate, all that he

did was insufficient. But Windham had yet to give a further and final proof of independence. For, when Pitt died, he joined Grenville's Cabinet, and when that ministry came to an end in the ensuing year, was fierce against Grenville and on the brink of an individual resignation.

All these changes, though they were nominal and not real, put him in the bad books of both political parties. He obtained the nickname of the " Weather-cock " ; the virulent and pedantic Parr called him the " Apostate." But the independent man in politics must accustom himself to harder knocks than nicknames. Windham was, indeed, the most consistent of politicians. He was neither Whig nor Tory, but always an anti-Jacobin, and always, as has been already said, a Burkite.

His oratory must have been remarkable, though his voice was ineffective. But he had presence and charm. He was not indeed handsome, yet his deportment was manly and dignified. " A tall, thin, meagre, sallow, black-eyed, penetrating, keen-looking figure." We have three volumes of his speeches, but reporting in those days does not seem vivid or exact, and latterly Windham, rushing, as his way was, to join an unpopular cause, quarrelled with the press, and henceforth went unreported. But he revised and published several of his orations from which a fair idea of his powers may be obtained. One of these, that in which as Secretary for War he developed his military proposals in 1806, was pronounced by Fox to be one of the most eloquent ever delivered. Fox's nephew, Lord Holland, who did not like Windham, gave him the highest praise as an orator. In fancy and imagery, in taste and above all in delivery, says Holland, he was far superior to the great god of his idolatry, Mr. Burke. In variety of illustration, in acuteness of logic, he scarcely yielded to Fox. In felicity of language he approached Pitt. In true wit and ingenuity he more than rivalled Sheridan. Testimony of this kind from a man who had heard Windham is worth a ton of criticism from the student who can only read him.

What a reader would say of his recorded efforts is that they are characterised by closely-knit and even philosophical argument, couched in the lofty style of those days. But their distinctive charm was originality, a felicitous agility and unexpectedness of mind, a raciness of expression and sudden bursts of pleasantry which probably drew to him fully as great a House as even Pitt or Fox could command. Of his quaint humour the best sustained example is the speech on the Repeal of the Additional Force Act in May 1806 ; its fun is still brisk and vivid. His most famous flash of fun was on the intention to take Antwerp by a *coup de main*. " Good God, Sir, talk of a *coup de main* with forty thousand men and thirty-three sail of the line ! Gentlemen might as well talk of a *coup de main* in the Court of Chancery." This drollery convulsed the House, and made, it is said, that grave and illustrious judge, Sir William Grant, roll from his seat with laughter. So happy a jest survives superior arguments on forgotten bills. Another sally, still more memorable, was that with which he slew a Reform

Bill, as with a smooth stone from the brook. "No one," he said, "would select the hurricane season in which to begin repairing his house " : a happy metaphor containing sound political truth. There is no doubt that Windham at his death was the finest speaker in Parliament ; the other giants had gone ; Sheridan was extinct, and Canning had not reached his full development.

What is most remarkable is the rapidity with which he reached a high parliamentary position. He delivered his maiden speech in the House of Commons in February 1785, and in 1787 he was considered of sufficient weight to be entrusted with one of the charges, and nominated one of the managers of the impeachment of Warren Hastings. Nine years after his first speech he was admitted to the Cabinet, a far greater and more limited distinction then than now, besides being in virtue of a minor office which had never before been associated with Cabinet rank. He was, moreover, the only Cabinet Minister in the Commons with Pitt and Dundas. So rapid a rise is seldom recorded, and proves a command of Parliament by eloquence and character such as few men of his standing can have achieved.

As a minister there is less to be said. He was always connected with the War Office, a territory which it is perilous for a civilian even in narrative to tread. It must be admitted that the few pebbles which he left on the shore of military history scarcely constitute a memorial cairn. But it must be remembered that during the first seven years of his administration he was not the Secretary of State, but a nominally subordinate

VII. minister, though with all the influence of Cabinet office ; and that he was only Secretary of State for a year. Still it was notorious that, though ardent and vigorous, he was a bad man of business. In his first office he was responsible for the disaster of Quiberon, which represented his personal policy of carrying on the war by supporting the French Royalists on the soil of France. During his second short tenure he countenanced the amazing scheme of despatching an inadequate army for vague purposes of conquest in South America, when we needed every man and every musket in Europe to grapple with Napoleon. This is no captivating record. On the other hand, it stands to his credit that he shortened the term of service in spite of the formidable resistance of George III. To the volunteers he was stoutly opposed, though he had a private but eccentric corps at Felbrigg in which he was the only officer. But few and rare are the British Ministers of War who have earned distinction, for the conditions of their office render success hardly possible. The nation which furnishes superb military material is absorbed in the primary interest of the fleet, and though it passively votes vast sums for its army never gives that active interest and support which strengthens the arm of the minister. The one great exception is Chatham. But Chatham, like Napoleon, wielded the whole strength of the Empire, political, financial, naval and military, and was backed by the confident enthusiasm of his country.

The real reputation of Windham, apart from his oratory, lay in the charm of his conversation.

In that vanished realm he was a prince. Testimony on the point is unanimous. It is safe to say that no one has recorded a meeting with Windham who is not a witness to his fascination. Miss Burney gives a lively account of her talks with him during the Hastings trial which enables us to realise in a measure how it was that he won, if not all hearts, at least sympathetic admiration. His expression was various and vivid. He was earnest, playful, and eloquent. He had the faculty, which is perhaps the most attractive of all, of appearing to give his very best to the person with whom he was conversing. Talk may be recorded, but its spell cannot. And so, though we rejoice in Miss Burney's record, we feel that we must rely on tradition, which, in so controversial a matter, must be held, when unanimous, to be an authority beyond dispute. The supreme judgement, from which there is no appeal, is that of Johnson. Windham had been elected to the famous Club when he was a country gentleman of twenty-eight, a sufficient tribute to his precocious repute. But in 1784, when the great man was near his end, Windham went far out of his way to spend a day and a half with him at Ashbourne. " Such conversation," writes the dying sage, " I shall not have again till I come back to the regions of literature ; and there Windham is *inter stellas Luna minores.*" Such a testimony from such a man is almost unique, but it is in truth confirmed by every witness.

Conversational fascination is apt to be a snare, and we are bound to hazard an opinion that

VII. Windham was a flirt. And yet there was no character that he condemned so strongly. Before going up in a balloon he addressed a testamentary letter to Cholmondeley, his closest friend, remonstrating strongly against Cholmondeley's conduct towards a certain Miss Cecilia Forrest. Cholmondeley, he declared, had ruined the girl's life, by inspiring her with a fatal affection of which he was unworthy. Thirteen years afterwards, with singular secrecy, Windham married the lady himself. He was then forty-eight and she past forty. And he completed this unusual transaction by making Cholmondeley one of his reversionary heirs. This is Windham all over. And we also learn that he had fallen, perhaps unconsciously, into the same error with which he had reproached his friend. He had engaged the affections of a daughter of Sir Philip Francis, and a lady endeavouring to console the unhappy girl told her that Windham had long hesitated between Miss Forrest and a devoted widow. In this one letter, therefore, we are confronted with three ladies whose hearts were captured by Windham. He had, moreover, come under the magic charm of Mrs. Crewe. To Mrs. Crewe, and Mrs. Crewe alone, he confided the secret of his marriage, and he records his agitation at meeting her immediately after the event. But perhaps the most authentic basis for conviction as regards Windham's attraction for the other sex is Lady Minto's remark on his resignation in 1801 : " I suppose he will return to his old line of gallantry." There let us leave the matter. It is worthy of observation as an essential part of a whimsical character. We may

be sure that Windham's flirtations were unconscious, honourable, and innocent.

Unhappily, he was fated to be something of a
suicide, for he dealt an almost mortal blow to his
own reputation. For we cannot doubt that it
would have stood much higher but for his Diary.
And yet he himself set store by it, as if, one would
think, he regarded it as a sure base for his future
fame. He left the fourteen quarto volumes of
which it was composed as an heirloom to pass
with the entailed estates, and yet any judicious
friend would have put it without hesitation
behind the fire. Extracts of this strange record
were published by Mrs. Baring in 1866, after the
estates and entail had all disappeared in the hands
of a hapless and irresponsible spendthrift. As
so much has been afforded, it is regrettable that
more should not be given. Lord Holland and
Charles Greville intimate that parts could not be
made public. But it seems clear that we have
not all the decorous portions of the fourteen
quarto volumes, and these we should possess to
complete a veracious and candid, though damaging, autobiography.

In the Diary, which is almost valueless as a
record of historical fact from the extreme vague-
ness of date and expression, we have an exact,
though painful, picture of Windham's character,
and an explanation of why it was that he did not
achieve more in public life. It is full of vacillation on the smallest points of conduct, full of
morbid self-reproach on every subject, and in a
minor degree disfigured by a lavish use of the
distressing substantive " feel," almost if not

VII.   quite peculiar to himself. Windham, indeed,
        though in public life he held firmly to his main
        convictions, in private life and in smaller matters
        was singularly variable. On the all-important
        question of marriage, as we have seen, he seems
        to have hesitated long. That may have been
        wise, but he records endless agitations about a
        ride, a walk, or a speech. Conscientious diaries
        are apt to make men morbid, and this one is
        certainly an instance in point. He seemed to
        worry himself with his pen. One passage, indeed,
        redeems the whole book : it is the pathetic
        description of his last interview with Dr. Johnson.
        That is classic. But it is counter-balanced by a
        denunciation of a literary " gem of purest ray
        serene," the delightful *Vicar of Wakefield.* We
        may surmise that this outburst may have been
        elicited by Windham's having heard it excessively
        praised, which would certainly drive him into
        extravagant reaction. Countless are the caprices
        of these strange journals. It had been better for
        his fame had this heirloom disappeared with the
        others.

            Still, with all deductions, he remains a noble
        figure. The influence of Johnson and Burke,
        grafted on to the stock of a fine and cultivated
        nature, could not but produce goodly fruit. His
        prime quality was independence, at once the
        choicest and the least serviceable of all qualities
        in political life. He was, on the other hand,
        excessive, like his great master, Burke : excessive
        in enthusiasm, excessive in resentment. To him,
        for example, when a manager of the great im-
        peachment, Warren Hastings was the vilest of

criminals.   But to him also, though their relations
were not always easy, Burke was among the gods.
There was, in truth, a want of balance in this
rare character which marred its great qualities.
It was this, from a fanciful fear of deterioration
in the British character, that made him preach
bull-baiting.   It was this which made him deem
it necessary, in the midst of the national grief for
Pitt, to stand up and oppose the funeral honours
proposed — a course which brought him many
enemies and which seemed in execrable taste.
But the mere fact of isolation was the same
temptation to him that the company of an overwhelming majority is to meaner minds.   His
argument, weak enough at best, for " 'tis not in
mortals to command success," was that Pitt's
policy had not triumphed, and that distinctions
denied to Burke should not be given to failure.
Most men who felt the same would at that
tragic moment have held their peace.   But
such a decent compliance seemed cowardice
to Windham ; so he wound his melancholy
horn.

This same irritable conscience made him an
uncomfortable colleague, and it is noteworthy to
observe how strenuously the idea of relegating him
to the House of Lords was pressed by Grenville, as
it had occurred to Pitt.   It was strange, as Windham himself remarked, that Grenville should be
so anxious to move the best speaker that his
ministry possessed in the House of Commons
out of that chamber into the House of Lords.
Promotion for another Grenville was no doubt
the urgent cause, but, as that could be managed,

VII.
  —

and was managed in other ways, there were probably reasons connected with Windham himself. Independence in a public man is, we think, a quality as splendid as it is rare. But it is apt to produce and develop acute angles. Now a colleague with angles is a superfluous discomfort. And independence in a great orator on the Treasury bench is a rocket of which one cannot predict the course.

His independence, then, admirable in itself, was a conspicuous bar to his success in politics. He was not, indeed, formed by nature for a politician in a country where party rules the roast. We will go a step farther, and hazard the opinion that his heart was never really in politics at all. He loved mathematics, he loved the classics, he loved reading, he loved country life ; but for parliament he had no natural propensity. From his first contact with politics in Ireland he instinctively shrank. His self-conscious, self-tormenting nature was indeed wholly unsuited for public life. But he loved oratory. From the moment when he found that he wielded that rare power over his fellow-men he delighted in exercising it. And he was imbued with one burning enthusiasm, the crusade against Jacobinism. He conceived himself to be the bearer of the sacred torch handed to him by Burke. This was his single purpose ; oratory and the French Revolution kept him in political life. Fox said cynically that Windham owed his fame to having been much frightened. But those who were apprehensive in that dark period were wiser than those children of light who, like

Fox, were content to watch the Revolution with blind and heedless favour.

Such, then, was Windham. A noble gentleman in the highest sense of the word, full of light, intellect, and dignity, loved and lamented. His best qualities, no doubt, as is often the case, he carried almost to excess ; for his cherished independence led to a morbid craving for isolation. But to the charge of vacillation in public affairs he was not obnoxious ; he was always true to his faith. He was, indeed, vitally influenced by two men. But he chose his masters well, Johnson and Burke ; the one gave him his religious, the other his political creed. In life he was brilliant and successful. In oratory, in parliament, in society, he was almost supreme. But he can scarcely be said to survive. He left no stamp, no school, no work. To those, however, who care to disinter his memory he displays character and qualities of excellence, rare at all times, rarest in these.

VIII

THE COMING OF BONAPARTE [1]

VIII. M. VANDAL has done me the signal honour of inviting me to write a few words, inadequate and superfluous though they be, to the English, or rather Scottish edition of his admirable book, *L'Avènement de Bonaparte*. It is a high distinction, for, so far as my limited range enables me to judge, he is the first of living historians. With great exactitude of detail he unites the large grasp, the power of spacious narrative, the gift of vivid portraiture, the sympathetic imagination which groups and illumines facts, the magnetic touch which gives light and life to every page ; in fine, the inborn qualities which distinguish the great historian from the arid chroniclers of dates and details.

His noblest book, to my mind, is the history of the contest between Napoleon and Alexander of Russia, because it represents a gigantic drama on a gigantic stage ; embodying as it does the secular antagonism between Europe and Asia ; the conflict of duplicity between the Corsican and

[1] This chapter appeared in English in the *Fortnightly Review*, July 1912, and in French as a preface to the edition of Vandal's *L'Avènement de Bonaparte* in the Collection Nelson.

the Greek of the Lower Empire, not unequally matched; the silent marshalling of races, from Spain to Siberia, for a superhuman struggle inspired by vast ambitions, nothing less than the planned partition of the world; Constantinople and the " Cat's Tongue " of the Dardanelles animating all. The fates seem almost visible, like the witches in *Macbeth*, beckoning to doom. Here is an ample stage for genius which would dwarf a lesser writer. The present book is not less consummate, but the scene is more limited, though full of interest. Here we see the first accession to power of Napoleon, and his first appearance as a ruler. New and wider horizons open before him, soon to be boundless. As the narrative proceeds we see the meagre conqueror disappearing and replaced by something larger. There is something looming, one can scarcely say what, which obliterates the craving soldier Bonaparte ; it is Napoleon in the egg.

The emerging of Napoleon from his uniform, and his first contact with civil government, are much the most interesting period of his career after his first triumphs. His success in administration must have seemed not more probable than if Joubert had been the Caesar, as he was intended to be ; not less doubtful than if Moreau or Masséna had been placed in such a position. But from the first, in the face of obstacles of all kinds, he is triumphant, and threads his way, through snares and ambushes and rancours, with unerring sagacity.

The difficulties were immense. No one perhaps can appreciate their magnitude without

VIII.

reading this book. The vague, popular apprehension of Napoleon's career is one of gigantic triumph and catastrophe. For a long period the success is so complete that it makes his achievements seem easy. The 18th of Brumaire seems to fit into this conception and to be a facile success. Bonaparte was a hero, the French Government was decrepit, the French people were eager for a change, and there you have the whole affair. M. Vandal's narrative shows how far this is from the truth. The premises are sound, but it was difficult to arrive at the conclusion. It might, indeed, have been easily missed.

There were no doubt in France a wretched Government, administrative and financial chaos, and a discontented people. Every one saw, except some of the Directors themselves, that this state of things could not last, and that revolutionary France was about to see another added to its long list of experiments in government. In May 1799 a new Director was elected in the person of Sieyès, a man of infinite shrewdness and skilled intellect, but timid and unsympathetic; who hated the aristocracy and despised the people; whose irksome fate it was to work unconsciously, like a bee, for others, but who promptly grasped the situation. He saw that a heroic figure was required; and, when the hero was found, indisposed as a soldier would probably be to the work of civil administration, proposed to administer for him. He would pull the wires of this noble puppet, and all would be for the best. Some even had further and wilder views. The puppet was in

good time to be displaced, and make way for a   VIII.
constitutional and Protestant monarchy under
a German Prince.

Had General Bonaparte been in Europe, the
choice must inevitably have fallen upon him.
But he was shut up in Egypt, without means of
escape, and with British fleets patrolling the
Mediterranean.   So Joubert, a noble and distinguished figure, was selected, and accepted the
nomination.   He was to return to France in
the glow of a great victory.   The intended battle
was fought.   He was to conquer Souvoroff, but
Souvoroff conquered him ;   and Joubert was
killed, some say by a Jacobin bullet.

So a new candidate had to be found.   Moreau
was thought of ; Macdonald was sounded and refused.   But at this moment the spell of disaster
ends.   Couriers bring the news of the victory
of Zurich.   " The Russian defends himself like a
mastiff," writes Masséna, " but I have him safe."
Souvoroff is indeed shattered, and retreats.
While the joy and relief are at their height, fresh
messengers arrive with tidings of Bonaparte,
announcing great victories in Egypt.   Following
fast on these comes the supreme apparition :
Bonaparte is actually in France.   His arrival
savours of the marvellous.   He has traversed
and escaped hostile fleets almost by a miracle,
revisiting his birthplace for the last time, and he
has arrived safe.   The Directory, with a grimace,
grudgingly announces the news.   The nation cares
little for the grimace so long as the news be
true.   There is unbounded enthusiasm ; legislation cannot proceed ; " suffocated with emotion,"

VIII. the legislators adjourn. In the streets, in the theatres, in the taverns, the people go mad with joy. So it is in the provinces. The cities through which the General passes are illuminated, his inn is beleaguered with delirious crowds, the peasants escort his postchaise with torches; and so the long, nervous strain ends in an ebullition of passionate ecstasy. The information reaches the conference where Sieyès is sounding Moreau. The conversation breaks off, for " There is the man you want," says Moreau, who had, indeed, little stomach for the enterprise; " he will do your business much better than I."

Why is there this remarkable outburst ? The answer is simple enough. It is not that the nation craves for fresh glory at the hands of the conqueror. What it demands is order at home, and peace abroad.

Order in the first place. For ten years they have been living on high aspirations varied by massacre, believing that legislation can effect everything, even transform human nature; and that taxation can be so adjusted by getting rid of the wealthy as to enrich and benefit the poor—worshipping, in fact, the silly gods that blight a nation. In five years 3400 laws had been enacted, enough to make the mouths of modern legislators water, enough to convert earth into heaven, were earth convertible by such means. All that had been produced was anarchy, poverty, and discontent. Nor had the finance of the system been more successful. The graduated tax on property had been a hopeless failure, and the Treasury was empty. The aspect of the provinces was little better. In Lyons, the second city of France, the Revolution had ravaged like an earthquake, and destroyed whole quarters of the town. In Marseilles, the third, we are told there seemed nothing surviving but hatreds. Brigandage reigned in some departments, civil war in others. It is not wonderful, then, that peace is the passion of the citizens, not only for itself, but because they feel that without peace the restoration of order is impossible. Other generals may gain victories, but the population has an ingrained faith that only Bonaparte can secure peace. He alone is victorious enough to terminate a war. And the only way to end the Revolution is to end the war.

At last the Man of Promise arrives obscurely in Paris. He appears before the Directory as it were incognito, dressed in the costume of a civilian, in a dark green greatcoat, with a Turkish scimitar. In this grotesque attire he seems sunburnt, emaciated, dried up ; only in his eyes is there life. He has returned with the determination to put an end to the Directory. His first idea is to become a Director himself, and gently rid himself of his colleagues. But a Director must be forty, and he is only thirty. Moreover, the simplest way seems the best : to get rid of the Directors as soon as possible and substitute himself. But he must be assisted by the victims themselves, who must be made to devote themselves unconsciously to their own immolation. For public opinion seems hostile to violent change.

He is disgusted with the fatuity of Barras, and turns to Sieyès. Sieyès is ready to co-operate,

VIII. and takes riding lessons so as to be on a more equal footing with Bonaparte on occasions of ceremony. Sieyès brings with him another Director. Two remain : Moulins, who does not count, and Gohier, who is reputed to be in love with Josephine. No time is to be lost. In three weeks from Bonaparte's arrival the blow is to be struck. Few are in the secret ; but the air is full of rumours, and action to be successful must be prompt.

The capital idea, as we have seen, was to employ the existing authorities in the task of their own demolition. The body with the absurd name of Council of the Ancients was at the disposal of the conspiracy, and had the power of ordering the removal of the Legislature from Paris to some calmer atmosphere. This was to be done under the not unfounded plea of a Jacobin conspiracy. The place chosen was St. Cloud. There the Council of Five Hundred, the popular body, was to be cowed or seduced into the acceptance of a new Constitution. How this was to be done was left in the vague. So was the Constitution. Sieyès was the author of the plan of campaign ; but even his brain, fertile in such schemes as it was, was not ready with a Constitution for the moment. It is so difficult to bind and restrain your hero, when you get him, by institutions, or saving clauses, or gilded chains ; so delicate to bleed him unobtrusively to extinction. All that was fixed was that there were to be three Consuls. To this Bonaparte listens in silence.

Moreau was gained over to the project. He

hoped that, if successful, Bonaparte would become a civilian, and leave the field of battle to him, exactly the reverse of the aspirations of Sieyès. Macdonald, Beurnonville, and Serurier offered themselves. The Egyptian companions of the young General, Leclerc and Murat, both his brothers - in - law actual or future, were eager and active. Bernadotte remained ambiguous, anxious as ever to play his own game. The army was, where not enthusiastic, not unfriendly. There remained a stiff and incalculable band, called the Guard of the Directory and of the Councils, rather police than soldiers, with a strong tinge of ruffianism, and devoted by interest to the existing order of things. What they might do was a subject of some anxiety.

Money, too, had to be found, and was found. Where no one knows. Bonaparte had returned empty from Egypt. A contractor named Collot seems to have found some ; perhaps other contractors had, under menace or persuasion, to yield part of their ill-gotten gains.

At last the memorable days arrived. The eve is spent by the General in giving the last touches. Sebastiani, Colonel of the 9th Dragoons, with the clannish spirit of a Corsican, is an enthusiastic adherent. His regiment is to play an important part. A magnificent horse, a necessary accessory of such occasions, even in later days, but almost too fiery for the purpose, is borrowed, strangely enough, from an Admiral. The night before the adventure the General dines with the cautious Cambacérès ; the guests are dull and preoccupied. Josephine sends a note to the amorous Director Gohier to bid him to breakfast. Bonaparte, at two o'clock in the morning, summons Moreau and Macdonald to come to him at dawn ; and invites himself to dinner with Barras for that evening, to throw that important Director off his guard.

In ninety burning pages M. Vandal describes the two dramatic days of the 18th and the 19th of Brumaire, the 8th and 9th of November. Here, where the complication is great, our historian is supreme. He marshals the actors, keeps the groups separate, and elucidates the facts with a master hand. No reader can begin this narrative and willingly lay it down. We breathe the air, we hear the tumult, we are led through the confusion by a sure guide. We are in the scene, though not of it.

Between five and six in the morning a picked selection of the Ancients are roused from their beds to attend an extraordinary session at seven. As the shivering members thread the dark streets, these are seen to be empty, though troops presently are on foot, marching for a purpose of which they are absolutely ignorant. The necessary decree is promptly agreed to. Briefly, the Councils are to meet next day at St. Cloud, and Bonaparte is entrusted with the execution of the mandate. Meanwhile, all the leading officers of the army are thronging to his house, outside which a squadron of dragoons forbids any one to leave. But Gohier has become suspicious, and has refused Josephine's invitation. Suddenly the door opens, and Bonaparte appears. Followed by a swelling crowd of officers, joined by Sieyès,

who has profited by his equestrian lessons, and
who is attended by two aides-de-camp, he rides
triumphantly to the Tuileries, where he finds
a joyfully expectant crowd. There he takes
the oath, somewhat incoherently, before the
Ancients, and that Council breaks up.

Then he enters the garden and faces his troops.
Here he is in his own atmosphere, and is coherent
enough. His wrath falls on a shuddering emissary
of Barras, come to watch events. " What have
you done with that France," he asks imperiously,
" which I left so brilliant ? I left you peace, and
I find war. I left you victories, I find defeats.
I left you millions from Italy, I find misery and
laws of spoliation. What have you done with
a hundred thousand Frenchmen whom I knew,
the companions of my glory ? They are dead."
And after this poignant exordium he proceeds,
in words scarcely less fervid, to proclaim that
a change is necessary and imminent. This short
speech produced a profound impression at the
time, and has survived to brand the Directory
with the opprobrium of history. It is, in fact,
the epitaph of that corrupt and disastrous
Government.

Meanwhile the work proceeds. The Five
Hundred assemble and are summarily relegated
by Lucien Bonaparte to St. Cloud. Barras
rolls away in a postchaise into space, with an
escort of dragoons, and a comfortable promise of
money. Gohier and Moulins, obstinate and inert,
are finally locked up. There is no symptom of
resistance. " We have never seen a more tran-
quil revolution," say the newspapers, which

VIII. had recorded so many in the last ten years. The
       Jacobins, no doubt, are seething. But their
       formidable name has lost its terrors. Sieyès
       proposes to arrest their chiefs, which Bonaparte
       summarily refuses. Bernadotte, however, joins
       them, and proposes that they shall appoint him
       as co-generalissimo with Bonaparte. Even this
       unselfish proposal fails to attract.

       The second day was far more critical, for
       everything had been left to the inspiration of
       the moment, and the result was nearly disastrous.
       Paris hurried to St. Cloud as to a great steeple-
       chase ; and, indeed, there were circumstances in
       that day not wholly unworthy of that sport. In
       the midst is Bonaparte, apparently cool and
       confident, escorted by dragoons, but followed
       by uneasy subordinates who feel that they are
       playing for their lives.

       When he arrives at St. Cloud he retires to a
       room, where, in a fever of impatience and agita-
       tion, he receives bulletins from the legislative
       field of battle, while Sieyès shivers by the fire.
       In the anteroom people murmur to each other in
       obvious anxiety. Some disappear. There are,
       indeed, vacillations and apprehensions. Sinister
       rumours begin to circulate. Emissaries, it is said,
       have been sent by the Jacobins in the galleries
       to Paris, in order to rouse the faubourgs to
       insurrection. At any moment there may be
       a Jacobin inundation, another 6th of October.
       Deputies are seen anxiously watching for some-
       thing or somebody. Sinister women are beginning
       to arrive, the knitters of the Revolution. Jourdan
       and Augereau, birds of ill-omen, are visible.

THE COMING OF BONAPARTE 171

The Five Hundred are being sworn in : a process which takes the first four hours of the afternoon. But Bonaparte feels that he cannot wait, he cannot leave these vague and mobile Assemblies any longer without personal control. There is danger in the air. So at half-past three, followed by his aides-de-camp, he marches straight to the Ancients, who hurry into their hall when the General is announced. His intention was to rally his friends and secure the Council. But his appearance is a failure. Before a civic assembly, in which are rude opponents, his inexperienced oratorical nerve not unnaturally fails. He hesitates and is lost. Disjointed fragments are heard, repetitions, incoherent accusations. The Ancients cease to listen, but in the tumult he continues speaking. At last he retires. It is almost a catastrophe.

But he calmly bids Bourrienne send an express to Josephine to say that all is going well, and then proceeds straight to the Five Hundred. The question may well be asked—M. Vandal asks it— why after one such failure did he hurry to a hostile assembly for a sure repetition of his oratorical disaster ? The answer would seem to be that his military instinct made him throw himself on the point of danger. It is clear, however, that he knew little what to do or say. Perhaps he only wished to excite the violence which should justify military intervention. And on this occasion he took a handful of grenadiers with him. He enters amid a throng of deputies and spectators, howling, " Down with the Dictator ; down with the tyrant." A free fight

VIII.

ensues; he is hustled and cursed. Stout Jacobins seize the little fellow and shake him like a rat. This violence unnerves him; he has to be rescued by friendly force from rough hands. There are probably no daggers, as was afterwards alleged, for then there would have been an end of him. The soldiers outside, hearing the tumult, burst into the Chamber, frantic at the outrage to their General. The contest around him becomes fast and furious. A huge deputy strikes him. At last he is extricated by his grenadiers, pale, fainting, almost suffocated; the gigantic legislator pummels the soldiers in the attempt to buffet the General himself. He has to retire amid general shouts of " Outlaw him, outlaw him." He has not been able to utter a word.

The situation seems compromised, if not lost. Pacific means have failed. The hero has failed to overawe. A providential man is required, and is found in Lucien. It is the supreme day of Lucien's life, and he had himself painted by Gerard at full length as he appeared on this critical occasion. His colleagues insist on proscribing his brother; they attempt to storm his presidential tribune. Lucien resists, insists on haranguing them to gain time; first he claims his right as President, then as Deputy; it matters little, no one listens to him or could hear him in the tumult.

Meanwhile Napoleon soon recovers; his physical faintness disappears in a burst of passion. He mounts his horse, but presents a ghastly figure. The skin of his face has become violently irritated, and he had scratched it to blood. His

ensanguined countenance, however, was an assistance and a stimulant.   For the rumour spread
at once that violence, even assassination, had
been attempted.   His wounded appearance corro-
borates the statement ; his furious words lash
his soldiery to rage.   But the Guards of the
Assembly remain dumb and ambiguous, even
hostile.   Sieyès, watching from a window, thinks
that he perceives a movement among them to
surround and seize him.   The tumult of the
Five Hundred is audible outside.   Some of the
members appear at the windows with frenzied
gestures, appealing to their Guards.   The short
November day is drawing to a close, and yet there
is no end.   There is wavering around the General.
The face of Talleyrand, pale but undismayed,
is visible, watching with anxiety the outcome
of this revolution—as it had to watch so many.
Inside, Lucien is still vainly struggling with his
colleagues.

   At last he sends in whispers a message
to his brother that the Assembly must be
broken up in ten minutes, or he can answer for
nothing.   Bonaparte sees that this is the critical
moment, and that he must make use of the
presidential authority by capturing the President.
Grenadiers enter and remove Lucien ; the arrest
of the President involves the dispersal of the
Council.   Outside he joins the General, and,
with the authority of President of the Five
Hundred, improvises in a passionate speech the
famous legend of the poniards with which an
attempt had been made to murder his brother.
The brother with bleeding face is by his side.

VIII. The time for action has come. Murat enters the
Orangery where the Five Hundred are assembled,
with drums beating and his soldiers. " Kick
these people out of doors," is his brief order,
quickly accomplished. " The petticoat crowd "
of futile senators in imitation togas is hustled
out to the relentless beating of the drums. The
soldiers lift the more obstinate from their seats
and carry them out like naughty children. These
lamentable and discredited tribunes are helpless
and become ridiculous. They scuffle out amid
the scoffs and scorn of the crowd. Scattered,
outraged, humiliated, they fly wildly in different
directions, traceable by the rags of their robes on
the bushes and the trees, and so are lost in the
mist of the evening.

This stormful drama, as set forth by M. Vandal,
in phrases which give the idea of actual presence,
is hot with the fumes, the emotions, the vicissitudes of that eventful day. But it leaves the
impression of a victory akin to a defeat. A cool
Jacobin or a concealed dagger might easily have
changed the history of France ; and, at the last,
it was only brute force that secured success.

The conquerors camped on the field of battle.
Through the long hours of the night they planned
and discussed. It was determined that the
violent dispersal of the Five Hundred scarcely
offered a sufficient constitutional basis for future
proceedings, and that some form of legality was
required. So ushers were sent forth to collect
what scattered members might be found. By
active and vigilant search in the wineshops and
in the inns, in private houses and in carriages

flying to Paris, a certain number of the fugitives
was collected ; Paris, with a laugh, said thirty,
calling them in mockery the Council of Thirty ;
M. Vandal thinks not far short of a hundred.
In any case, they passed the requisite formulas,
as well as votes of thanks to the generals who had
ejected them. The Ancients, too, collected. At
two o'clock in the morning, before the Rump of
the two assemblies, the provisional Consuls Bonaparte, Sieyès, and Ducos took the oaths. And
then all, Consuls, Deputies, troops, and spectators,
hurried back to Paris through the dark November
morning, all but the initiated believing that
they had saved the Republic. The troops, too,
tramped back to the familiar, yet no longer
appropriate, " Ça ira."

Next morning at ten o'clock the General took
possession. Paris is calm and even satisfied, a
rare condition in that turbulent city at moments
of crisis. But the tranquillity was easy to explain.
It was felt that insecurity, the curse of revolutionary agitations, had disappeared ; there was
now some guarantee for the future ; men could
buy and sell and work in peace. Still, the work
of reorganisation required infinite tact and
patience, and here Bonaparte reveals himself
in a new character. He is eminently tactful
and imperturbable. He has to keep vigilant
watch in three directions where there is danger :
he has to watch the Royalists, the Jacobins,
and the army, which is Republican. He has to
balance, to conciliate, to inspire confidence on
the one hand, without exciting jealousy and
distrust on the other.

VIII.

The first difficulty, as always, is money ; the Treasury is empty, and everything is in arrear. At the War Office things are little better. The outgoing Minister is questioned. " You pay the army, give us the pay-sheets." " We don't pay the army." " Well, then, you feed the army ; tell us what you pay for food." " We don't feed the army." " Well, at least you clothe the army ; what is the cost of that ? " " We don't clothe the army." All is chaos.

Sieyès, who had dreamed that Bonaparte would leave civil administration to him, is quickly undeceived. The young General — for he is only thirty years old, how incredible that seems ! — haggard and emaciated, toils feverishly for eighteen hours a day, sees every one of every party, works to bring order out of confusion. Of this prodigious operation no epitome is possible ; the reader must have the pleasure of studying it in the vivid and entrancing pages of the historian.

Then there is the Constitution, no light task. Sieyès now has one ready, ingeniously contrived so as to reduce Bonaparte to a pompous nullity. It is not safe as yet to dispense with Sieyès, so a compromise has to be found between the plan of the ex-Director, who wants Bonaparte to be a " pig for fattening," and that of Bonaparte who means to be everything. The work is at high pressure, the committee breaks down. He himself survives, indefatigable, vigorous, feverish with anxiety to get the Constitution settled. Sometimes he has moments of fierce impatience. He gnaws his nails, stamps his feet, yields to an irrepressible outburst. But he soon recovers himself. At last it is settled that there are to be three Consuls, two with a deliberative voice, but that the decision of the First Consul is to be final. This, of course, settles the question of who is to be master. Sieyès is consoled by the presidential chair of the new Senate, and by a rich estate. He also by a touch of Corsican finesse is made to nominate the three Consuls, who should have been elected. The process is comically unscrupulous, in Bonaparte's latest style. On this occasion the illegality signifies little. The man or woman in the street, as so often happens, says the last word on the Constitution. It is being proclaimed in the streets. " I have not heard a word," says one. " I have not lost a word," says the other. " What is in the Constitution, then ? " asks the first. " There is Bonaparte," replies the second. A Constitution, said the First Consul later, should be short and obscure ; this one was apparently short and clear.

The living and admirable part of the Constitution, besides the First Consul himself, is the Council of State, the ideal helpmate of the ideal Dictator. It is composed of men of all parties. " I use those who have the will and capacity to work with me," says the First Consul. The Council is his laboratory, his palace of truth ; there he tests, experiments, consults, discusses vigilantly and precisely all projects, and produces his own for criticism. Such a department, severely and conscientiously worked, is a priceless critic and assistant for a strong ruler. Moreover, as auditors of this body, he trains the choicest

VIII.   young men for the service of the State. Fortunate
——   is the country which is privileged to possess such
an institution, worked and developed as it was by
Napoleon.

His main determination is to restore order,
to put an end to violence, uncertainty, and civil
war. He puts out feelers of conciliation in every
direction. He has long talks with the Royalists ;
he buries the Pope with dignity, and Turenne with
splendour ; he allows priests, and opens the
churches ; he shuts his eyes, or gives open toleration, when emigrants return ; " Nous autres
nobles," once escapes his lips. But all this
has to be done with extreme caution before the
closing but suspicious eyes of the Revolution.

His eyes are beginning to pierce clearly into
the future. He must have a church to conciliate
France, even though it displease a loud minority.
France in its depths, M. Vandal tells us, was still
Catholic, and the movement towards the recognition of Christian faith proceeds of its own accord.
Décadi gives place unofficially to Sunday. In
churches where there are no priests, peasants
assemble spontaneously for common prayer,
" pour faire le geste religieux." France is nearly
ripe for the Concordat. And, as the churches
open, the emigrants creep back. They wander
sadly about trying to localise the Paris they
remember. " Vous souvenez-vous ? C'était là.
C'était ici," are murmured everywhere. All this,
with a wealth of fascinating detail, gleaned from
an entire literature, M. Vandal sets before us.

In the centre of all there is the Ruler, watchful,
prudent, far-seeing. He is seldom seen, except

once every ten days, when he holds an inspection
of troops in the Carrousel. His only relaxations
are the austere sittings of the Institute, and the
week-end parties for the Décadi holiday at
Malmaison, where he plays prisoners' base like a
boy. When seen he is scandalously ill-dressed;
Royalists say ugly; all say short, save when he
raises his head and glances with his eye, then
he seems suddenly to tower up. He is always
learning and absorbing. All France seems to
flow into that self-contained vessel. What is
fermenting inside ?

Then he sees that the success of his work
depends too much on his own life—a life so
precarious and exposed. Thus he is led to
dynastic ideas, perhaps not unwillingly, for " il
avait l'imagination républicaine, et l'instinct
monarchique," shrewdly remarks our author.
He has no child, so he must adopt an heir. There
are his brothers. Joseph and Lucien he discards;
one is too easy, the other too personal and
ambitious. At last his choice rests on Louis !
Louis at this time is sweet-tempered, affectionate,
docile. But how the First Consul could dream
that this gentle being could ever be the Aeolus
to control the winds and storms of tumultuous
France remains a mystery. It is less surprising
that Josephine should favour the project. She
pushes it with the idea that Louis shall marry
Hortense, unite the two families, and eradicate
the idea of divorce. She succeeds with disastrous
success. She produces the most unhappy of
marriages. The chosen heir, ill, hypochondriac,
impossible, irritates every one connected with

VIII.

him by obstinacy, suspicion, and conceit ; and at last outlaws himself, as it were, so as to escape from his brother, his wife, and his throne. But we are looking too far ahead.

The dynasty for the present must take care of itself, there is too much to do. What will not wait is a Code of Laws. There is a noble monument to put one's name to ; and the General sets to work. He has in his Second Consul Cambacérès a skilled and efficient jurist. With him and other experts he labours. He animates, superintends, and moulds the operations ; *fervet opus.* It is a work of fusion and compromise between the old and the new, between the philosophical and juridical spirit, between tradition and written law. Its effect is to codify the Revolution. " Il ne crée pas le progrès, il l'enregistre et le fixe, le stabilise. En lui l'ardente matière se concrète sous forme solide, indestructible ; par lui en cette partie la Révolution se fait bronze et granit."

The work is not set about in earnest until after Marengo, so that it scarcely comes within the limits of the book. But we cannot be too grateful to M. Vandal for including it, and for the eloquent pages he gives to it, summing up with the just phrase : " Napoléon, comme Rome, en perdant l'Empire sur les peuples, leur laissa ses lois."

From this vast work of reorganisation the First Consul is suddenly called by an irresistible summons. He sniffs war, and cannot resist the call of the battlefield. Austria is stubbornly in arms, contained, indeed, by Moreau on the eastern frontier, but far too strong for Masséna in Italy. There are two great difficulties. One is to take part of Moreau's army from that frigid and jealous chief. He will not let Bonaparte come to his army; with difficulty he cedes thirty thousand men. The other obstacle is this : the Constitution appears to forbid the First Consul to command in the field. That, too, is surmounted ; he will only inspect and review. Then, with the army of reserve, he crosses the Alps and throws himself into Italy. At his departure conspiracies once more raise their head ; indeed, his own friends have to consider his successor in case of his death ; for his enemies his defeat will be enough. He leaves all this scornfully behind. As they plot or prepare, they are electrified by the news that he has entered Milan. This eclipses the announcement that Masséna has had to evacuate Genoa with all the honours, and more than all the honours of war. But still this reverse swells the hostile army by freeing the besieging force.

On the very day that the news of the capitulation of Genoa reaches Paris the decisive battle is raging. After a day of desperate fighting the French are everywhere repulsed. Mélas, the Austrian General, sends a courier to Vienna to announce his victory. If the hundred expectant heads of faction in France only knew! But Desaix, one of Napoleon's few friends, perhaps his dearest, arrives with fresh troops ; Kellermann with his cavalry completes what the charge of Desaix had begun ; the fortune of battle turns, and Marengo is won.

VIII.   Six days afterwards Paris is waiting in trepidation.   A rumour had reached the Government of a great battle fought—first lost and then gained. But there is no official news. Are, then, the tidings true ? Does the absence of a despatch mean that Bonaparte is dead ? If so, Carnot must be presented as the official candidate for his place. But the Second Consul keeps Joseph in reserve. The night passes in feverish suspense ; then about eleven o'clock three couriers successively arrive, and the great news is circulating on every lip. Bonaparte, who, as Vandal says, was a born journalist, sends home a masterpiece of his art. He admits his defeats, but describes the recovery of the battle and the charge of Desaix in language full of colour and heat. Then he comes to the tragedy : Desaix is dead, in the flush of victory. In the style of the ancients, he composes the dying speech of the hero and his own reply.

Paris goes mad with joy. The Tuileries, palace court, and garden are open and thronged. The workmen are roused to enthusiasm. It is the first spontaneous rejoicing that has taken place for nine years. Marengo is, says Vandal, one of the rare events in history which has vibrated through all the various masses of the French nation. Marengo to them spells peace.

His friend is dead, but the conqueror may not tarry ; Patroclus is killed, but there is no rest for this Achilles ; he cannot remain with his army ; he must return to the volcanic soil of Paris. Thither he returns, unexpectedly and quietly as from Egypt, and, hereafter, from Russia and

Elba. But all the capital illuminates as soon as it learns his presence. The sinister source of revolutions, the Faubourg St. Antoine itself, is a blaze of light ; it pours its turbulent artisans in throngs to the Tuileries ; but the General will not show himself.

Marengo has changed him; he has become master, his tone is curt and imperious. He knows that whether the fatal battle has brought peace or not, it has given him supreme power. Even on his way home he has done what he could not have done before, he has opened negotiations for a Concordat. He is now master of France, ready to be master of Europe. What he said long afterwards of his earlier victories is true at least now : " Dès lors j'ai prévu ce que je pourrais devenir ! Je voyais déjà le monde fuir sous moi comme si j'étais emporté dans les airs ! " Yes, France has found the man she sought, to rid her for the time at least of Revolution. But she has also found a master. And on Europe his hand will be not less heavy. It will take the Continent fourteen years and a generation of mankind to get rid of him.

M. Vandal in his early pages finds Bonaparte an aspirant to absolute power; he leaves him in possession of it. He shows us in gross and in detail what the difficulties have been, how nearly the enterprise failed, or became ridiculous—which is much the same thing. And when it succeeded the complications were scarcely less, only to be surmounted by a patience, tact, and prudence which seem alien to the hero.

If any doubting student shall be led by these

VIII.   words to this history I shall be well rewarded, and so will he. I have already been repaid by running through the book again in order to write this notice ; he will be led through a succession of stirring and momentous scenes by a keen and fascinating spirit.

*

IX

SIR ROBERT PEEL [1]

THE historical monument to Sir Robert Peel [2] is now almost complete, and three massive volumes set forth fully, but not redundantly, the career of a statesman who ended or commenced an epoch.

Almost, but not quite. In the first place, the present work does not pretend to be a complete biography, for it scarcely notices what has appeared elsewhere—such as the correspondence with Croker; the speeches; the appeal from Cobden on Peel's resignation and the reply to it, which is the most striking, passionate, and vivid letter of Peel's that we possess. This last we regret, though the editor has, on the whole, exercised a wise discretion; for to have taken any other course would have swollen the volumes to an intolerable bulk. What is here attempted and achieved is the selection of all that is characteristic and interesting from the Peel papers,

[1] This chapter, which originally appeared in the *Anglo-Saxon Review*, was published by Messrs. Cassell & Company as a booklet in 1899.

[2] *Sir Robert Peel, from his Private Papers, edited for his Trustees by Charles Stuart Parker.* 3 vols. 1891-99. John Murray.

IX. and so the delineation of Peel's career by himself and his correspondents.

Again, the monument to Peel will never be complete without a new edition of his speeches. The published collection in four volumes is, we believe, the least common of such publications. It contains much of permanent interest, and some models of parliamentary speaking. But it is vilely printed, and cannot be said to be edited at all. Two or three volumes of fair type and respectable paper would contain all that it is necessary to preserve. It is not much of a tribute to pay to the man who gave his fellow-countrymen " abundant and untaxed food, the sweeter because it is no longer leavened by a sense of injustice "; and without it the record of his career is still inadequate and unfair.

The course of the present biography has been strange. Six or seven years after Peel's death there appeared two volumes, prepared for publication by himself, which embraced the three capital crises of his life. Then we wait for forty years. The chests of his papers, bequeathed in solemn trust, slumber in silence : there are rumours of documents which affect living statesmen and which impose reserve : the statesmen die, and yet there is no sign : the trustees themselves die, and are replaced by others : an eminent author dips into them, and brings up a magazine article : the appetite of posterity remains whetted and unappeased : the documents remain, an unexplored treasure of political history.

There is a story that Sir Robert, in the last

year of his last administration, appeared late
at night in the bedroom of Cardwell, and paced
up and down without saying a word, Cardwell
watching with amazed perplexity from his bed.
At last he broke silence. " Never destroy a
letter," he oracularly said. " No public man who
respects himself should ever destroy a letter."
He then turned on his heel and left the room.
It was understood that he was referring to the
solace which might be derived, under the philippics
of an alienated supporter, from the possession of
the orator's applications for office.   Be that as it
may, we may be sure that as Sir Robert preached,
so did he practise.   He preserved his papers, and
so the most exact revelation of himself.

But now at last we have the papers, or a
careful selection of them, and we feel that we
have only gained by having to wait for them,
as the editor may be cited as a chief among the
rare masters of that fastidious calling.   Laborious,
conscientious, and fair, Mr. Parker is anxious
never to obtrude himself on the reader's attention.
We might, indeed, wish that he had given us
more illustrations derived from his close intimacy
with Lord Cardwell, one of the original trustees.
But with one exception—the essay at the end
of the volumes—Peel is allowed to speak for
himself.   It must, therefore, be felt that that
essay, clever and interesting as it is, is out of
place.   Without it, the direct and majestic delineation of the statesman is consummate and
complete.   The piety and enthusiasm of his
descendant jar with the austere self-revelation
of the man.

IX.

A portrait such as this can only be produced of one of the princes of mankind. They gain by that scrutiny which would kill and damn lesser beings. Nothing personal to them can be spared or omitted—not the wart of Cromwell, or the burlesque mask of Gibbon, or the deformed foot of Byron. It is at once their glory and their penalty, for it is only the great in spirit and in truth that must and can endure the glare of minute biography.

How does Peel bear this test? To that question there can be, we think, but one answer—that few can endure it so well, that we have here the picture of a public career, happily not unique, but illustrious and unalloyed. It is little derogation to add that he had lived in the searchlight of the world, or prepared for it, from the beginning of things. The tradition goes that on his birth his father, in a transport of pious gratitude, had on his knees vowed the baby to the service of his country, and had expressed the hope that his child might tread in the steps of his political idol, William Pitt. From his childhood, then, when he repeated to his father critical abstracts of the sermons he had heard in church, in order to strengthen his memory in view of a political career, the little Robert lived, as it were, devoted to the public, in the very eye, so to speak, of the Muse of History.

So far back as we can discern him at all, we find him from the outset the same able, conscientious, laborious, sensitive being that we leave him at his death. But this preparation for politics was not wholly an advantage. It was carried on under the auspices of his father, who called himself a Pittite, when that name was monopolised by High Tories and High Protectionists. Peel, then, found his creed prepared for him without an option. He was sworn to Toryism before he understood the meaning of the oath. This was unfortunate, for Toryism was by no means congenial to the character of his mind. He was a representative of the great middle class, commercially a Liberal, with no aristocratic prejudice or tradition to hamper his examination of any question on its merits. His habit of mind would thus, had he been left untrammelled, have made him a Whig, but a Whig who would have developed in the popular direction. At one time, indeed, it seemed possible that a Whig he might actually become. Arbuthnot told the Duke of Bedford that the old Sir Robert Peel had once uttered a significant warning that, if Robert were not secured by high office, he would go over to the Whigs, and be for ever lost to the party. This story, on the face of it, does not seem improbable, and derives a shadowy support from a letter which the father wrote to Mr. Perceval. It is likely enough that young Peel, had he remained a free-lance, would have broken loose from the Toryism of that day. Greville, as he relates the anecdote, makes his own characteristically acid comments : " Never," he says, " did any father do a greater injury to a son, for if Peel had joined a more congenial party, he might have followed the bent of his political inclination, and would have escaped all the false positions in which he has been placed.

IX.   . . . As it is, his whole life has been spent in doing enormous mischief, and in attempts to repair that mischief." But it was otherwise fated, not perhaps for his own welfare or happiness.   He was in 1829 to deal High Toryism an almost mortal blow ; to reconstitute a new Toryism by patience and labour ; and to shatter all in 1846.

But throughout life there was in him a streak of what we call Liberalism.   The inner habit of his mind, though essentially cautious, was indeed essentially Liberal.   Even in opposing the Reform Bill of 1832 he urged, as one great objection to it, that it confined the franchise to the higher and middle classes and excluded the labourers, disfranchising those possessed from time immemorial of the privilege.   This was not the objection of his party, or even akin to their objections.   It is, indeed, safe to say that these volumes do not present the portrait of a Tory, as Toryism was then understood.   They contain the constant protests and struggles of a candid mind against class prejudice and class jobbery.   What he had in common with the old Toryism was the historical apprehension of a man born before the French Revolution ; and obvious traces of this feeling may be found in a letter he wrote to Goulburn in August 1836.   It is probable that he clung to this abstract and negative principle as a base of support for the reactionary attitudes which he was sometimes compelled to assume.   But it may safely be said that in the everyday business of life, in the distribution of patronage, in the dealing with abuses, Peel worked in a spirit of severe public duty, and of constant protest against privilege, or bigotry, or jobs—a spirit alien to the older Toryism. It must, indeed, be admitted that in 1825 he wrote to Liverpool asking for preferment in the Church for one brother, and for secular promotion for his brother-in-law, so that another brother might occupy the post held by the brother-in-law. This letter in the light of these days reads oddly enough, but then it must be read by the light of those. Peel's general stand against High Tory ideas of patronage is none the less clear and strong. And there is further to be noted, in the words of Mr. Gladstone, that, as there were two Pitts, so there were two Peels : the Peel before and the Peel after the Reform Bill. To put it otherwise, before the Reform Bill Peel was a Tory ; after it he was a Conservative. He recognised the new conditions resulting from that Bill ; he endeavoured to shape his policy and adapt his party to them. In this attempt he bent his party to the breaking-point ; but for a time, by his parliamentary skill and the loyalty of Wellington, the catastrophe was averted.

Nothing, indeed, appears more clearly in these volumes than the fact that it was only the climax of the disruption of the Tory party that was reached in 1846. Since the death of Lord Liverpool there had been an increasing fissure. In 1834–35 there was a momentary closing of the ranks against further reform, and in support of the spirited stand made by Peel. The old Duke of Newcastle—the very pontiff of High Toryism — mindful, perhaps, that Peel had

IX.

defended him in the House of Commons, had tendered to Peel an elaborate support, and had offered, with superfluous ardour, to accompany him to the scaffold. At the same time, being against every description of reform, wholesale and retail, his " satisfaction at seeing Peel at the head of affairs was not pure and unmixed." When, however, a Newcastle could affect even a moderate contentment with Peel, High Toryism could support him with apparent cordiality. But, between the fall of Peel's Government in 1835 and his return to office in 1841, the difficulty of combining the extreme and moderate sections of his party taxed all his resources. Peel himself in his later years, after his final resignation, wrote as follows : " On reflecting on all that passed, I am much more surprised that the union was so long maintained than that it was ultimately severed." And in July 1845, Prince Albert, a shrewd and close observer, writes to Stockmar : " In politics we are drawing near the close of one of the most remarkable sittings of parliament. Peel has carried through everything with immense majorities, but it is certain that he has no longer any stable parliamentary support. His party is quite broken up, and the Opposition has as many different opinions and principles as heads." He had to experience, as Pitt had before him, the difficulties that attend a Liberal Minister governing by a majority of old Tories ; while his strength lay, negatively, in a Liberal opposition, distracted by multifarious principles and conflicting chiefs.

By the word " Tory " no reference is, of

course, here intended to the party now existing,
which is sometimes called by that name. The
old Tory party can scarcely be said to have
survived, even in a languishing condition, the
cataclysm of 1846, and it finally disappeared
in 1867. Since then there have been Tories in
name, or Tories of a different kind. Lord
Beaconsfield loved to call himself a Tory, so
did Lord Randolph Churchill. But the followers
of this last were commonly identified as Tory-
Democrats, a conjunction of terms which sufficiently explains the change. What would Sidmouth, or Eldon, or Sir Robert Harry Inglis
have said to such a combination ? An imaginary
conversation between one of them and a Tory-
Democrat would transcend the imagination of
a Landor, unless indeed he resorted to the
compendious forms of the Commination Service.
No : what is meant by Tories, relatively to Sir
Robert Peel's career, is a party opposed to the
Whigs ; and the Whigs of 1840 would be considered by many Tories of to-day to be retrograde
and fossil politicians. The Tories of Sir Robert's
time cherished the names of Eldon, Sidmouth,
and Inglis. He himself acknowledged the dis-
crepancy between himself and them by adopting
the term " Conservative."

From the time of Roman Catholic Emancipation, if not earlier, there had reigned an atmosphere of distrust round Peel. His reserve,
his awkwardness, a certain slyness of eye, which
appears in some of his portraits, may account
for this as much as the suspicion of Liberal
tendencies, though this also prevailed. That

IX.

expression of the eye is noticed by Disraeli in the study of Peel which he wrote for his *Life of Lord George Bentinck*. " The eye," he says, " was not good : it was sly, and had an awkward habit of looking askance." It does not appear that anything in Peel's public or private career justifies the imputation of slyness. His shyness may have given him occasionally the " awkward habit of looking askance." The sly expression of the eye was probably the indication, not of cunning, but of humour. For even on public and solemn occasions Sir Robert was known not to be deficient in that saving salt, though its full abundance has only been revealed in these last years. His reputation in that respect rested on the famous passage in the speech of May 18, 1841, often quoted, but too good to leave unquoted as we pass :

" Great as is my commiseration, I cannot assist you. I view with unaffected sympathy the position of the right honourable gentleman the Chancellor of the Exchequer. It has been remarked that a good man struggling with adversity is a sight worthy of the gods. And certainly the right honourable gentleman, *both with respect to the goodness of the man and the extent of his adversity*, presents at the present moment that spectacle. Can there be a more lamentable picture than that of a Chancellor of the Exchequer seated on an empty chest, by the pool of bottomless deficiency, fishing for a budget ? I won't bite : the right honourable gentleman shall return home with his pannier as empty as his chest."

That passage is classical. But during the last decade there has been abundant proof that the humour lurking in Peel's eye represented a strong but severely repressed characteristic of the man. Carlyle, who was, at any rate, an admirable portrait-painter, had noticed this. " A warm sense of fun, really of genuine broad drollery, looks through him : the hopefullest feature I could clearly see." Rogers, too, who had seen everybody and noticed everything, was alive to the occasional flashes of Peel's humour. Once, he tells us, at a meeting of the Trustees of the British Museum, some one mentioned young Tomline's costly purchases of pictures, adding, " What would the Bishop say, if he could now look up ? " " I observe," remarked Peel, " you don't say ' look down ' ! " But perhaps it finds its most frequent vent in his letters to Croker, written at the time when he trusted Croker. Mr. Parker too, especially in his first volume, gives several letters with that same happy note ; nor is it even absent during Peel's last desperate session as Prime Minister, when, in the House of Commons, he bantered the Recorder of Dublin with regard to the housemaid : " Ne sit ancillae tibi amor pudori." Sir William Gregory, who saw him often at this period, has told of his fun, sometimes broad, his ready stories, his robust fits of laughter, and quotes Lord Strangford to a similar effect. Even in the solemn moment between his resignation and resumption of power in December 1845, Greville tells us that Peel was full of jokes and stories, enlivening a hilarious Cabinet. All this

IX.
seems worth notice, for it does not represent the ordinary view of Peel.

With regard to another force of Peel's nature, equally strong and almost equally suppressed— his fiery temper—Mr. Parker adds something to what was already known. He records how Peel called out Townshend, his opponent at Tamworth in the 1837 election. He tells us what is to be told of the abortive duel with O'Connell. He gives us the correspondence in which Peel called Hume to account for " expressions not consistent with the usages of Parliament "; and that in which he exacts an apology from Hobhouse. He narrates the painful scene in the House of Commons when Peel lost his self-control under an attack by Cobden, ill-timed and ill-expressed; but not that when, with inexplicable fury, he repelled a contemptible cannonade from Cobbett. There is, moreover, we have always understood, but little doubt that at one time he had it in contemplation to challenge Mr. Disraeli; though on this point the papers are silent. But scarcely in the Irish Parliament, or in Lever's novels, is there any memory of so peppery a politician with so constant an inclination to the " saw-handles." There is, indeed, ample documentary proof, besides the tradition of those who knew him, that the cold, cautious exterior of Peel concealed a highly-strung, nervous temperament, and a prompt pugnacity which we can scarcely realise in these days.

But, except in regard to these two points, there is nothing in these volumes to vary materially the popular conception of Peel's habit of mind. To work hard had always been his practice. " Work," Dean Cyril Jackson had early exhorted him, " work like a tiger, or like a dragon, if dragons work more and harder than tigers." And in his last tenure of office Peel speaks of himself more than once as working seventeen hours a day. Even with that desperate diet of labour it seems difficult to understand how Peel accomplished all that he did at that time.

For he was the model of all Prime Ministers. It is more than doubtful, indeed, if it be possible in this generation, when the burdens of empire and of office have so incalculably grown, for any Prime Minister to discharge the duties of his high post with the same thoroughness or in the same spirit as Peel. To do so would demand more time and strength than any man has at his command. For Peel kept a strict supervision over every department : he seems to have been master of the business of each and all of them. He was conversant with all departmental questions, and formed and enforced opinions on them. And, though he had an able Chancellor of the Exchequer, in whom he had full confidence, ·he himself introduced his great Budget of 1842 and that of 1845. The War Office, the Admiralty, the Foreign Office, the administrations of India and of Ireland felt his personal influence as much as the Treasury or the Board of Trade.

In the House of Commons he, with Graham, mainly bore the burden, so much to the exclusion of even so brilliant a colleague as Stanley that we find this last demanding his removal to the

IX. House of Lords, on the ground that business in the House of Commons was done entirely by Peel, Goulburn, Graham, and Gladstone, and that he had therefore become a cypher: an extraordinary testimony, when we reflect that this Stanley, for whom no use could be found, was incomparably the first debater in Parliament. Charles Villiers, an opponent, but even then a practised parliamentarian, offered evidence of equal weight: " See how those two men (Peel and Graham) do their business and understand it." It is probable, then, that no Prime Minister ever fulfilled so completely and thoroughly the functions of his office, parliamentary, administrative, and general, as Sir Robert Peel; though it may perhaps be found that Peel's greatest pupil followed in his footsteps during the famous administration which began in 1868. But in these days of instant, continuous, and unrelenting pressure, the very tradition of such a minister has almost departed; indeed, it would be impossible to be so paternal and ubiquitous. A minister of these days would be preparing or delivering a speech in the country, when Peel would be writing minutes of policy for the various departments. Which occupation is the better or more fruitful is not now in question: it is sufficient for our purpose that the difference exists.

Nor, perhaps, would such a minister be now altogether welcome to his colleagues. For Peel was in name and in deed that functionary so abhorred and repudiated by the statesmen of the eighteenth century—a Prime Minister. With

a collection of colleagues perhaps unparalleled
for ability and brilliancy, he stood among them
like Alexander among his Parmenios and Ptole-
mies. In these days we have returned, perhaps
necessarily, to the views of the last century. A
Prime Minister who is the senior partner in every
department as well as president of the whole,
who deals with all the business of government,
who inspires and vibrates through every part,
is almost, if not quite, an impossibility. A first
minister is the most that can be hoped for, the
chairman and on most occasions the spokesman
of that board of directors which is called the
Cabinet, who has the initiation and guidance of
large courses of public policy, but who does
not, unless specially invoked, interfere depart-
mentally.

Peel, himself, in 1845—more than half a
century ago—had arrived at the conclusion that
the task of a Prime Minister in the House of
Commons, as he understood the office, had
become almost impossible. In August 1845 he
writes :

" I defy the minister of this country to perform properly the duties of his office—to read
all that he ought to read, including the whole
foreign correspondence ; to keep up the constant
communication with the Queen, *and the Prince* ;
to see all whom he ought to see ; to superintend
the grant of honours and the disposal of civil
and ecclesiastical patronage ; to write with his
own hand to every person of note who chooses
to write to him ; to be prepared for every debate,
including the most trumpery concerns ; to do

IX.   all these indispensable things, and also sit in
the House of Commons eight hours a day for
one hundred and eighteen days.

" It is impossible for me not to feel that the
duties are incompatible and above all human
strength—at least, above mine.

" The worst of it is that the really important
duties to the country—those out of the House
of Commons—are apt to be neglected.

" I never mean to solve the difficulty in one
way—namely, by going to the House of Lords.
But it must be solved in one way or another.
The failure of the mind is the usual way, as we
know from sad experience."

This is surely a striking pronouncement. His
detail of his duties, his speaking of himself as
" the minister of this country," which defines
in a phrase his view of his position, his indication
of the real danger, long since realised, that
administrative must necessarily be neglected for
parliamentary duties, his allusion in the last
sentence to Liverpool and Castlereagh are all
noteworthy. So is his declaration that he would
never take refuge in the House of Lords. In
Martin's *Life of the Prince Consort* (i. 266) it is
stated, on the authority of Mr. Anson and Lord
Aberdeen, that Peel had come to the conclusion
that the Prime Minister should be in that House.
The question has scarcely more than an historic
interest, since the conditions are no longer the
same. But it is impossible, even as a matter of
historic interest, altogether to ignore any definite
opinion on such a subject, pronounced by so
consummate a master of his craft.

What is a Prime Minister ?   That is a question
which it would require a pamphlet to answer,
but in a few sentences it may be possible to
remove a few hallucinations.   For the title
expresses much to the British mind.   To the
ordinary apprehension it implies a dictator, the
duration of whose power finds its only limit in
the House of Commons.   So long as he can
weather that stormful and deceptive ocean he
is elsewhere supreme.   But the reality is very
different.   The Prime Minister, as he is now
called, is technically and practically the Chairman of an Executive Committee of the Privy
Council, or rather perhaps of Privy Councillors,
the influential foreman of an executive jury.   His
power is mainly personal, the power of individual
influence.   That influence, whatever it may be,
he has to exert in many directions before he can
have his way.   He has to deal with the Sovereign,
with the Cabinet, with Parliament, and with
public opinion, all of them potent factors in their
various kinds and degrees.   To the popular eye,
however, heedless of these restrictions, he represents universal power ;   he is spoken of as if he
had only to lay down his views of policy and to
adhere to them.   That is very far from the case.
A first minister has only the influence with the
Cabinet which is given him by his personal
arguments, his personal qualities, and his personal weight.   But this is not all.   All his
colleagues he must convince, some he may have
to humour, some even to cajole :   a harassing,
laborious, and ungracious task.   Nor is it only
his colleagues that he has to deal with :   he has

IX. to masticate their pledges, given before they joined him; he has to blend their public utterances, to fuse as well as may be all this into the policy of the Government; for these various records must be reconciled, or glossed, or obliterated. A machinery liable to so many grains of sand requires obviously all the skill and vigilance of the best conceivable engineer. And yet without the external support of his Cabinet he is disarmed. The resignation of a colleague, however relatively insignificant, is a storm signal.

Nothing, indeed, is more remarkable than the cohesion of Cabinets, except that strange institution itself. To the Briton, who found it existing at his birth, it seems the natural if not the inevitable form of government. To the inquiring foreigner, however, nothing can seem more extraordinary, in a country with so much of democracy about it, than the spectacle of a secret council, on the Venetian model, and sworn to absolute silence, conducting the business of a nation which insists on publicity for everything less important. The secrecy of the Cabinet in such a condition of things would resemble, one would surmise, the secrecy of the ostrich—the material fact would be visible to all while a shallow head was embedded in the sand. But it is not so. The secrets of the Cabinet are, as a rule, preserved. After the sharpest internal discords the members will present a united, even if a silent and sullen, front. Whether the system of Cabinet government be an efficient one or not is not now the question : whether the collection of the heads of departments at sparse intervals to discuss hurriedly topics, for which they are often unprepared, be a good arrangement for business is not the point : but what may confidently be asserted is that of all anomalous arrangements for executive government in an Anglo - Saxon community, during the present epoch and under the present conditions, the strangest is the government of the British Empire by a secret committee. That it works well, on the whole, is a tribute less to the institution itself than to the capacity of our race to make any conceivable institution succeed.

Of course, it may be said that the public and the Press are excluded from the counsels of all executives. But it will be found not infrequently elsewhere that the conclusions at which executives have arrived are announced to the public. In Britain it may safely be said that this is never, or scarcely ever, the case. Nor is even the subject of discussion ever known, though enterprising editors make spirited conjectures on the subject, which sometimes take the form of authoritative paragraphs. Practically, then, during the whole of the parliamentary recess at least, we have not the faintest idea of what our rulers are doing, or planning, or negotiating, except in so far as light is afforded by the independent investigations of the Press. This is said in a spirit, not of criticism or deprecation, but rather of meditation—which, however, must not be allowed to allure us too far from our subject.

Of this secret committee, such as it is, the Prime Minister is the chairman. He is also the channel by which its decisions reach the Sove-

IX.

reign. We do not know how Peel acquitted himself in the first capacity, though we think it probable that he left something to be desired ; but in the second he acquitted himself admirably. He had, in 1841, to surmount perhaps some memories of the difficulties which had prevented his accepting office in 1839 ; though between 1839 and 1841 these had been removed by the tact and wisdom of the Prince Consort, acting on behalf of the Sovereign. But nothing is more delightful than the account of his relations with the Queen and her young husband. There is a paternal, tender note which seems infinitely graceful in a man of his cold and awkward reserve. Had he been more genial, more tactful, more a man of the world, the difficulty of the Household in 1839 would have easily been overcome. But as the relations of the Sovereign and the minister became more constant and definite, when the one was able to see how warm a heart, how wise and generous a nature was concealed under a formal exterior, when the other realised that no natural prepossessions would prevent fair play to the new Government, mutual appreciation was easy and complete ; until it culminated in the scene of December 20, 1845, when the Queen required the minister to remain in her service, and the minister replied, as he records himself, " I want no consultations, no time for reflection. I will be your minister, happen what may. I will do without a colleague rather than leave you in this extremity." Comment or addition would only mar so chivalrous a picture.

The relations with the Sovereign are, however, only a part, though they may be the pleasantest part, of the Prime Minister's personal relations. He has, as has already been pointed out, to keep in such touch with his Cabinet that they may act cordially with him.

Here Peel in one great instance may be said to have been less successful. He did not, indeed, owe everything, but he owed much, to the Duke of Wellington. Without Wellington, Catholic Emancipation could not have been carried in 1829. Wellington consented to act as warming-pan for Peel in 1834. He helped Peel loyally, sometimes against his own convictions, in conducting Opposition from 1835 to 1841. Without Wellington it is safe to say that Peel could not have maintained himself in 1845–46. The loyal old soldier acted not from any particular sympathy for Peel, but from a stern resolve that the Queen's Government should be carried on. This is not to say that he was an altogether easy colleague, but it is to establish that Peel was bound to him by every tie of gratitude and interest. These volumes, however, teem with proofs that Peel took little pains to keep the Duke in a good humour, that he communicated with him as little as possible, that their relations were sometimes strained, and that Arbuthnot, the Duke's bosom friend, was instant at all seasons to try and bring about more intimate consultation. Over and over again he intimates in various forms, as if the statement were a startling novelty, that the Duke, " if he has a weakness," has the weakness of liking to be

IX.

consulted. Peel on one occasion answers that he knows of no pleasure comparable to that of consulting the Duke. But he showed a singular self-denial in availing himself of this gratification. Sometimes common friends intervene. On one occasion, in answer to such expostulation, Peel confesses himself aggrieved, and states with his usual moderation the causes of offence. But in any case the result is always the same : renewed want of intercourse, renewed complaints, and, at most, communication through the channel of Arbuthnot.

One short correspondence is, however, so fascinating that it deserves to be noticed. Sir Robert's second son, William, then a midshipman —afterwards, in the Crimea and in India, so famous and beloved—writes home to his father an account of the naval operations on the coast of Syria in 1840. Peel, breaking through his habitual reserve, sends the letter to the Duke, who returns it with rare commendation. The delight of the father is as irrepressible as it is charming, and forms a grateful oasis in his relations with his illustrious colleague.

Strangely enough, if one turns to Greville, one finds almost the same complaint of the Duke. In 1841 Wellington had, it seems, fallen into strange and morbid ways. Once so accessible, he would see no one. Once so fond of being consulted, he avoided everything of the kind —indeed, all communications with his fellow-creatures. He retired for a time into a gloomy and silent solitude, denying access to every one with passionate and almost brutal vehemence.

It is not probable that this fit lasted long. But
it is only fair to note the fact in the controversy
as between Peel and the Duke.

That there were faults on both sides is probable. It is impossible, however, not to feel that
Peel was the more to blame. The position and
qualities and age of Wellington were such as
demanded an attention little short of homage.
When Peel was still a Harrow schoolboy, Wellington had won Assaye. When Peel entered
Parliament, Wellington had stemmed the universal dominion of France, and before Peel was
eight - and - twenty, had put an end to it. He
was incomparably the first, the most illustrious,
the most venerable of living Englishmen. What
his political services had been to Peel has already
been stated. He had, moreover, for many years
endeavoured to bring a hostile House of Lords
into harmony with Peel's views, and by his
matchless authority had succeeded. Peel, it is
clear, should have taken endless pains to gratify
and conciliate the supreme old man. If he took
any, or any but the slightest, it does not appear
in the present biography.

With others of his colleagues he laboured
more effectually. For example, Ellenborough
had proceeded to India as Governor - General.
Even before his arrival at Calcutta, the restless
and exuberant vanity of the new Viceroy had displayed itself in an ominous manner. After he
had landed a few weeks it developed a thousand-
fold. His predecessor he offended by the careless candour of his egotism. He outraged two
successive Presidents of the Board of Control.

He flouted the Court of Directors. His generals, Nott and Pollock, he openly denounced as incompetent; but afterwards arrogated, or seemed to arrogate, to himself the merit of their achievements. He wished to have a commission that would enable him to command the army himself. Without it, he followed the army with the pomp and parade of a Xerxes. He undertook daring, and in Peel's judgement unjustifiable, measures of policy without consultation with any home authority. In one part of a letter to Hardinge he hints at a march to the Dardanelles, in another at the conquest of Egypt. In fine, there never was, it would appear, with all his ability, so impossible a Governor-General.

But to read Peel's correspondence with him, and with Fitzgerald and Ripon, his official chiefs, is a lesson in itself. The tact, the sagacity, the patience, are as rare as they are admirable. Swollen with arrogant importance, Ellenborough disdained the post in the Cabinet offered to him by Peel when he returned from India, intimating that Cabinet office was beneath the notice of one whose mind was devoted to sublimer subjects. Peel turns away with a smile.

With Stanley, if we may judge from this biography, he was never cordial. Nor is this wonderful, for perhaps no two men were ever endowed with more opposite natures than these two Lancashire leaders; though it seems probable, fiery as was Stanley, that Peel's was the more fiery nature of the two. So, too, they both had humour. But Lord Dalling reports a tradition that Peel suffered much under the irrepressible banter of Stanley—to such an extent, indeed, as to have resolved to be rid of him. It has been remarked by an eminent writer that a difference of taste in jokes is a great strain on the affections. But we doubt if it has ever seriously strained those of a Cabinet ; we feel sure that it never produced a schism in Peel's. Indeed, the tradition is in itself a joke. Nor do we find any trace of intimacy between the not less brilliant Lyndhurst and the Prime Minister. Ripon and Fitzgerald have to be soothed under the irritating vagaries of Ellenborough, and are dexterously appeased. Of Mr. Gladstone we catch only glimpses, mainly at the time of his resignation in 1845. Then he perplexed his chief, who complains of sometimes finding great difficulty in exactly comprehending what he means. But that was not wholly surprising. Mr. Gladstone's resignation was based on a high and honourable refinement, arrived at during a period of stress, if not of transition. It was consequently not easy to explain. Moreover, first ministers usually find a difficulty in understanding the intellectual processes of colleagues who wish to resign.

Yet Gladstone writes of Peel in 1853 as " my great master and teacher in public affairs." The younger Newcastle, too, declares : " *He* is my leader still, though invisible. I never take a step in public life without reflecting, how would he have thought of it." But with three exceptions we only see the ministers dimly. With these three, however, Peel's relations were warm and intimate.

Lady Peel, in the exquisite letter which she

IX. addressed to Lord Aberdeen a month after her bereavement, says : " My beloved one always talked of you as *the friend* whom he most valued, for whom he had the sincerest affection, whom he esteemed higher than any." From this testimony there can be no appeal (though it may be contrasted with Peel's letter to Graham of July 3, 1846), but it finds little support in the present biography. Aberdeen inspired the warmest regard in those who penetrated beneath a somewhat cold and taciturn exterior. Both the Queen and Mr. Gladstone seem to have felt for him an affection which it is rare for statesmen to attract. But in the correspondence with Pcel this is not so apparent. Indeed, there was once a crisis. For Aberdeen felt so complete a trust in France and the government of Louis Philippe that he and Guizot were, it is complacently stated, on the footing rather of colleagues than ministers of different countries ; they showed each other their despatches, and exchanged their secret letters. This anticipation of a political millennium seemed to the British Cabinet premature. At any rate, they declined to allow it to extinguish a modest scheme of national defence. Thereupon Aberdeen tendered his resignation : " a policy of friendship and confidence " had, he thought, " been converted into a policy of hostility and distrust." On the other hand, the Cabinet agreed with the Duke of Wellington in thinking that nothing would so much contribute to friendly relations with France as the placing ourselves in a position of efficient security. Guizot protested, and declared that " the ancient maxim,

' si vis pacem, para bellum,' had become dangerous and absurd." Peel summed up the controversy with tact and judgement. The ancient
maxim might be unwise, but he certainly doubted
if the converse were true. " I do not believe
that there would be security for peace by our
being in a state which would unfit us to repel
attack without several months' preparation."
The controversy is worthy of attentive study,
for it relates to a subject of capital and permanent
interest. But the point on which it touches our
present purpose is that the note of the correspondence does not seem very close or cordial,
though Peel declares that he should consider
the loss of Aberdeen as irreparable.

That lack of expansiveness would not, perhaps,
be so noticeable did we not read the correspondence with Aberdeen beside that with Graham
and with Hardinge. Had it not been for the
letter of Lady Peel quoted above, it would appear
to the impartial reader that the colleague whom
Peel most trusted was Graham, and most loved
was Hardinge.

Constant consultation on all points of policy
and administration point to Graham as Peel's
right-hand man. So, too, does their close concurrence of view. In 1842, for example, they
seem to have been agreed that the repeal of the
Corn Laws was only a question of time, and of
a short time. But on all questions, day by
day, Peel and Graham keep in touch. " I have
never doubted for a moment," wrote Graham
in 1845, " your kind support in every difficulty.
It has never failed me, and happily the most

cordial agreement in feelings and in opinions prevails between us." And, when the battle was over, and the minister had gloriously fallen, Peel writes to Graham : " With what pleasure shall we talk over the stirring events of the last five years. Your cordial support and entire and unreserved confidence have been my chief stay." And Graham replied : " I shall remember our past union with pride, and I hope that till the end of our lives we may never be divided."

But the correspondence of Peel and Hardinge touches a still more exquisite note. There had always been a peculiar closeness of friendship between the two men. On at least two occasions Hardinge had been named as Peel's second in his projected duels. One would, indeed, infer from Hardinge's letters that there is no service that he would have refused to one for whom he felt the most generous form of hero-worship. When Hardinge goes to India as Viceroy, the Prime Minister finds time to write to him constantly in terms of confidence and affection, which distinguish these from all his other letters, and which, as the recipient declares, " give me energy to work." One ends " most affectionately yours," a rare form with Peel ; another, in the heat of the Corn Law struggle, written from the Cabinet, " God bless you, my dear Hardinge. Excuse my hurried letter. I am fighting a desperate battle here ; shall probably drive my opponents over the Sutlej : but what is to come afterwards I know not." One almost, as one reads, hears the beating of the writer's heart. And the correspondence as between Viceroy and

minister closes with an almost impassioned testimony of sympathy and devotion from Hardinge.

If any letters more noble in themselves, or
more creditable to the writers and their school,
have passed between two public men, we cannot
call them to mind. Nor is it difficult to understand why such letters should be rare. There is
never a calm on the political ocean : its most
serene temper is the ground swell which follows,
or the grim stillness which precedes, the storm,
often more awful than the storm itself. The
unresting waves seldom permit politicians to
remain in close cordiality for any length of time.
The billow that bears one friend buoyantly on
its bosom lands the other high and dry, sometimes
among strangers, sometimes among enemies. Constant changes of atmosphere produce constantly
new combinations. And so the correspondence
of statesmen who have survived their first ingenuous enthusiasm is apt, in view of possible
contingencies, to be clouded with a forbidding
wariness.

With politicians at large Peel was not exuberant. He was beset by the busy attentions of
Croker ; and his letters to Croker before 1827
are the happiest specimens of his youthful period.
He was tormented in his later years by the
irrepressible amity of Brougham, from which
he disengaged himself with tact and skill. Of
his relations with Disraeli it is only necessary to
say this much—apart from the famous correspondence itself—that Disraeli was, probably,
in every way, in appearance, in style, in manner,
profoundly antipathetic to Peel ; and that Peel

IX.

not improbably was wholly wanting in that cordiality or attention which might have appeased a pique which became implacable. Peel can scarcely be blamed for not perceiving, as Lyndhurst did, the wild and strange genius which was concealed under the rings and the ringlets, the velvets and the waistcoats, of the young Jewish coxcomb. There was something in all this too Bohemian and garish for Sir Robert. But, at any rate, he must have understood that the pen of Disraeli was a power, that he was a member of the House of Commons having influence with other young members, and that, even if unwilling to try him in political harness, it was worth the while of the leader of the House to attempt to keep him in good humour. Such an effort seems to have been repugnant, or impossible, to Peel. And the complaint of Disraeli is not without dignity and even pathos : " Pardon me if I now observe, with frankness but with great respect, that you might have found some reason for this [deficiency in hearty goodwill] if you had cared to do so, in the want of courtesy in debate which I have had the frequent mortification of experiencing from you, since your accession to power." The applications for office and the subsequent denial of them are happily outside our scope. But, as to the philippics arising from Peel's refusal, it may perhaps be felt by politicians that it would be a churlish and mawkish morality which would deny to baffled ambition the natural outlet of invective and lampoon.

There is another aspect of a Prime Minister's

relations with mankind scarcely less difficult
than his communications with colleagues, political
writers, and members of Parliament. Patronage
Peel always detested, or believed himself to
detest. " The odious power which patronage
confers," he calls it in his famous letter to Cobden.
But the Prime Minister is the guardian of the
honours of the Crown, and he discharged this
duty with a fidelity, a wise caution, a pervading
sense of responsibility, of which the very traditions have almost faded away. What is perhaps
most important of all, he remembered that each
case was capable of becoming a precedent of
the largest and most distorted application. And
so the chapter on patronage reads to us like a
dream, like a chapter dropped from the annals
of some Utopia or Atlantis. In five years Peel
only recommended the creation of five peerages
—all for marked public service. His last great
Government of 1841 has not left a single name
on the British baronage. We can scarcely, as
we read, believe that this period occurred only
fifty years ago. Peel had adopted this super-
human strictness owing to the " immense addi-
tions recently made to the House of Lords."
What would he have said had he lived in the
last quarter of the century ?

And yet, even as it was, he felt that the
whole world was bursting prematurely into
blossom. " The distinction of being without
an honour is becoming," he writes with sardonic
gravity, " a rare and valuable one, and should
not become extinct." And again : " There would
not be a simple squire in the land, if the fever for

IX.

honours were not checked. I never yet met with a man in Ireland," he adds, " who had not himself either refused honours from the Crown or was not the son of a man, or had not married the daughter of a man, who had been hard-hearted enough to refuse the solicitations of the Government. In general it is a peerage that has been refused."

To Monckton Milnes he writes : " You will quite understand me that it is from the unfeigned respect I have for the talents of your father that I advise him to retain the distinction of not being a baronet." This is cynical enough, but it is the cynicism of a purpose to maintain a principle, which is perhaps better than the cynicism which neither investigates nor refuses.

To Hallam, to the father of Mr. Gladstone, and to Sir Moses Montefiore he offered baronetcies. To Wordsworth and Tennyson and Owen he gave pensions. Death interposed to prevent a similar favour to Hood. " Dear Sir," wrote Hood, " we are not to meet in the flesh " ; and adds with pathetic pleasantry, " it is death that stops my pen, you see, not a pension." The care and delicacy and conscience with which he treated his patronage seem to us not the least of Peel's claims to our admiration as a minister.

We have endeavoured thus briefly and hastily to consider him from his administrative and personal aspects as Prime Minister, but even thus we have left ourselves little space to consider him from the aspects which mainly appeal to the public—policy and Parliament. Still an attempt must at least be made to consider Peel as a parliamentary and political leader.

In a country like ours, great and, indeed, disproportionate importance attaches to a minister's faculty of public speaking. The greatest of statesmen, the most consummate administrators, the most sound and fertile projectors of public measures, avail little in a parliamentary nation without the power of explaining and, so to speak, advertising themselves. This in itself is not a subject for complacency. Nations are built up in silence. Their addiction to oratory is usually a sign of decadence. But in any case the fact remains, and makes it necessary to examine for a moment this part of Peel's equipment.

It is almost sufficient to say, in a sentence, that his speeches represent the best and most potent style of speaking for the days in which he lived and the parliaments in which he sat : grave, dignified, weighty, with the roll of phrase which veils so many defects, and which in an argument acts as a permanent saving clause. There are no alarming flights, and no shivering falls ; no torrents or cascades, but an ample flow, clear and strong and abiding. Speeches, as a rule, even the best, are as evanescent as fireworks or thistle-down ; they are explored for untimely quotation during the speaker's life, and when that useful purpose ceases at his death, they cease to be opened at all ; they are even less read than old sermons, which possess an elect public of their own. There are, however, a few of Peel's speeches which are still classical,

IX.

still consulted by experts, such as the speech on Repeal of the Irish Union in 1834, or on the Currency in 1844, or on Free Trade in 1849. There are, too, such speeches as that in 1817 on Roman Catholic Emancipation, the subjects of which have lost something of their savour, but which are read by those who desire to study great parliamentary arguments. A great parliamentary argument is a noble work of art, and one that Peel could always achieve. But beyond that limit he could not pass. It is not possible to conceive his arousing enthusiasm, or rising to the tender or the sublime. An acute and experienced journalist used to say that it was always possible to tell when Peel was beginning the peroration which he had written or prepared —there was a mechanical change. To a generation which has glowed with the gradually swelling perorations of Gladstone and of Bright this suggests a shortcoming, and, indeed, these efforts of Peel's do not much impress the reader—not even the most famous of all, that on his resignation in 1846. But, when all is said and done, any wise leader of the House of Commons would gladly surrender all chance of an occasional inspiration of the highest eloquence for so consummate a parliamentary instrument as the speaking faculty of Sir Robert Peel.

Of his voice Disraeli says that it was admirable; on the whole, the finest heard in his day, except, perhaps, the thrilling tones of O'Connell. But with all its excellence it may be doubted if it attained the rich and melodious tones of his son, the late Sir Robert, which have been extolled as supreme by both Mr. Gladstone and Lord Beaconsfield. " With such an organ," said the last, " he might have achieved anything." " I have only known two perfect things," the former is reputed to have said, " the handwriting of Lord Palmerston, and the voice of (this) Sir Robert Peel."

As a leader in the House of Commons, on either side of the House, he had great excellences. His knowledge of that gregarious, wayward assembly was complete, and his tact when dealing with it, except on the rare occasions when his passion mastered him, unerring. But his manner with his followers was, it is said, shy, ungraceful, and ungenial. This is the commonest charge brought against leaders, and it is easy to understand how often, when oppressed with cares known only to themselves, they find it difficult to assume a genial briskness in the lobby. There can, however, be little doubt that Peel, reserved with his closest colleagues, was not expansive to his followers, and that the twin curses of shyness and self-consciousness condemned him to that awkward manner, " haughtily stiff, or exuberantly bland," to which his party never accustomed itself.

One or two lights on the more important side of his parliamentary tactics are, however, obtainable—partly from himself. He was in the first place extremely careful as to the perfection of the measures which he proposed to Parliament. He made it, we are told, a point of honour to prepare his bills so that they should pass with little amendment. And consequently he was able,

just after he had finally left office, to write :
" I pique myself on never having proposed
anything that I have not carried." A proud
and perhaps unrivalled boast, founded on elaboration and foresight, never likely to be repeated
in these more listless and slatternly times.

Disraeli, whose brilliant sketch of Peel seems
to us, with some reserves, neither ill-natured nor
unfair, thinks that he carried this pride in his
measures too far. He tells us that, even after
the election of 1834, Peel, though in a minority,
did not despair. " I have," he said, " confidence
in my measures." His commentator justly in-
sinuates that the bills proposed by an archangel
in office would not conciliate an opposition in a
majority. This is true enough, and pity 'tis
'tis true. But there is a spirit in Peel's remark,
unworldly though it be, which is not ungrateful
to that great controlling mass of the nation
which eventually puts measures before majorities :
though it may be admitted that the Tadpoles
and the Tapers, wriggling under their exhausted
receivers, can never understand it.

Another light on Peel's qualities as a leader
is afforded by himself. " I would not," he writes
in March 1845, " admit any alteration in any of
those bills. This was thought very obstinate and
very presumptuous ; but the fact is, people like a
certain degree of obstinacy and presumption in
a minister. They abuse him for dictation and
arrogance, but they like being governed." There
is probably much truth in this, but it indicates
a sort of veiled autocracy in Peel, which is also
perceptible in his readiness to stand alone in 1828

and 1846 : the result of an honest self-confidence, but significant also of his aloofness from his party.

Aloof from his party he certainly was. In the Tom, Dick, and Harry business, as it may be called, he was certainly deficient : it is the charge brought against all great ministers. But he had one crowning merit, which finds its place in any view of him as a parliamentary leader. He had disciples : he made men : he formed a school. Of no other minister since Pitt can this be said, and even of Pitt only in a lesser degree. What men he shaped ! What a creed of honest work he left with them ! What a tradition of public duty ! Graham, Gladstone, Hardinge, Dalhousie, Canning, Cardwell, Sidney Herbert, and Newcastle. These men stood together after his death like the last square of a broken army, firm in their faith, in their leader, in their cause. To be a Peelite was a distinction in itself : it denoted statesmanship, industry, conscience. In the course of years the froward currents of politics tumbled them hither and thither ; death dealt hardly with them, for only two of those we have named were in public life a decade after Peel's death ; but to the end they bore the marks of Peelism, the high sense of public duty, the unlimited estimate of labour and devotion. Such men and their principles were a precious national possession : nothing of the kind, so far as we know, has ever taken their place. Our wolves are not, it is to be supposed, of the breed that suckled them.

So much for Peel in Parliament and as regards the stamp he left on part at least of Parliament.

IX.

With regard to Peel as a statesman there is one preliminary remark which must be made. He was at his greatest, not in power, but in a minority. This, so far as we know, is peculiar to him : it can be said of no other Prime Minister. Yet no one who examines Peel's life can doubt that, of the two epochs in his life when he stood supreme, the first was the period in 1834–35 when England waited breathlessly for his return from Rome, when he formed a Government, and, after a hopeless struggle against a party overwhelming in numbers, elated by enfranchisement, and drunk with victory, he retired from office the foremost statesman of his country. The second was the period of four years that elapsed between his resignation and his death, when, although he had nothing left of his former army but the staff, although he was detested by the mass of his former followers, although he was aloof from and indeed above party connection, his voice was the most potent and trusted in the country. But when he was in office with a majority behind him, though he achieved great things, he was always in a false position, always marching with confident utterance and intrepid bearing to an inevitable abyss. There were in consequence two great catastrophes. In 1828 he had been the principal opponent, as he had been for many years, of the Roman Catholic claims, and in 1829 he was the minister who ·passed through Parliament a measure for the satisfaction of those claims. In 1841 he commenced his term of office as the champion and leader of the Protectionist party, and concluded his term of

office in 1846 by putting an end to Protection IX.
and the party.

With regard to these two salient points there
will always be a controversy as eternal as the
Junian or the bimetallic, that of the Iron Mask
or the candlesticks of Hugo's saintly bishop. It
is not denied that on both occasions the policy
was right, though, strangely enough, seventy
years after the interment of one of these questions,
and fifty years after the funeral of the other,
there appear to the attentive observer more
symptoms of anti-Romanist and anti-Free Trade
fanaticism than at almost any period in the
interval. But though it is not denied that the
policy was right, it is, and always will be, stoutly
contested whether Peel was the minister to carry
it out. It is not our intention to examine this
discussion in detail. Neither party to it will
ever convince the other, so in itself it is fruitless
and endless. Moreover, before engaging in it,
it is necessary to examine not merely the history
of each question in detail, but also the nicest
issues of political conscience, and even political
casuistry. Still, it is impossible to pass it by
altogether, as it is capital in any survey of Peel's
career. One point at any rate is clear, that a
favourable verdict on the first transaction does
not necessarily imply a favourable issue on the
second, and, to some apprehensions, makes it
more difficult. Granted that he was right in
the first transition, he should not have repeated
it : the character of public men cannot stand
two such shocks : we incline, as it were, to the
old verdict of " Not guilty, but don't do it again."

The briefest recital of the familiar facts will
suffice. Wellington, with the concurrence of
Peel, had in January 1828 formed a ministry
on the plan of Liverpool's, leaving open the
question of Catholic Emancipation. Three
months afterwards, the section favourable to
Emancipation resigned—a resignation, it should
be noted, which could easily have been averted
by Wellington, who, in his military fashion,
treated the disquieted Huskisson as a deserter.
Peel declares that but for this resignation he
should himself have resigned, in consequence
of a narrow vote in the House of Commons
favourable to the Roman Catholics. The resignation of the " Catholic " ministers from power,
strangely enough, resulted obliquely in Emancipation. For one of the offices they had resigned was accepted by Vesey Fitzgerald, who
had in consequence to vacate his seat and
seek re-election for Clare. He polled all the
forces of ascendency, the gentry to a man, and
the fifty-pound freeholders : the constituency
was held by an overwhelming military force.
But O'Connell, though incapable of a seat
in Parliament, was returned, on a wave of
national uprising, at the head of the poll.
This one election let the ocean through the
Protestant dykes, and made further resistance,
in the opinion of Peel and Wellington, impossible.

The philosophical observer cannot help here
turning his gaze for a moment fifty-eight years
forward. In 1828 one Irish election was held
to warrant Peel in a great change of policy : in

1886 eighty-five were declared insufficient to justify Mr. Gladstone.

To return to Peel. He came at once to the conclusion that the election opened up the whole Irish question. He considered it, to use the words in which Cornewall Lewis concisely summarises his views, " as a national and not a religious question. Not merely the removal of disabilities from a body of religionists, but the pacification of Ireland was at issue." At the same time he determined to resign. These views he communicated to the Duke of Wellington in August 1828. The Duke answered briefly, and did not combat Peel's desire to resign ; indeed, he expressly acquiesced in it. And so matters went on through that dark and distracted autumn, varied only by the removal of the Lord High Admiral and the Viceroy of Ireland ; for the Duke, from high notions of discipline, had in those days a passion for removals. But the dismissal of Anglesey in no degree affected the resolution of Peel and Wellington that the Roman Catholic question must be settled, nor the apparent agreement that Peel himself must go. A strange incident now made Peel waver as to his resignation. In January 1829 the Duke endeavoured, at an interview, to persuade the Primate and the Bishops of London and Durham to acquiesce in a measure for Catholic Emancipation. The prelates refused. Thereupon Peel, in an evil hour, as we think, for his own fame, fearing that the King was behind the Bishops, or might base a veto on the Bishops, wrote to Wellington to offer to continue in office should his retirement, in the Duke's opinion, be an insuperable obstacle to the prosecution of his policy. The Duke, of course, eagerly replied that it would be, and Peel remained.

We are here compelled to part company for a moment from Mr. Parker. He thinks that the Duke's letter left Peel no option. But it was, in truth, Peel's own letter that had this effect. He made the offer to remain when the Duke had long agreed that it was necessary that they should part. Conscious as he was of enormous difficulties, Wellington eagerly clutched at Peel's suggestion ; it is not too much to say that in common politeness he could scarcely have done otherwise. It was not the Duke who bound Peel, but Peel who bound himself. To us, anxious as we are to concur with so real an honesty of character and purpose, it seems that the reasons adduced by Peel are inadequate to explain or condone his course. In May 1828 he had been the champion in Parliament against the Roman Catholic claims ; somewhere between May and August 1828 he had been convinced that those claims must be admitted ; in August 1828 he was not less convinced that he could not decently be the minister to settle them, and remained in that conviction till January 1829. Then the attitude of the Bishops made him fear a declaration of *non possumus* from the King, and so he agreed to remain. In the letter itself it may be noticed that there is no mention of such an apprehension. That does not appear to have transpired till 1831, when Peel alluded to it in the House of Commons. And he proceeded to ask what, had he resigned, and the King had said to him, "You advise this course, and ask me to sacrifice my opinion and consistency, why will you not make the same sacrifice ? " he could have replied. As the speech is reported his point is not clear, for the sacrifice of opinion and consistency would be made by Peel whether in or out of office. But it is obvious that the King was supposed to intimate that, as he was compelled to sacrifice his convictions and remain King, Peel, in making the same sacrifice, should remain minister.

All this seems to us shallow reasoning, and to indicate some self-delusion on the part of Peel. It is, in the first place, obviously irrational to confuse the positions of a constitutional Sovereign and a constitutional minister. Constitutional Sovereigns are often compelled to agree both to measures and to men of whom they disapprove ; but there is no question of their retirement. But a minister who considers a measure inevitable, which he has always opposed, has no other course honourably open to him. This Peel himself felt both in 1828 and 1845, though on neither occasion did he definitely withdraw.

But Peel urges, or seems to urge, that, had he retired, the King would have found the courage to declare publicly that he would never consent to Emancipation. We see, we confess, but little grounds for such an apprehension. Unnerved as he was, with the fear of rebellion in Ireland, with the army open to doubt, with the great captain of his country and the Protestant champion both against him, with no one, indeed, to rely upon but the forces of fanaticism, not more

IX.

violent than feeble, we do not believe that the King would have done anything of the kind. The Duke of York had, indeed, made such a declaration, printed on silk, stamped on pottery and pocket - handkerchiefs, applauded at the banquets of bigots. But the Duke of York was both less responsible and more intrepid than the King. The only reason, in fact, which Peel seems to give for his belief is that the King would have founded such a veto on the hostility of the Bishops, and, of course, the House of Lords. For this hypothesis we can find no foundation whatever. Nor in any case can we see how the question whether Peel was in or out of office when supporting the Bill could have made any material difference in the King's attitude. It is rather our firm conviction that Peel out of office could have given the Bill a much more potent advocacy than as a minister : his arguments would have been as efficacious ; his conviction more manifestly pure ; he would have prevented the cancer of personal suspicion, and he would have maintained beyond all question his character as a public man. In fine, we agree with Peel in August 1828 and disagree with his recantation of January 1829.

In point of fact we can scarcely doubt that Peel deluded himself. He sincerely believed, as all men do at times, and as some, like Althorp, do really and always, that he disliked office. In December 1845 he speaks of his loathing of office. But we believe, on the contrary, that he was unconsciously attached to office, and for the highest motives ; that he enjoyed official work, knowing how well he did it ; that he liked leading the House of Commons, because he knew how well he did it ; that he greatly preferred the fruitful task of administration to the spent candour of criticism ; that, to sum all, he was convinced that as a minister he could render excellent service to his country. He did not go so far as Chatham and believe that he alone could save the country, but he felt that his rectitude and capacity would always tide his country over a difficult crisis.

Then, as the session drew near, he began to realise that the great measure would have to be framed by another, and carried through the Commons by another, certainly inferior, hand. Under the mastery of these feelings he wrote to Wellington, and offered to remain. It does not seem to have occurred to him that out of office he could have taken as great a share as he chose in constructing the Bill, and that out of office he could have taken a much more weighty part in carrying it than he could as a minister. He could, in fact, as a private member have sheltered and assisted the Duke's Government, just as from 1846 to 1850 he sheltered and assisted the Government of Lord John Russell.

All this, it may be said, is pure hypothesis. But in a discussion of this kind, where hidden motives and inconsistent action have to be considered and reconciled, it is necessary to have recourse to conjecture ; we cannot, indeed, when the documents are exhausted, employ any other guide.

In 1845–46 the circumstances were somewhat

IX.

different. Peel resigned, not because of the
inconsistency of his proposing the abolition of
the Corn Laws, which his party was sworn to
defend, but because he thought that he required
a unanimous Cabinet to help him to carry his
measure. In 1828 he had written : " I have
been too deeply committed on the question—
have expressed too strong opinions in respect
of it . . . to make it advantageous for the King's
service that I should be the individual to originate
the measure." In 1845–46 he does not seem to
have felt this difficulty. And having resigned,
and the Whigs having failed to form a Government, he may have felt that he was on stronger
ground. In any case, he resumed office with
buoyancy, and, as we have been told on high
authority, confidently reckoned on carrying his
party with him. So far, it may be said that
the Whigs had had their chance, and that it
therefore became a matter of absolute necessity
that Peel should return and carry the measure to
avert a famine. It is difficult to resist this
view. Nor is it necessary to weigh whether
Peel might not have given larger promises of
support to Russell, for Russell inexplicably re-
nounced his task, because he could neither
satisfy Grey nor proceed without him. Russell
seems, if we may judge from his explanation at
the opening of the session, to have required two
conditions to enable him to form a Government :
stronger assurances of support from Peel, and
complete unanimity among his own colleagues.
Both requirements denoted a sanguine nature.
But, so far as Peel was concerned, it must be

felt that, in view of the crisis and of the fact that Russell was in a considerable minority, his assurances of support should have been as ample as possible. Russell, however, failed, and Peel returned.

There seems, then, a clear case of necessity. But it is impossible to avoid the feeling that there is something extremely unfortunate, if not sinister, in the fate which drove Peel a second time to carry, as minister, a measure of which he had been the principal opponent. And it is obvious from the remarkable letter which Graham addressed to Peel in December 1842 that Peel and his closest intimates had foreseen for three years the inevitable change, and had viewed it calmly. " The next change," wrote Graham, " in the Corn Laws must be to an`open trade " : this seventeen months after Peel had entered office as the last hope of the Protectionists. " But," he adds, " the next change must be the last ; it is not prudent to hurry it ; *next session is too soon* ; and, as you cannot make a decisive alteration, it is far better to make none." We have not the answer to this, or the letter which elicited it. But it is impossible to doubt that it represents the views of Peel.

Peel, therefore, amid every outward semblance of political prosperity, was doomed. The leader of a party pledged to Protection, with the clear consciousness that his next step, which might at any moment be taken, must be to Free Trade, he was, in 1842 and for three years onwards, standing on gunpowder ready to explode. He was pontiff of a church with the conviction of being in truth a heretic. It is possible, or even probable, that he felt confident that the course of events would soon convince his followers as well as himself— that he was only anticipating that conviction. If so, we can only say that he little understood the temper of the agrarian knights behind him. They, at any rate, knew what they wanted and what, so long as was possible, they intended to maintain. They did, indeed, suspect their leader's hesitation. But they were determined that their force should not merely intimidate the enemy, but keep that leader, whether willingly or not, in his place. Should he falter, their weapons should prick him forward, or, if necessary, hew him as a traitor. So when he suddenly appeared before them, not in their uniform, but in the clothes he had a second time appropriated from the bathing Whigs, they had no thought but revenge. We can hardly, then, be surprised at the attacks which were made on him in 1846. Lord John Russell summed it all up in his dry, drawling way :

" I cannot express surprise or wonder at any warmth or vindictive feeling being directed against the right honourable gentleman, because in his political career he has done that which perhaps has never happened to so eminent a man before. He has twice changed his opinion on the greatest political question of his day. Once when the Protestant Church was to be defended and the Protestant Constitution rescued from the attacks of the Roman Catholics, which it was said would ruin it, the right honourable gentleman undertook to lead the defence. Again, the

Corn Laws were powerfully attacked in this House and out of it. He took the lead of his party to resist a change and to defend Protection. I think, on both occasions, he has come to a wise conclusion, and to a decision most beneficial to his country ; first, when he repealed the Roman Catholic disabilities, and secondly, when he abolished Protection. But that those who followed him—men that had committed themselves to these questions, on the faith of his political wisdom, on the faith of his sagacity, led by the great eloquence and ability he displayed in debate—that when they found he had changed his opinions and proposed measures different from those on the faith of which they had followed him—that they should exhibit warmth and resentment was not only natural, but I should have been surprised if they had not displayed it."

Peel, in the memoir which he himself prepared, has left us his defence. It amounts simply to this : that his duty to the nation was greater than his duty to the party. As regards the grave but minor charge, that he did not try and take his party into his confidence, his defence seems to us to be words, and merely words, a fog through which there flashes the one clear sentence, " I should have failed in carrying the repeal of the Corn Laws." It was obviously, then, as a question of strategy that he refused his confidence to his followers. He had no right to be surprised that they withheld theirs from him. Nor is it pleasant, bearing in mind our conviction that Peel's unconscious attachment to office was greater than he knew, to remember the remark inferred or recorded by the Prince Consort : " Peel . . . says to himself, ' the minister who settles the Corn Laws is not so easily turned out.' " We would rather he had said, " History will wish to forgive anything to the minister who settles the Corn Laws."

But we return to the larger issue. Peel held that his duty to the nation was greater than his duty to his party. So stated, the proposition is a meritorious platitude, and one of which party men cannot be too often reminded. But all depends on the application, for it may be employed for the basest as well as the sublimest purposes. We can conceive a minister thinking it his duty, in some agony of his country, to sacrifice his party, his future, his fame, nay, his good name, as Brutus sacrificed his sons. On the other hand, such a maxim might easily be utilised to cut at the very root, not of party alone, but of political honour. A political knave or a political mountebank might perennially dwell on the same note to excuse every tergiversation. " Pledges, my dear sir, promises, nay, even principles, what are they in comparison with my duty to my country ? " Peel, with a high consciousness of his aims and character, saw nothing of this. To himself he was saying, " Perish my party, let me save my country." But parties do not like perishing, and always see more available and comfortable methods of saving the country.

So the year 1846 was destined to be fatal to high principle in politics. Peel, with the view of saving his country, betrays his party. His party revenges itself on him by a coalition as discreditable as that of North and Fox. And the mischief does not end with the moment. Twenty-one years afterwards, Peel's bitterest censor, from the point of view of political consistency, imitated his tactics with that fidelity which is the sincerest form of flattery. " First pass the Bill and then turn out the Ministry," said Mr. Disraeli in 1867. This was Peel's attitude in 1846. The year 1846 scarcely seemed perilous to political principle, the retribution was so swift and severe. But it produced 1867. From the transactions of 1867 English public life received a shock which it has scarcely recovered.

Our view is that Peel did not exhaust the alternatives before returning to office. We think that he should have reasoned thus : " Nothing but Free Trade in bread-stuffs, promptly given, can avert a famine in Ireland, but I am the last person who should pass the measure ; for I cannot a second time be placed in the position of a minister betraying his political position. All that I can do, I will do. I will co-operate with any Ministry that will take the necessary steps, and give it my cordial support. If I am consulted, and I must inevitably be consulted, I will give my best counsel. I will do anything and everything, except remain in office." We cannot doubt that, had Peel used this language, Lord John Russell would have disregarded or overcome the hesitations of Grey, would have formed a Government, and have passed the Bill. In any case, we hold that it was Peel's duty to try every conceivable and inconceivable combination to obviate the necessity of his remaining minister, and so lowering the standard of English public life.

Peel thought differently. He considered himself absolved and freed by a genuine resignation, followed by the failure of the Opposition, and the apparent impossibility of any other combination. Nor is it possible to judge him hardly. It is difficult for a minister to exercise an absolutely clear and unbiassed judgement when the horror of famine is upon him, and when the literal rules of the political game appear to have been observed. Moreover, he had hoped not to break up his party but to carry it with him; he had also to remember that he was the rock and pillar of essential Conservatism, not merely in Britain alone, but in Europe. This was no light trust and responsibility, and it made him, we doubt not, reluctant to relinquish his post.

So he judged, and we will not judge him. If he deceived himself, he deceived himself nobly, and he wrought an immortal work. He paid, moreover, the full penalty; he redeemed his reputation by his fall; his political sins or errors, if sins or errors at all, were condoned by the affection and gratitude of the nation. On the night of his resignation a silent multitude awaited him as he left the House of Commons, and, with bared heads, escorted him home. As he lay dying, a sadder crowd surrounded that home day and night, waiting breathlessly for the tidings of the father of their country. This was his reward. And his expiation became a triumph. The two extremes of political party combined to overthrow him. Both, to use a familiar expression, turned their backs upon themselves, in order to secure his defeat; and both acquired those fruits of victory which they coveted. The Protectionists obtained the desert apples of revenge, the Whigs the more succulent substance of office. Lord John Russell and his followers, including Grey, who now sacrificed his scruples, occupied Downing Street, but propped and overshadowed by Sir Robert Peel. For then, and now, and for all time, above and beyond that Government and the perished passions of the time, there looms the great figure of the great minister, with feet perhaps of clay as well as iron, but with a heart at least of silver, and a head of fine gold.

X

DR. CHALMERS [1]

x. WE Scotsmen do well to take every opportunity of revering and burning incense before the memory of Dr. Chalmers. For he was one of the greatest of our race : a commanding character, a superb orator, the most illustrious Scottish churchman since John Knox. His memory remains green and vivid with us when statesmen, writers, and philosophers are, if not forgotten, languishing in the shade. It is a noble and blessed life, none more enviable.

But it is specially in Glasgow that it is fitting to commemorate him, for it is here that his most fruitful years were spent. Here he revealed himself not merely as preacher and divine, but as a statesman. Here he tried that great experiment which sought to preserve the thrift and independence of the Scottish character. The experiment failed in practice, because it required a Chalmers to carry it out; nay, a score of Chalmerses. This in his modesty he always vehemently denied. Nevertheless it was the truth. We know that the plan continued in

[1] An Address delivered on April 14, 1915, in commemoration of the centenary of his first connection with Glasgow.

238

operation to some extent after his departure,
in no slight degree probably an aftermath of his
harvest, but no one but himself could have continued his system for long in face of the overpowering influences against it.   Could even he ?

What was his plan ?   It was in principle
simple enough.   Division into districts and, if
necessary, into sub-districts, with benevolent
supervision by deacons, strict separation of the
deserving from the undeserving poor, a large
scope afforded for the charity and co-operation
of the poor themselves, which was heartily
given.   He refused all public grants and aids,
yet he reduced the expenditure on the poor in
his parish of St. John from £1400 to £280.
Moreover, as a proof, though not a conclusive
proof, that the plan was acceptable, nearly
twice as many people came into the parish as
left it during his administration.   At any rate,
Chalmers's successor, the Rev. Dr. Macfarlane,
was able to testify that the poor, excepting the
worthless and profligate, were in better condition,
more contented and more happy, than the poor
in the other parishes of Glasgow.

This was his scheme, combined with Christian
education and the multiplication of churches,
for both of which he made marvellous efforts ;
it embodied his policy.   But the plan for the
relief of the poor which I have just described,
even had it been practicable without a genius
or a collection of geniuses to carry it out, was
doomed to failure.   The municipal authorities,
who, as Chalmers quaintly put it, " flounce
in the robes of magistracy," did not smile on

x. it ; in those days they seldom smiled on anything, except perhaps the punch - bowl. But
that indifference might have been gradually
worn down by the force of public opinion. There
was, however, no public opinion of sufficient
strength behind him. Indeed, public opinion
has developed in exactly the opposite direction.
He lived to see the arrival of the Poor Law,
which was the end of Chalmersism. State aid,
which he combated, has been increasingly sought.
It may be from some relaxation of character ;
it may be from a feeling that where large sums
are annually exacted in taxation the community
should get as much out of them as possible ; it
may be that Socialism, Christian or un-Christian,
for there are both kinds, has gained strength,
but the fact remains. Individual independence,
for which Chalmers fought, and in which he
believed as the backbone and strength of our
rugged Scottish character, has almost ceased to
operate as a factor. That may be right or may
be wrong, but there will always be a faithful few
to adhere to the creed of Chalmers, and to range
themselves under his tattered but glorious banner.
He seems now to us to have been baling out the
Atlantic ; but the attempt was worth making,
even though the Atlantic did not run dry.

But, if he nobly failed in this enterprise, he
succeeded in another and perhaps a greater.
He warmed Glasgow. He found Glasgow cold,
wealthy, and material. It would not be true to
say that it was spiritually dead, for in the course
of eighteen years the stipends of the city clergy
had been augmented no less than four times by

the Corporation, in spite of a condition of city
finance which almost approached bankruptcy. A
few new chapels or churches had been built,
notably that for Dr. Wardlaw. Nevertheless
the city was not spiritually alive, partly perhaps
from an ecclesiastical conservatism which Dr.
Chalmers considered as specially indigenous in
the West. The church organ, for example, long
banned by the presbyteries, was banned with
especial bitterness in Glasgow. Indeed, the city,
growing by leaps and bounds in population and
commerce, showed little of the same eagerness
in spiritual matters. Chalmers appeared, and
all was transformed. He breathed a new soul
into the community. Laymen rallied round him
with money and personal service. New places
of worship and new schools were erected. And
after three years at the Tron he himself gave an
inspiring example by leaving that historic church
for the new and not very attractive district of
St. John's, that he might work with free hands at
organising a parish according to his view of what
a parish should be.

   Ah, gentlemen, when we think of Dr.
Chalmers's work in Glasgow we are irresistibly
reminded of the origin of your motto. That
was an ancient inscription, " Lord, let Glasgow
flourish through the preaching of Thy Word and
praising Thy Name." The next edition was,
" Lord, let Glasgow flourish by the preaching
of the Word." And the last and only authorised
heraldic form is " Let Glasgow flourish "—a
sensible and wholly secular aspiration. But may
we not say that when Chalmers reigned in

x.   Glasgow his motto at any rate was the earlier
        form that I have quoted, and that his ambitions
        and ideals for Glasgow were wholly spiritual and
        exalted ? For with him those quaintly pious
        words were a living truth. He believed in no
        other means and no other aim. Even those
        whose creed is weaker will pause to admire his
        glowing and single-minded faith and to marvel
        at all that it achieved.

        His instruments for this high work were
        twofold : his preaching and his personality.

        As to the splendours of his preaching, the
        overwhelming power of his oratory, we possess
        conclusive proofs. One is, of course, the sermons
        and speeches which remain to prove themselves.
        He had a lavish gift of diction, a profusion of
        powerful and gorgeous sentences which gathered
        an irresistible momentum and impetus as they
        rolled on. He began, we are told, weakly and
        almost inaudibly, dull-eyed and lifeless, so that
        strangers prepared themselves to be disappointed.
        But in a few moments he warmed up, presently
        he glowed, and soon he was hurling with stormy
        vehemence thunderbolts of eloquence from the vol-
        canic heights of his soul on an audience almost
        paralysed with emotion. He would indeed pause
        from time to time to allow human nature to
        recover itself from the strain. Then breath
        would be drawn, the suppressed coughs would
        be released, and after a space the orator would
        proceed with the same fervour until again he
        had to allow a minute or two of relaxation. This
        to a congregation occupying every inch of space
        right up into the pulpit, which had waited for

hours, and which remained steaming and breath-   x.
less under the wand of the enchanter, through
sermons of an hour and forty minutes or more.
And, what makes the effect still more remarkable,
these sermons were read. Chalmers's ordinary
manuscript was almost illegible. What must
his peculiar shorthand have been! Yet these
discourses seem to have been delivered from this
impenetrable script. His accent, too, was the
broad Doric of Fife, and his pronunciation often
original, yet he controlled his English audiences
as much as his Scottish. These mannerisms
indeed assisted rather than marred his effects.

His appearance must also have aided them.
The huge forehead, which seemed to crush down
by its weight the sweet and mobile mouth, must
have been a formidable adjunct to his eloquence.
His eye, however, had not the glint of oratory,
it was inanimate and leaden. But he had what
Americans call a Daniel Webster head, and
tradition tells how his class students whenever
they got the chance would try on his hat, with
humiliating results. One fancies that the impression produced by his appearance was that
of commanding intellect and an unaffected,
benevolent simplicity.

I like to be told that he had not many sermons,
that he concentrated himself upon a comparatively few, and advised other ministers to do the
same. So that he preached nothing but master-
pieces, whether in the little church at Kilmany
or to the excited audiences of Glasgow and
London. And each time that he repeated them
he gave them new life. He gave, in fact, at all

x. times of his best, and disdained to offer anything less.

The other substantial proof of his immense oratorical power was his audiences. When he preached in London for the Missionary Society, though the service began at eleven the Church was packed at seven, and many thousands turned away. This you may say was anticipation, but it was anticipation so fully realised that though he was so exhausted in the middle of his sermon that he sat down while two verses of a hymn were sung, one of his auditors wrote that he was still under the nervousness of having heard and witnessed the most astounding display of human talent that perhaps ever commanded sight or hearing. It was at this visit to London that Canning, the most brilliant and fastidious orator of his day, was moved to tears by the preaching of Chalmers, and declared " the tartan beats us all." Again, on this visit, but on another occasion, Chalmers himself could not penetrate the crowd, and had almost abandoned the idea of preaching, when, as it would appear, he was admitted over a plank through a window.

I take these examples from London, which might be supposed to be indifferent, but it was always the same pressure in Glasgow. Here, even when he preached on Thursdays, the tide of the whole city seemed to flow into the doors. Here, too, his church was constantly taken by storm, and at his last sermon in St. John's, a strong force of police having failed to stem the torrent, the military had to be called in. We who have seen the great mass meetings, wonderful as they were, addressed by Mr. Gladstone at the height of his fame and popularity have nothing to record like this. There can be but few parallels to it in history.

Oratory must, then, have been one main secret of his amazing power. Energy was another. Tenderness, the tenderness of sympathy, was another. Read the story of his connection with young Thomas Smith and you will hear his heart beating aloud. But his base was character. Through all the splendours of his speech, through all his activity of administration, through all his powerful and voluminous writings there flamed the glory of a living soul: a supreme, unquenchable, fervent soul. For him Christianity was everything; his faith inspired every action of his life, every moment of his day, every word that he uttered, every letter that he wrote. That was the real secret of his power, that drew all hearts willingly or unwillingly to him, and that gave a mystery of inspiration to his discourse. He wrote enormously, he spoke continually, he revealed his inner self in every possible way; but after his first struggles and victory every word that remains on record seems instinct with a pervading, undoubting, eager Christian faith. There was an unconscious sanctity about him which was, as it were, the breath of his nostrils; he diffused it as his breath, it was as vital to him as his breath. This is what we mean by a saint, and if ever a halo surrounded a saint it encompassed Chalmers. It is not breaking the tenth commandment to covet his spirit, though one may despair of the intellect which it animated.

x.   But this sanctity was by no means innate.   It
is, indeed, a consolation to weaker mortals to
know that it had not always been so.   Till he was
past thirty, as we know, the faith of Chalmers,
such as it was, sat lightly on him.   Then he was
principally a mathematician, a philosopher, a
cordial neighbour, giving his Church and his
parish what remained of his time after secular
study had been adequately accomplished.   It
was in these early Kilmany days that he enlisted
in the St. Andrews volunteers, became Chaplain
and Lieutenant ;   and it is recorded that he
preached a war sermon with such violence of
gesture that he tore his gown aside and revealed
the uniform beneath, exclaiming in words which
come home to us now :   " May I be the first to
ascend the scaffold erected to extinguish the
worth and spirit of the country ;   may my blood
mingle with the blood of patriots ;   and may I
die at the foot of that altar on which British
independence is to be the victim."   So he said
with regard to the threats of Napoleon, and so
we say with regard to the menace of far mightier
hosts than Napoleon ever dreamt of.   Then an
illness lifted him into a higher sphere, and he
soared aloft.   There he remained to the end in
communion with the Divine ;   from that time
he was what he continued till death, a unique
personality of prodigious powers, all devoted to
sole purpose of service to God.

Again, it should be said that this saintliness
was not that of an anchorite brooding in religious
solitude.   Here was a man, bustling, striving,
organising, speaking and preaching with the dust

and fire of the world on his clothes, but carrying his shrine with him everywhere.

He did not shrink from his fellow-men: on the contrary, he sought them, for it was the business of his life to permeate them with his message. Yet, like the Duke of Wellington, he had no small talk. Mr. Gladstone, who accompanied him on some of his pastoral visits, said that he sat embarrassed and almost silent. In Glasgow, too, he would perhaps only utter a blessing or a short prayer on such occasions. But his visits were prized, for he radiated benevolence.

I have almost entirely confined myself in what I have been saying to the eight years of his Glasgow life. And yet do not rend me if I say I am not sure if his whole heart was ever in Glasgow. His energies were there, his love for the people was there, the field for beneficence in which he delighted was there, his fame rose there. But you asked too much of your minister in the way of secular business, you made too many extra parochial calls on his time, you paid him too many visits; dare I say it, I am not sure that he relished the climate. And though he resolutely shook off the shackles to which I have alluded, he imposed on himself others not less heavy until he found the burden too much for him to bear. Nor do I think that his heart was in Edinburgh, or St. Andrews. I believe that he was always faithful to his early love, and that his true affections were centred in Anstruther or Kilmany.

Was he able to keep clear of politics—by

which I mean party politics ?   Yes, I think that
that may be claimed for him, though there are
occasional signs that he knew something about
parties, at least their names.   In writing to Peel,
for instance, in 1832, he says, " I am a thorough
Conservative," and in 1835 we are told that at
this period Dr. Chalmers " was in the habit of
expressing in no measured terms his distrust of
the Whigs."   When he was greatly disappointed
with Lord Melbourne's Government for refusing
money to build churches in Scotland, he met a
young friend and said in an accent which my
friend Lord Guthrie has endeavoured to com-
municate to me, " I have a mōral lŏthing of these
Whugs—and espeēcially Fox Mȧȧl."

But whatever party name he may have given
himself, he could not descend enough from his
altitudes to understand the forces which necessarily sway and impel politicians, and so it may
safely be said that he never was in any real sense
a party politician himself.

This seems the proper place to ask what,
outside Church questions, were this great man's
aims and policy.   I do not pretend to have
read the manifold volumes of his works, but
that is not necessary to form a conclusion.   It
is sufficiently clear that the ideal was to raise
the nation by Christianity, by Christian co-operation, Christian education, Christian worship.   He
thought that by these means he would be able
to rear a character and race which would disdain
State aid or State patronage, and be independent
of all but the faith.   It was a sublime vision, and
though he could not accomplish it, it animated

him to do great things while working for it, and   x.
it gave an inspiration to his smallest acts.

The rush of time and events, the torrent that
sweeps human effort into eternity, may have
effaced much of Chalmers's practical work. The
world creeps on in its blind course through the
centuries, we know not whither, but it certainly
does not seem to tend towards the aims of
Chalmers. That, however, does not obliterate
the glory of the effort and the enterprise. He
was, indeed, the Moses of his country, pointing
to a land of promise into which neither he nor
his countrymen entered or were destined to enter.

As to his oratory and its quality, what are we
to say ? This is not the occasion on which to
award the palm to the great pulpit orators of
the nineteenth century. That would require far
greater knowledge and far ampler time than I have
at my disposal. But I have said enough already
to indicate the prodigious effect of his sermons.
If only for his speech on Roman Catholic Emancipation, however, he may claim a high place
among the secular and political speakers of his
time. Perhaps the chief of these were Canning
and Plunket, while others might rank Brougham
and Irving with them in spite of the terrible
drawback of extreme prolixity. Bright and
Gladstone had hardly reached their highest point
when Chalmers died. Mr. Gladstone, however,
it may be remarked in passing, though so strong
an Anglican and High Churchman, was a diligent
disciple. We rarely drove between Edinburgh
and Dalmeny without Mr. Gladstone pointing
out with affectionate interest the spot where,

x.   when they were walking together on the Queens-
ferry Road, Dr. Chalmers's hat had been blown
off across a dyke, and the future statesman
had had to run a considerable distance to
catch it.

But let us return to the orators. The great
fault of Chalmers's oratory was his diffuseness,
arising from a diction of inexhaustible opulence,
always affluent, and always swelling, until it
sometimes overflowed its banks. For this reason
his discourses are sometimes tedious to read.
But then Charles Fox said that a speech which
read well must be a bad speech, which implies
that the converse may often be true. Be that
as it may, we cannot judge of Chalmers's oratory
when divorced from his overpowering and irresistible delivery. That, which combined action,
passion, and soul, with an accent which, as we
have seen, might in cold blood excite a smile,
was evidently half his secret. The interminable
sentences which are often irksome in print came
rolling on like successive billows in a storm,
each driving in the effect of the last. This is not
to underrate the rich splendour of the speech or
sermon itself, but to explain the unique effect
that was produced. The others who have been
mentioned may have been more terse and so
more pointed, but it is to be doubted if any
other orator in Great Britain has ever wielded
the sublime thunder of Chalmers.

Perhaps among all his greatest oratorical
effects the most powerful was that produced by
his speech on Roman Catholic Emancipation. Is
it too familiar to quote ? Surely not on an

occasion like this, for it displays a sane liberality as well as the highest eloquence.

" It is not by our fears and our false alarms that we do honour to Protestantism. A far more befitting honour to the great cause is the homage of our confidence ; for what Sheridan said of the liberty of the Press admits of most emphatic application to this religion of truth and liberty. ' Give,' says that great orator, ' give to ministers a corrupt House of Commons ; give them a pliant and a servile House of Lords ; give them the keys of the Treasury and the patronage of the Crown ; and give me the liberty of the Press, and with this mighty engine I will over-throw the fabric of corruption, and establish upon its ruins the rights and privileges of the people.' In like manner, give the Catholics of Ireland their emancipation ; give them a seat in the Parliament of their country ; give them a free and equal participation in the politics of the realm ; give them a place at the right ear of majesty, and a voice in his counsels ; and give me the circulation of the Bible, and with this mighty engine I will overthrow the tyranny of Antichrist, and establish the fair and original form of Christianity on its ruins." Here we have the striking effect produced by quoting a fine passage of eloquence from Sheridan, and over-topping it by his own.

Of his pathos in the pulpit the most familiar and perhaps the most perfect example is that from his sermon in aid of the orphan children of clergymen, where he describes a minister's children obliged to leave their home on their father's death :

x.

" With quietness on all the hills, and with every field glowing in the pride and luxury of vegetation—when summer was throwing its rich garment over this goodly scene of magnificence and glory, they think, in the bitterness of their souls, that this is the last summer which they shall ever witness smiling on the scene which all the ties of habit and affection have endeared to them ; and then this thought, melancholy as it is, is lost and overborne in the far darker melancholy of a father torn from their embrace, and a helpless family left to find their way, unprotected and alone, through the lowering futurity of this earthly pilgrimage."

Dean Ramsay, who heard the sermon, says that the preacher's tears dropped like raindrops on the manuscript.

To illustrate the variety of his power I would only allude to another sermon, where he described a hunting-field, " the assemblage of gallant knighthood and hearty yeomen," " the high-bred coursers " and " the echoing horn," " the glee and fervency of the chase," " the deafening clamour of the hounds," with such vivid energy that Lord Elcho's huntsman who was present had difficulty in restraining himself from giving a " view holloa." This is the sort of passage that might have been written by Walter Scott himself. Let us here recall that one of the rare occasions when the great Sir Walter was touched by praise was when he was told of the admiration of Chalmers.

And now, in conclusion, let me leave Glasgow behind, and come to what may be considered the fifth act of his magnificent career.

The 18th of May 1843 was one of the most
memorable days in the history of Scotland; it still
thrills the nation to its core. When in the course
of affairs it is recalled, it moves our hearts with a
faint remote harmony like that which the evening
breeze evokes from the aeolian harp. It matters
not to-day who were in the right or who were
in the wrong on that immortal occasion. But
the sight of more than four hundred ministers
proceeding from St. Andrew's Church, leaving
behind them their manses, their kirks, their
homes; casting on the waters the daily bread of
themselves and their families; separating themselves from the Church in which they had minis-
tered so devoutly, from beloved traditions, from
precious friendships; marching resolutely into
the wilderness, and all for conscience' sake, was
one which will never be obliterated from the
minds of their countrymen. They may have
been right, they may have been wrong; still those
who made so glorious a sacrifice cannot have been
wholly wrong. That, thank God, matters little
now, for all parties at this stage can afford to
admire and applaud the apostolical procession,
in which Dr. Chalmers followed the protesting
Moderator, Dr. Welsh. "He had been standing,"
we are told, "immediately to the left. He
looked vacant and abstracted while the protest
was being read. But Dr. Welsh's movement
awakened him from the reverie. Seizing eagerly
upon his hat he hurried after him with all the air
of one impatient to be gone." That has always
struck me as a living portrait.

Since then much has happened, and we have

x.   found the law-courts discussing what were Dr. Chalmers's real views and policy on that occasion. To us now that is of no consequence, for we are approaching, if we have not actually reached, a happier time. Those controversies are dying, if not dead. We meet in temples of concord to bury them and to proclaim peace over their graves. And may we not feel that from our present brotherly discussions, too tardy and elaborate though laymen may feel them to be, but which perhaps require full time in order to lay strong, ample, and compact the bases of a restored and permanent structure, the benediction of Chalmers is not absent? Nay, is it presumptuous to believe that, if departed souls are ever permitted to revisit the scene of their activities in this life, there may be present in the congress of the Fathers of the Church, striving for Christian fellowship and Christian harmony, the spirit of Chalmers, rejoicing with the pure ecstasy of an angel in the blessed prospect of the completed unity of our National Church?

XI

MR. GLADSTONE[1]

I am here to-day to unveil the image of one of the great figures of our country. It is right and fitting that it should stand here. A statue of Mr. Gladstone is congenial in any part of Scotland. But in this Scottish city, teeming with eager workers, endowed with a great University, a centre of industry, commerce, and thought, a statue of William Ewart Gladstone is at home.

But you in Glasgow have more personal claims to a share in the inheritance of Mr. Gladstone's fame. I, at any rate, can recall one memory— the record of that marvellous day in December 1879, nearly twenty-three years ago, when the indomitable old man delivered his rectorial address to the students at noon, a long political speech in St. Andrew's Hall in the evening, and a substantial discourse on receiving an address from the Corporation at ten o'clock at night. Some of you may have been present at all these gatherings, some only at the political meeting. If they were, they may remember the little incidents of the meeting—the glasses which were

[1] A Speech delivered at the unveiling of the statue at Glasgow, October 11, 1902.

255

XI.

hopelessly lost and then, of course, found on the orator's person—the desperate candle brought in, stuck in a water-bottle, to attempt sufficient light to read an extract.   And what a meeting it was— teeming, delirious, absorbed !   Do you have such meetings now ?   They seem to me pretty good ; but the meetings of that time stand out before all others in my mind.

This statue is erected, not out of the national subscription, but by contributions from men of all creeds in Glasgow and in the West.   I must then, in what I have to say, leave out altogether the political aspect of Mr. Gladstone.   In some cases such a rule would omit all that was interesting in a man.   There are characters from which if you subtracted politics there would be nothing left.   It was not so with Mr. Gladstone.

To the great mass of his fellow-countrymen he was of course a statesman, wildly worshipped by some, wildly detested by others.   But, to those who were privileged to know him, his politics seemed but the least part of him.   The predominant part, to which all else was subordinated, was his religion ;   the life which seemed to attract him most was the life of the library ;   the subject which engrossed him most was the subject of the moment, whatever it might be, and that, when he was out of office, was very rarely politics. Indeed, I sometimes doubt whether his natural bent was towards politics at all.   Had his course taken him that way, as it very nearly did, he would have been a great churchman, greater perhaps than any that this island has known ; he would have been a great professor, if you

could have found a university big enough to hold
him ; he would have been a great historian, a
great bookman, he would have grappled with
whole libraries and wrestled with academies, had
the fates placed him in a cloister ; indeed it is
difficult to conceive the career, except perhaps
the military, in which his energy and intellect
and application would not have placed him on
a summit. Politics, however, took him and
claimed his life service, but, jealous mistress as
she is, could never thoroughly absorb him.

Such powers as I have indicated seem to belong
to a giant and a prodigy, and I can understand
many turning away from the contemplation of
such a character, feeling that it is too far removed
from them to interest them, and that it is too
unapproachable to help them—that it is like
reading of Hercules or Hector, mythical heroes
whose achievements the actual living mortal
cannot hope to rival. Well, that is true enough ;
we have not received intellectual faculties equal
to Mr. Gladstone's, and cannot hope to vie with
him in their exercise. But apart from them,
his great force was character, and amid the vast
multitude that I am addressing, there is none
who may not be helped by him.

The three signal qualities which made him
what he was were courage, industry, and faith :
dauntless courage, unflagging industry, a faith
which was part of his fibre—these were the levers
with which he moved the world.

I do not speak of his religious faith—that demands a worthier speaker and another occasion.
But no one who knew Mr. Gladstone could fail

XI.

to see that it was the essence, the savour, the motive power of his life. Strange as it may seem, I cannot doubt that while this attracted many to him, it alienated others, others not themselves irreligious, but who suspected the sincerity of so manifest a devotion, and who, reared in the moderate atmosphere of the time, disliked the intrusion of religious considerations into politics. These, however, though numerous enough, were the exceptions, and it cannot, I think, be questioned that Mr. Gladstone not merely raised the tone of public discussion, but quickened and renewed the religious feeling of the society in which he moved.

But that is not the faith of which I am thinking to-day. What is present to me is the faith with which he espoused and pursued great causes. There also he had faith sufficient to move mountains, and did sometimes move mountains. He did not lightly resolve, he came to no hasty conclusion, but when he had convinced himself that a cause was right, it engrossed him, it inspired him, with a certainty as deep-seated and as imperious as ever moved mortal man. To him, then, obstacles, objections, the counsels of doubters and critics, were as nought; he pressed on with the passion of a whirlwind, but also with the steady persistence of some puissant machine.

He had, of course, like every statesman, often to traffic with expediency; he had always, I suppose, to accept something less than his ideal; but his unquenchable faith, not in himself—though that with experience must have waxed strong—not in himself but in his cause, sustained him among the necessary shifts and transactions

of the moment, and kept his head high in the
heavens.

Such faith, such moral conviction, is not
given to all men, for the treasures of his nature
were in ingots, and not in dust. But there is,
perhaps, no man without some faith in some cause
or some person : if so, let him take heart, in
however small a minority he may be, by remembering how mighty a strength was Gladstone's
power of faith.

His next great force lay in his industry. I do
not know if the aspersions of " ca' canny " be
founded, but at any rate there was no " ca' canny "
about him. From his earliest schooldays, if
tradition be true, to the bed of death, he gave
his full time and energy to work. No doubt his
capacity for labour was unusual. He would sit
up all night writing a pamphlet, and work next
day as usual. An eight-hours' day would have
been a holiday to him, for he preached and
practised the gospel of work to its fullest extent.
He did not, indeed, disdain pleasure ; no one
enjoyed physical exercise, or a good play, or a
pleasant dinner, more than he ; he drank in
deep draughts of the highest and the best that
life had to offer ; but even in pastime he was
never idle. He did not know what it was to
saunter, he debited himself with every minute
of his time ; he combined with the highest
intellectual powers the faculty of utilising them
to the fullest extent by intense application.
Moreover, his industry was prodigious in result,
for he was an extraordinarily rapid worker.
Dumont says of Mirabeau that till he met that

XI. marvellous man he had no idea of how much could be achieved in a day. " Had I not lived with him," he says, " I should not know what can be accomplished in a day, all that can be compressed into an interval of twelve hours. A day was worth more to him than a week or a month to others." Many men can be busy for hours with a mighty small product, but with Mr. Gladstone every minute was fruitful. That, no doubt, was largely due to his marvellous powers of concentration. When he was staying at Dalmeny in 1879 he kindly consented to sit for his bust. The only difficulty was that there was no time for sittings. So the sculptor with his clay model was placed opposite Mr. Gladstone as he worked, and they spent the mornings together, Mr. Gladstone writing away, and the clay figure of himself less than a yard off gradually assuming shape and form. Anything more distracting I cannot conceive, but it had no effect on the busy patient.

And now let me make a short digression. I saw recently in your newspapers that there was some complaint of the manners of the rising generation in Glasgow. If that be so, they are heedless of Mr. Gladstone's example. It might be thought that so impetuous a temper as his might be occasionally rough or abrupt. That was not so. His exquisite urbanity was one of his most conspicuous graces. I do not now only allude to that grave, old-world courtesy, which gave so much distinction to his private life ; for his sweetness of manner went far beyond demeanour. His spoken words, his letters, even when one differed from him most acutely, were all

marked by this special note. He did not like
people to disagree with him—few people do; but,
so far as manner went, it was more pleasant to
disagree with Mr. Gladstone than to be in agreement with some others.

Lastly, I come to his courage—that perhaps
was his greatest quality, for when he gave his heart
and reason to a cause, he never counted the cost.
Most men are physically brave, and this nation
is reputed to be especially brave, but Mr. Gladstone was brave among the brave. He had to
the end the vitality of physical courage. When
well on in his ninth decade, well on to ninety, he
was knocked over by a cab, and before the by-
standers could rally to his assistance, he had
pursued the cab with a view to taking its number.
He had, too, notoriously, political courage in a
not less degree than Sir Robert Walpole. We
read that George II., who was little given to
enthusiasms, " would often cry out, with colour
flushing into his cheeks, and tears sometimes in
his eyes, and with a vehement oath : ' He
(Walpole) is a brave fellow ; he has more spirit
than any man I ever knew.' "

Mr. Gladstone did not yield to Walpole in
political and parliamentary courage—it was a
quality which he closely observed in others, and
on which he was fond of descanting. But he had
the rarest and choicest courage of all—I mean
moral courage. That was his supreme characteristic, and it was with him, like the others,
from the first. A contemporary of his at Eton
once told me of a scene, at which my informant
was present, when some loose or indelicate toast

XI.

was proposed, and all present drank it but young Gladstone. In spite of the storm of objurgation and ridicule that raged around him, he jammed his face, as it were, down in his hands on the table and would not budge. Every schoolboy knows, for we may here accurately use Macaulay's well-known expression, every schoolboy knows the courage that this implies. And even by the heedless generation of boyhood it was appreciated, for we find an Etonian writing to his parents to ask that he might go to Oxford rather than Cambridge, on the sole ground that at Oxford he would have the priceless advantage of Gladstone's influence and example. Nor did his courage ever flag. He might be right, or he might be wrong—that is not the question here—but when he was convinced that he was right, not all the combined powers of Parliament or society or the multitude could for an instant hinder his course, whether it ended in success or in failure. Success left him calm, he had had so much of it; nor did failures greatly depress him. The next morning found him once more facing the world with serene and undaunted brow.

There was a man. The nation has lost him, but preserves his character, his manhood, as a model, on which she may form, if she be fortunate, coming generations of men. With his politics, with his theology, with his manifold graces and gifts of intellect, we are not concerned to-day, not even with his warm and passionate human sympathies. They are not dead with him, but let them rest with him, for we cannot in one discourse view him in all his parts. To-day it is enough

to have dwelt for a moment on three of his great
moral characteristics, enough to have snatched
from the fleeting hour a few moments of communion with the mighty dead.

History has not yet allotted him his definite
place, but no one would now deny that he bequeathed a pure standard of life, a record of lofty
ambition for the public good as he understood it,
a monument of life-long labour. Such lives speak
for themselves; they need no statues; they face
the future with the confidence of high purpose
and endeavour. The statues are not for them
but for us, to bid us be conscious of our trust,
mindful of our duty, scornful of opposition to
principle and faith. They summon us to account
for time and opportunity; they embody an
inspiring tradition; they are milestones in the life
of a nation. The effigy of Pompey was bathed
in the blood of his great rival : let this statue
have the nobler destiny of constantly calling to
life worthy rivals of Gladstone's fame and character.

XII

LORD SALISBURY [1]

I DO not know that I was ever in a more difficult position in the whole course of my life. It
seemed easy enough, in the leafy month of June,
when you invited me, some time in November,
to perform the duty of to-day, to say " Yes " to
the invitation so gracefully proffered. But now,
when I come face to face with the facts, I begin
to think I was the very last person who ought to
have been chosen for this duty. I am in a three-
fold difficulty. In the first place, it is too near
the time at which we lost the statesman whom
we commemorate to-day to be able to appreciate
fully and entirely his position, his historical
position, in the annals of his country. Secondly,
it seems to me that the duty should have been
confided to one who was more closely connected
with him, to one who could speak with more
experience of his private life, and to one who,
at any rate, had had the pleasure of being his
colleague or his follower. Perhaps it was with
a pleasant sense of paradox that you, Mr.
President, threw the handkerchief to me. But

[1] A Speech delivered on unveiling the memorial bust in the Oxford
Union, November 14, 1904.

my third difficulty is even more formidable. XII.
It is that I am now making my maiden
speech in this assembly.   I joined the Union
eight - and - thirty years ago.   I did think that
in that time I had got through all the maiden
speeches it was possible for me to deliver.   But
now I find myself, deep in middle age, before an
audience all of whom, I presume, have delivered
successful maiden speeches within these hallowed
walls, listening to a maiden effort of my own.
I hoped and believed I should go to my grave
without delivering that maiden speech at the
Union, because, when one has become stiff in one's
joints, oratorically speaking, one has lost that
sense of bashfulness, that anxiety to please, that
tone of classical erudition which distinguishes
the maiden speech of any one taking part in the
debates of the Oxford Union.   Now I have done
with my excuses, and will say a few words on the
topic to which you have invited me to-day.

One thing is most manifest about the career
of Lord Salisbury.   It was not a career of promise
cut short before performance was possible ;   it
was not prematurely severed.   No.   His life was
drained to the last drop, and drained in the
service of his country.   Never, indeed, was a
life more complete.   We can speak of him without
a feeling of regret.   Happy those who have so
long mixed in public life of whom that may be
said.   There are two other points, dominant
points, in Lord Salisbury's career which in a
complete study of his life could not be left un-
noticed, but which I must pass over to-night for
reasons obvious enough.   There are those here,

his sons, who can speak of them with more of the truth of eloquence than I can pretend to ; and when I mention his devout religious feeling, his devoted churchmanship, I think you will feel I am alluding to topics on which it would be almost ,sacrilege for a mere acquaintance to intrude. And again, when I speak of what I believe was his dominant happiness, his family and domestic life, there again I think you will feel that we should be wise to leave that untrespassed. I have heard that it was his custom, that it was his special relaxation all through his laborious Parliamentary life, to gather round him on Sunday evenings at dinner every member of his family who could be collected for the purpose, and those who have assisted at these reunions have told me that never was Lord Salisbury seen to such advantage as among those he so dearly cherished and so deeply loved. Well, then, we come to points on which it is more permissible to touch.

I suppose that Lord Salisbury wielded the most brilliant pen of any Prime Minister of the nineteenth century with the exception of Canning, and with Canning's and with Lord Beaconsfield's I think that Lord Salisbury's pen may be reckoned. We have constantly heard stories of how in his youth he maintained himself largely by his pen. I do not doubt that that was a fact. To the end of his life he never wrote a despatch which did not show pre-eminently the literary gift. In speaking, at one time he rose to great heights of eloquence. I do not think that it was oratory in the highest sense of the word, but it always shone, perhaps because it showed so pre-

eminently the literary faculty. Lord Salisbury's
sentences were always polished, his speeches were
always literary gems, and although towards the
end he was no longer equal to himself, those who
have heard him in his prime will feel that there
was nothing that appealed more to their intellect
and to their admiration than that deep, rich voice
rolling out brilliant sentence after brilliant sentence
as if the fountains of eloquence could never run
dry within him.

There was one other point, I think, on which
Lord Salisbury differed from most men—his
absolute scorn of wealth and honours. The
luxuries purchased by wealth, the swell of honours
and titles, that mean so much to most men,
meant absolutely nothing to Lord Salisbury.
They were dross to him. I doubt if he ever took
the slightest count of them. I do not feel confident, but here I speak under correction, that
he even appreciated as much as many men would
the magnificent palace which he had inherited
at Hatfield. Nor were his diversions those of
a great prince or of a wealthy man. His only
relaxations that I know of were science, and
reading, and the love of his family ; and through
all, above all, never failing, ardent, uncompromising work. I suspect, if the truth were
known, it would be found that he was one of the
hardest workers of his time.

There was another point of his character in
which he was almost unique—his hatred of
anything like advertisement. In these days, to
find a statesman who dislikes advertisement is
to try to find a creature that rarely exists. In

XII. these days, a great many of us seem to spend
our lives in puffing, or in being puffed. Nothing
was so abhorrent to Lord Salisbury. All the
little devices, the scattered portraits, the carefully
announced hours of departure and arrival, all
the little stimulants to mechanical enthusiasm
so much in vogue, found their most uncompromising opponent in Lord Salisbury. He only
asked to do his work and to be left alone. And,
I take it, no man ever disliked so much as he did
the pomp of public occasions, when as Prime
Minister he was compelled to play a conspicuous
part.

Of course, there are criticisms. He was
thought to be a proud man. Was he a proud
man ? If he were, he was too proud to show his
pride. Was he a shy man ? There I should
plead guilty for him. He was certainly a shy
man. Had you met Lord Salisbury in the streets
of London you would have taken him to be some
learned literary recluse hurrying, after a visit to
the British Museum, back to the study he had
regretted leaving.

He was charged with cynicism. What is
cynicism ? I have never been able to arrive at a
definition of cynicism. In speech it seems, at
any rate, to amount to this, the parching up of a
subject by the application to it of a wit so dry
as to be almost bitter. And is not that often a
very convenient faculty ? Is it not a priceless
advantage when some untimely or importunate
question is put, or some subject is advanced
which it is not desirable to discuss, to have the
acid, the corrosive cynicism, to apply to it, to

dissolve it, at any rate for the moment ? My impression is that that was the character, to a large extent, of Lord Salisbury's cynicism. I have sat on committees with him, and I am convinced that a great part of that valuable faculty to which I have alluded was used for the purpose which I have indicated.

But it is said he was a pessimist ; he was so cynical as to be a pessimist. Well, I will admit so much. I think Lord Salisbury was a pessimist as regards the effects of legislation. He took too broad and wide a view of human affairs and the course of human history to set very much emphasis on the efforts of passing legislation. He viewed the progress of humanity as a whole, and saw in that progress how very little direct effect legislation has had. If I may say so, I think he forgot in that survey that legislation in a democracy is more often an effect than a cause, and that men are not always able to take so broad and exalted a view as he did, but are anxious in their time and in their generation to effect by legislation some step onward in the path of progress. Well, I do not think there could be much in his pessimism or much in his cynicism, because no one, even one who had so little to do with him as I had, would fail to be touched and warmed by the essential kindness of his heart. I can recall kindnesses that he did for me, though I do not think I ever voted in the lobby with him in my life ; and if he was so kind to me, how much kinder must he have been to those who were closely associated with him ?

And now, if I have not detained you too

long, I am going to approach the thorny path of politics. I am not going to perform an egg dance, for the satisfaction of anybody, among contemporary eggs. The eggs which I shall approach are so ancient as to indicate the decay which I believe characterises the eggs that are used for the purpose of argument at elections. I want to take three epochs in Lord Salisbury's life which, in my appreciation of him, are the three critical epochs of his career.

The first was in 1867, when he resigned office rather than agree to a Reform Bill which he thought was an outbidding by the Conservative party of what had been proposed by their Liberal opponents. He had no language to spare for those who were guilty of what he considered to be a breach of trust in the Conservative party. It perhaps is a strange observation to make, but I think you will find it to be true, that a man of high ideal and exalted standards is apt to reserve his chief bitterness of language for his own party, or to use it with more satisfaction than he does with regard to his opponents. And the reason is simple enough. The honour, the interest, the welfare of his own party are part of himself, part of his being, his own life ; and when, therefore, he sees his party, as he thinks, playing false to him, then it is that he pours over them the vials of his bitterest wrath. The party with which he is not connected may have their own code of honour, their own principles, their own methods of action, but they do not affect him, they are matters for themselves ; he may criticise them with asperity, but the bitterness of his heart goes out to those who, he thinks, have betrayed his own honour and his own party. That was the case with Lord Salisbury, and when the Reform Bill of 1867 was passed, he used language of absolute despair. He retired from office ; it seemed as if he were to retire from political life. He said in his place in Parliament that the monarchical principle was dead, the aristocratical principle was doomed, and the democratical principle was triumphant. He lived to see every one of those prophecies falsified. Before he died the monarchical principle was infinitely stronger than it was in 1867, the aristocratical principle was so much stronger that it seemed almost to have assumed a permanent predominance, and the democratical principle, which he thought would govern the country from 1867 onwards, has had a rather sickly time of it since. In a book published recently—which perhaps is already in the library of the Union— *The Life of Lord Coleridge*, you will find confirmation of this despairing attitude of Lord Salisbury. The year afterwards, in 1868, he writes to Lord Coleridge : " My opinions belong to the past, and it is better that new principles in politics should be worked by those who sympathise with them heartily." That seemed like a formal abdication of politics.

From 1867 to 1874 his position in politics was ambiguous and difficult. He had quarrelled formally with the leaders of his party, he had cursed them with bell, book, and candle (and his curse had a certain potency in it), and it did not seem possible that the quarrel would ever be made

XII.

up. Then came the great Conservative majority of 1874, and Lord Salisbury had to make a supreme choice—whether he would stand on that bed-rock principle on which he had placed himself in 1867 and would remain isolated, almost a political hermit, for the rest of his days, or whether he would join the Government of Mr. Disraeli, who, he considered, had in 1867 betrayed his party. Now the choice was a very difficult one. I am not at all sure—I speak entirely from surmise—I am not at all sure that if Lord Salisbury had consulted his own wishes he would not have taken the first course, and remained permanently outside the new arrangement. But he had this to consider, that he was living in a world, not of abstract principles, but of practical work, and that if he were ever to apply his high abilities to the public service it was now or never, though he must in doing so, no doubt, abandon something of the rigidity of his original principles. Well, I have endeavoured to put the choice before you as it appears to me. I myself think he chose rightly. The country would have lost enormously if he had remained an isolated figure, a prophet of woe, in the midst of Parliament. We know now by his subsequent career how much we should have lost. But still, it was a difficult choice to make, and it appeared bifurcated before him. He chose the path of work, the path of party action, and he became for the rest of his life a strong, effective, and successful party man.

That was the second epoch to which I said I would call your attention. The third will only demand a sentence. I think that he reached the

greatest moment of his life in 1878. It was not
that he returned from the Congress at Berlin
in that year with flowers, acclaiming of crowds,
illuminations, and " peace with honour." The
great moment of Lord Salisbury's life, to my
mind, the moment in which he set his stamp on
his country and on his own fame, and achieved
for himself a European reputation, was when he
went to the Foreign Office, succeeding Lord
Derby, shut himself up in a room, and then and
there, without, as far as I know, any assistance
whatever from the staff of the Foreign Office or
any external source, wrote that famous despatch
on the provisions of the Treaty of San Stefano
which, whatever may be thought of its substance
and policy, will, I believe, remain for long generations to come one of the historic State papers
of the English language. From that time, the
time when he joined the Government of 1874,
and still more from the time when he established
himself by that despatch as a European statesman, Lord Salisbury's career ran on greased
wheels. He was to see a Government succeed
his in 1880 by no means happy in its performances
or in its results. He was to see, the year after
that Government ended in 1886, the party of
his opponents deprived of all power for at least
eighteen years, and during all that time, from
1885 up to the moment of his death, or retirement,
Lord Salisbury remained the predominant factor
in English politics.

There let us leave him. It is not for a contemporary hand to probe any deeper than that
into a career so lately ended. It is not to-day

XII.

or to-morrow that we can ascertain the place and the niche in which his honoured memory will repose. He loomed large in the history of his country. He exercised a singular and prolonged influence over her destinies. He held the highest position in the State for a longer time, I think, than any statesman since Lord Liverpool. Whether he was one of those whom history for one reason or another stamps as great, history alone can say. This much is certain, that he was an able, loyal, untiring servant of his Sovereign and his country. He was a public servant, if I may so express myself, of the Elizabethan type, a fit representative of his great Elizabethan ancestor. And he was a man of pure, exalted, and laborious life. May there be many in this assembly—inspired by his example—who will endeavour to emulate his career. They cannot all be Prime Ministers, they cannot all be Chancellors of this ancient University, but they can at any rate give themselves as loyally and entirely as he did to the work that lies to their hand to do for the service of their King and their country.

XIII

LORD RANDOLPH CHURCHILL [1]

I

SHORTLY after Lord Randolph Churchill's death, his mother asked me to write something about him. I excused myself as it was then too near his time. It may be still too near, at least to arrive at a cool and impartial estimate : that in any case can scarcely be done by a personal friend. But now that his *Life* has appeared I may perhaps venture to acquit myself of what I feel to be in some sort a debt. In any case it is a melancholy satisfaction to set down what I can properly publish of one of the most remarkable men, with perhaps the most remarkable career, of my time.

This much in preface. But it may be urged, Why write at all, when so much has been written so recently and so well ? My answer would be that I knew my friend as a contemporary ; and the knowledge of a contemporary and that of a son are essentially different. I do not in any sense compete with what his son has produced. His book is a careful and authoritative life. Mine at most is only a reminiscence and a study.

[1] First published by Mr. Arthur L. Humphreys, 1906.

275

XIII. Little indeed can be added to the *Life.* Lord Randolph Churchill is fortunate in his son and his biographer ; for the *Life* is a remarkable book, and, considering the difficulties that beset the author, it is little less than marvellous.

To no one could the task of narrating Lord Randolph's career be easy ; to write it ten years after his death required no common courage. But to a son bound by all the ties and truth of filial devotion, yet who may be said not to have known his father, politically speaking, at all ; who was determined to write as impartially as possible ; who has himself taken the step from which his father shrank, and has exchanged Toryism for Liberalism ; and who has therefore to face some hostility on both sides, Liberal antagonism to his father and Tory resentment towards himself, the work presented obstacles that might well have been insuperable. But Mr. Winston Churchill has overcome them all. Tactfulness has not perhaps been considered the strongest element in his Corinthian composition ; but tact was the first requisite of his enterprise, and it has not failed him. It was not easy to be fair, yet he has held the balance surely. He may have unwittingly trodden on some secret corns, but he was threading a living crowd. He has not probably been able to unveil every transaction ; he has assuredly not been able to delineate nakedly every character on his scene. But he has been bold and candid, as bold and candid as it was possible to be. He has, more-over, not drowned his subject's personality in contemporary history ; of that he tells enough

and not too much. The story of those times has XIII.
yet to be written in its entirety, but few will
quarrel with Mr. Churchill's presentation of its
dominant features.

That the book would be brilliantly written,
readers of Mr. Churchill's books and speeches
would expect with confidence, and they have
not been disappointed. There is a pleasant
flavour of irony, there are passages of high
eloquence. As an example of the first quality,
I would cite the description of the Aston
riots ; [1] and of the second, the metaphor of the
old battlefield.[2] If there be a flaw, if there be
a want unsatisfied, it is perhaps that we are not
treated to more of Randolph's crisp, pointed, and
delightful letters. The reason is, no doubt, that
they were too crisp, pointed, and delightful for
present publication. What a fascinating volume
could be provided by his voluminous correspondence with Lord Salisbury, himself so skilful with
his pen ! But this, for the present generation
at any rate, is, I presume, forbidden fruit. The
intimate interchange of thought between high
Ministers of State should not be lightly or prematurely published. Here Mr. Churchill is wise,
though we are the sufferers. Those who are
young to-day may lick their intellectual chops
in joyful anticipation ; for their elders there is,
very properly, no hope.

But we cannot help wishing for more letters
of the earlier period, for he was an admirable

[1] *Life*, i. 362. [In these references I propose, for brevity, to mention
the biography as the *Life*, which, though not the actual title, is sufficiently descriptive.]

[2] *Life*, ii. 49.

writer even in his school days. How excellent is the description, given in the *Life*, which he wrote from Eton of the marriage of the Prince and Princess of Wales : one runs and shouts with him, and is left with him breathless and hatless in the road.[1] When he grew up, his letters to his friends were usually couched in a style of ironical or pungent banter, which would require marginal notes of explanation. Mr. Churchill has had the bold wisdom to narrate his father's matrimonial negotiations, and to this we owe some excellent letters. Occasionally, however, Randolph could mount the high epistolary horse and write with all the pomposity of the eighteenth century. Of this, a good example is given in the biography : a letter to Mr. Tabor, the eminent schoolmaster of Cheam, asking for " a holiday for those young gentlemen who are now deriving from you similar advantages to those which befell me." [2] It would seem that these paroxysms of solemnity usually seized him on his accession to office, for this letter was written when he went to the India Office, and I remember another written when he became Chancellor of the Exchequer, which was pitched even higher. The truth perhaps is, that the constant exercise of irony made sometimes a confusion as to whether he was writing seriously or not. I well remember a letter in his undergraduate days couched in terms of some severity which I believed to be ironical, but which I afterwards found to be seriously meant. As Randolph's disease grew upon him his letters grew

[1] *Life*, i. 9.   [2] *Life*, i. 426.

longer and longer, and yet the tremulous writing betrays what an effort they must have cost him ; but in substance and language they were still excellent, though the few I have left seem still too personal for publication.

There is, however, one letter published in the *Life* which is of supreme interest to Randolph's friends and admirers : a letter the pathos of which, to those who knew him, it is not possible to exaggerate ; it is almost an epitaph. " So Arthur Balfour is really leader," he writes to his wife from Mafeking in November 1891, " and Tory Democracy, the genuine article, is at an end. Well, I have had quite enough of it all. I have waited with great patience for the tide to turn, but it has not turned, and will not now turn in time. In truth, I am now altogether *déconsidéré*. . . . No power will make me lift hand, or foot, or voice for the Tories, just as no power would make me join the other side. All confirms me in my decision to have done with politics, and try to make a little money for the boys and ourselves. . . . More than two-thirds in all probability of my life is over, and I will not spend the remainder of my years in beating my head against a stone wall. I expect I have made great mistakes ; but there has been no consideration, no indulgence, no memory or gratitude—nothing but spite, malice, and abuse. I am quite tired and dead-sick of it all, and will not continue political life any longer. I have not Parnell's dogged, but at the same time sinister resolution ; and have many things and many friends to make me happy without that

horrid House of Commons' work and strife." [1]
Surely a tragic letter, the revelation of a sore and
stricken soul. He was sick of heart and body
when he uttered this burst of melancholy candour.
And yet, had he thought a moment when he
confessed to the mortal conviction that the tide
would not turn in time, he must have seen that
he hardly gave the tide a chance when he refused
all contact with either party. In all that may
be written about the tragedy of Randolph's life
there will be nothing so sad as this letter of his.
About the same time he copied out for himself
that passage of Dryden which ends with

Not Heaven itself over the past hath power;
But what has been has been, and I have had my hour. [2]

Strong lines, with a pang of solace.

On the other hand, while regretting the
paucity of letters, a different regret may be
expressed with regard to speeches. Two personal
attacks are quoted at length which Randolph
deliberately omitted from the revised collection.
It is not a matter of great moment; it must be
a subject of supreme indifference to the objects;
but these extracts are by no means the best
instances of his humour and invective. Under
these circumstances the discretion of the orator
himself might have been imitated with advantage. But this, after all, is a small blot, if blot
it be; and, in fine, the author is to be congratulated on a consummate achievement. He has
under great difficulties produced a fascinating
book, one to be marked among the first dozen,

[1] *Life*, ii. 452.   [2] *Life*, ii. 213.

perhaps the first half-dozen, biographies in our   XIII.
language.

II

Sincere and honest as it is, Mr. Churchill's
Memoir cannot be a complete disclosure. It is
quite possible, for example, that it will not, as
the biographer seems to desire, eradicate the
impression that the relations between Randolph
and the Irish party up to June 1885 were in the
nature of a close understanding little short of
an alliance. For in the *Life* itself we find
adequate evidence of an agreement amply sufficient for its purpose, although not drawn up on
paper ; as nobody, indeed, supposed that it was.
Mr. Churchill draws too large an inference from
the fact that no document " directly or indirectly
referring to the subject has been preserved." A
suspicious man of the world would perhaps draw
from this very circumstance a directly opposite
conclusion. Neither Parnell nor Randolph was
likely to commit his negotiations to writing ;
political negotiations rarely or never are so
recorded. It is, however, " certain," says Mr.
Churchill, " that he (Randolph) had more than
one conversation with the Irish leader ; that he
stated to him his opinion of what a Conservative
Government would do should it be formed ; and
that he declared that he considered himself
precluded by public utterances from joining a
Government which would at once renew the
Crimes Act." [1]   Randolph's own statement was
that " there was no compact or bargain of any

[1] *Life*, i. 394.

XIII.

kind : but I told Parnell when he sat on that sofa that if the Tories took office and I was a member of their Government, I could not consent to renew the Crimes Act. Parnell replied, ' In that case, you will have the Irish vote at the elections.' " [1]

Mr. Churchill's view of all this is that it was not in any sense a bargain, as it was not certain that his father would form part of the next Tory Government. This reasoning does not seem very conclusive, and it certainly did not weigh with Mr. Parnell. That shrewd politician knew well not only that Randolph must inevitably form part of any substantial Tory Government, but that within or without the Government he was incomparably the most formidable Tory in the House of Commons, and probably in the country. A promise by such a man was of inestimable value. Parnell did not hesitate a moment, and in return for the pledge given at once promised the Irish vote at the General Election. " I will do so-and-so," said one party. " In that case I will do so-and-so," said the other. This may not be called a compact, but it is remarkably like one. To the principals, at any rate, this exchange of engagements was quite sufficient, and did not need the compromising accessories of parchment, paper, or seal.

It is the easier and pleasanter to believe in this compact, as both parties were perfectly honest and sincere. There was nothing, in truth, of which either party as individuals need be ashamed. Randolph really believed that any

[1] *Life*, i. 395.

form of what is technically known as " coercion "
was at that time unnecessary, and Parnell
naturally gave his support to a view which was
entirely his own.

Randolph, moreover, from his official experience in Ireland, had imbibed a serious distrust
and dislike of " coercion." " People sometimes
talk too lightly of coercion," he said in one of his
earliest speeches ; [1] " it means that hundreds of
Irishmen who, if laws had been maintained
unaltered, and had been firmly enforced, would
now have been leading peaceful, industrious, and
honest lives, will soon be torn off to prison without
trial ; that others will have to fly the country
into hopeless exile ; that others, driven to
desperation through such cruel alternatives, will
perhaps shed their blood and sacrifice their lives
in vain resistance to the forces of the Crown ;
that many Irish homes, which would have been
happy if evil courses had been firmly checked at
the outset, will soon be bereaved of their most
promising ornaments and support, disgraced by
a felon's cell and a convict's garb ; and if you
look back over the brief period which has been
necessary to bring about such terrible results,
the mind recoils in horror from the ghastly
spectacle of murdered landlords, tenant-farmers
tortured, mutilated dumb animals, which everywhere disfigures the green and fertile pastures of
Ireland." [2] These, I doubt not, were his innermost and sincerest views. Has any orator even
of Irish race protested more strongly against exceptional administration for his people ? That

[1] *Speeches*, i. 19.   [2] *Speeches*, i. 18.

XIII. being so, Randolph can scarcely be blamed as an individual for his compact with Parnell.

Randolph's official account of all this gives to the renunciation of coercion a much more deliberate and concerted character. In a speech delivered at Sheffield in September 1885, he stated that some weeks before the fall of Mr. Gladstone's Government in the previous June, Lord Salisbury and his immediate political friends took counsel together as to what they should do in the event of Mr. Gladstone's defeat. The gravest question, he said, that they then had to consider was " whether Ireland could or could not be governed by the ordinary law. That subject was considered with great deliberation. *We* had many facilities for gaining information." These facilities, put briefly, were the advice of Lord Ashbourne and " many other sources of accurate information." And the result was that some weeks before Mr. Gladstone's defeat " Lord Salisbury and his friends came to the conclusion that in the absence of official information—that was the important saving clause—there was nothing which would warrant a Government in applying to Parliament for exceptional laws for the administration of Ireland " ; and he proceeded to say that when they did have access to official information there was none that warranted their departing from their previous view.[1] The " we " that has been italicised seems to prove that Randolph formed part of this council. In a memorandum drawn up during later years, he says that the " question had been

---

[1] *Speeches*, i. 258.

more than once discussed in small *conciliabules* before the fall of Mr. Gladstone's Government, and a sort of decision arrived at. . . . But the former semi-decision did not help Lord Salisbury much when the actual crisis came. . . . Mr. Gibson in this difficulty was the real arbiter." [1] We must all regret that the minute is too confidential to be given in its entirety, for there is an alluring suspicion of withheld piquancy about the printed extracts.

It is easy to believe that he urged his view, but that he did not mention his momentous conversation with Parnell. As to the facts, it is only necessary to observe that the " official information," which made Lord Spencer, with his matchless experience and knowledge and his liberal Irish views, insist on some coercion, did not produce the same effect on the new ministers. Whether they took any great pains to examine the " official information " is doubtful. Randolph certainly gave me to understand that the abandonment of coercion was one of the two conditions he made for his joining the Government.

There can be, I think, no question in any impartial mind that there was a valid, though unwritten, understanding with the Irish leader, of which many in high position among the Tories may have been unconscious, and of which Randolph was the medium and the channel. The result was apparent in a memorable scene, when, in the House of Lords, the new Prime Minister, after setting forth his political programme, handed over, against all precedent, to Lord

[1] *Life*, i. 409.

XIII.

Carnarvon, the new Viceroy, the task of announcing the Irish policy of the Government. No one who was present on that occasion will ever forget it, or can have carried away the belief that this Irish policy was congenial to the head of the administration. Nor indeed did Lord Carnarvon perform his task with any peculiar relish. The two ministers seemed rather to resemble penitents in a public act of contrition than advisers of the Crown commencing with hope and confidence a new departure. The last may have been the truth, I can only record the impression.

It may perhaps be held, without doing him any injustice, that Randolph was prepared to concede almost all Irish demands, except that which is popularly and sentimentally known as " Home Rule." But on that issue he was immovable. I never heard him use but one language with regard to it—that it was impossible. In 1891 he stated this with great emphasis in a public letter. " I have always been of opinion that however attractive Home Rule for Ireland might be in theory, it was an absolute impossibility to put Home Rule into a bill. You might as well try to square the circle." [1] He never varied in this opinion, and was insistent on this point from the beginning. " Now mind," he said in September 1885, " none of us must have anything to do with Home Rule in any shape or form." [2] Yet, strangely enough, and unknown to him, his own Viceroy had for two months past been handling the accursed thing with some familiarity. Before this Government of eight months had ended,

[1] *Life*, ii. 508.   [2] *Life*, i. 461.

Lord Carnarvon was indeed to intimate that unless the Government could move in the direction of Home Rule he could not continue to hold office.[1] The answer was the promise of a strict Coercion Bill.

In later years Randolph drew up a memorandum in which he blamed himself for his compact with Parnell. " I believe," he says, almost innocently, " that the decision not to attempt to renew the Crimes Act, more than any other event, finally determined Mr. Gladstone no longer to resist Repeal." This can scarcely be called a new light, for it is obvious that this decision was the starting-point of the new Liberal departure. But it is not necessary here to enter into the polemics of that critical and stormy period. Randolph ends by saying that " looking back on those events after January 1886, and after the resolution arrived at by Mr. Gladstone to introduce a measure for the Repeal of the Union, I came to the conclusion that in June 1885 we had been most unfortunately inspired. I can trace a clear connection of cause and effect between Lord Salisbury's accession to office in 1885 and Mr. Gladstone's new departure in 1886." [2]

Two comments may be made on this somewhat belated discovery.

The first is that Lord Carnarvon was more clear-sighted than his colleagues, and perceived at once that if, rightly or wrongly, coercion was at that time to be discarded, the only alternative was to make concessions to the Irish demand

[1] *Life*, ii. 21.   [2] *Life*, i. 409, 411.

XIII.

for self-government. So immediately after the Government was formed and the abandonment of coercion announced, he obtained an interview with the Irish leader. This was no doubt an imprudent step ; but its purpose in itself was quite legitimate, and, though absolutely unknown to the Cabinet, it was expressly sanctioned by Lord Salisbury. Lord Carnarvon sought to ascertain whether the essential demands of Mr. Parnell were impossible of concession. The result was reported to Lord Salisbury. Lord Salisbury remained hostile to Home Rule, and had to return to the other alternative of coercion. Lord Carnarvon remained averse to coercion, and proceeded onwards towards Home Rule.

The second comment that may be made is this : Had Randolph and his colleagues made, in June 1885, the discovery that the abandonment of coercion would drive Mr. Gladstone to a Home Rule policy, would that necessarily have changed their policy ? From his memorandum you would think so, but I greatly doubt the fact. What is there in party warfare so exalted and so refined as to make party leaders recoil from driving their opponents to a course at once perilous and open to the most sensible of all reproaches ? [1] Such a proceeding is not in the least inconsistent with the tactics and devices which are inevitable under the conditions of British political life. Even had the Tory leaders foreseen that the Home Rule policy would break up the Liberal party, and keep the legitimate remnant out of power for a score of years, would that painful

[1] Cf. *Life*, ii. 21, 28.

prospect have deterred them ? The question answers itself. The rules of warfare do not proscribe, they rather prescribe, the forcing an adversary to take up an exposed and untenable position.

And Randolph, when he wrote his penitent memorandum, must have forgotten that he had been in 1885 a fierce and zealous party chief, by no means careful to discriminate between legitimate and illegitimate methods of warfare. He fought with any weapon that came to hand, intent on the end rather than on the means of the contest. It is difficult to believe that he did not realise to some extent that he was forcing Mr. Gladstone on to the horn of fresh concessions in the Irish dilemma. But it is quite within the bounds of probability that in afterwards writing this minute, when his judgement had cooled, this fact was no longer present to his mind.

III

No such attempt to write a biography of a fiercely controversial politician soon after his death has been made since Disraeli published his *Life of Lord George Bentinck*. But there is an essential difference between the two cases. Disraeli had to justify the part that he himself had taken by the side of Lord George Bentinck in violent polemics, and had determined to do this without mentioning his own name or the personal pronoun with regard to himself. This he thought he could do without affectation, and, it may be said, he succeeded. Moreover, the issue between the followers of Peel and Bentinck was still burning at the time he wrote. The book therefore was something of a party pamphlet. Here there are no such bias and no such difficulty. From another point of view, also, Mr. Churchill's task is easier. Lord George Bentinck was, from the political point of view, a difficult figure to drape with picturesque effect. No one was better aware of this than his biographer; so, to lighten the scene, he made his book a political treatise in which Lord George plays but a minor part, and introduces a glittering chapter on the Jewish faith to illuminate the whole. Bentinck indeed, when living, was a notable and almost dramatic figure, for he was a man of splendid presence, marvellous industry, and a tragic vindictiveness. Vindictiveness was his sombre motive power; he could neither forgive nor forget. For the man who once injured him or any whom he loved, there was no possibility of pardon or even of mitigation. The fierce impression upon him of a wrong remained as vivid to the last moment as it was at the first; and he could not rest until he had wreaked a remorseless revenge on the offender. His bitter attacks on Sir Robert Peel were inspired not by any personal injury, but by the conviction that Peel had deserted Canning, his relative, near a score of years before. As to the rest, he was the dreariest of speakers—a fact which troubled him little, if at all, for he only sought to lay before his audience the bare and bony appeal of statistics. But had he had tact, and some power of blandishment, or at least of reticence in rancour, he would

have been more valuable to his party than many
orators. His stately person, his lineage, his
application, his ability, his unstinted devotion
to the cause in hand, even though that cause
seemed to be personal animosity, would have
made · him a leader of the highest value to
any party, more especially to the Tories. But,
strangely enough for one who had spent his best
years on the turf, he seems to have had no knowledge of men, no consideration for their feelings,
no power of give and take. And so, after a
few months of leadership, he disappeared in a
huff.

On the other hand, Randolph's personality was
one full of charm, both in public and in private
life. His demeanour, his unexpectedness, his fits
of caressing humility, his impulsiveness, his tinge
of violent eccentricity, his apparent dare-devilry,
made him a fascinating companion ; while his
wit, his sarcasm, his piercing personalities, his
elaborate irony, and his effective delivery, gave
astonishing popularity to his speeches. Nor were
his physical attributes without their attraction.
His slim and boyish figure, his moustache which
had an emotion of its own, his round protruding
eye, gave a compound interest to his speeches
and his conversation. His laugh, which has been
described as " jaylike," was indeed not melodious,
but in its very weirdness and discordance it was
merriment itself. All this comes back to a friend
as he reads this book—the boyhood, the manhood,
the mournful and gradual decay. He may be
pardoned if he draws for a little on his memory
with regard to this brilliant being.

IV

XIII.

I first saw Randolph Churchill at Eton—a small boy in an extremely disreputable hat. Now, the hat was at Eton in those days almost as notable a sign of condition as among the Spanish nobility. Moreover, his appearance was reckless—his companions seemed much the same ; he was, in a word, but a pregnant word at Eton, a Scug. His elder brother had left Eton before I came, because, I think, of some difference with the authorities as to the use of a catapult. Randolph looked as if he too might differ with the authorities on any similar issue.

I was some two years senior to him, and I scarcely knew him till he went to Oxford, little perhaps beyond saying " good-night " at " lock-up " — the equivalent of an adult nod. I remember only one story of him : probably a myth founded on fact. He boarded at Frewer's, an obscure house, where, it was said, the inmates consisted of some sixteen lower boys. And it was rumoured that as soon as Randolph got into fifth form, he, without waiting for the higher refinement of " fagging division," assumed . the whole remaining fifteen as his personal fags.

At Oxford he was a member of Merton and I of Christ Church. There we saw a great deal of each other and became close friends ; for, largely owing to the unifying quality of the Bullingdon Club, he lived much with the Christ Church set, which at that time saw regrettably little of the rest of the University.

He was now quite unlike his Etonian self :

he was spruce, polished, but full of fun.   He was   XIII.
the idol of his parents and sisters, for he was the
son that lived with them and loved his home
better than any place on earth.   Through him
I came to be much at Blenheim, and to see him
in his family as well as in his Oxford life.

At this time he did not read much in the
regular way, though he took a degree in the then
undivided school of Law and Modern History.
He bought books, and read outside the course of
recognised study.   But his main literary passion
was Gibbon.   To Gibbon's immortal work he
gave what leisure of reading he had to give,
and this literary devotion lasted to the end.
One story I remember, and believe to be true.
There was pending an election at Woodstock,
then practically a close borough of the Dukes of
Marlborough, and his Merton tutor took an active
part in opposition to the Blenheim candidate.
In the course of one of his speeches he told an
anecdote which appeared to reflect severely on
the Duke.   After this Randolph ceased to attend
his lectures, and this systematic neglect was laid
before the Warden.   Randolph's excuse was
absolute and overwhelming.   " How, Sir, could
I attend the lectures of one who had called my
father a scoundrel ?   How could I reconcile
attendance at his teaching with my duty towards
my parents ? "   Tradition said that he got the
best of it.

It is perhaps enough to say that at Oxford
he did not differ much in his habits from those
of other young men of his class, save in his
affection for the *Decline and Fall of the Roman*

xiii. *Empire*, and, of course, in his frequent visits to Blenheim.

After we left Oxford we drifted in different directions : he, I suppose, much at home with his pack of harriers, when he directed that famous sarcasm against a Master of Hounds who had offended him, which still echoes in admiring chuckles among the sportsmen of Oxford and Berkshire. Then, still very young, he almost simultaneously entered Parliament and married his beautiful wife : two great events in his life, of which one, however, seemed then almost insignificant to him, for his happiness in his marriage completely eclipsed his election for Woodstock. Not long afterwards he became involved in a question of severe social stress, in which, so far as I remember, he took the part of a near relative with more zeal than justice or discretion. This for a time almost isolated him. Friends fell off ; acquaintances disappeared ; he was left naked, but not ashamed. That he felt this ostracism deeply cannot be doubted. And yet he seemed to me as gay and cheerful as ever when he met an old friend ; sobered perhaps, and apt to be a little absent, but essentially unchanged.

This, however, was the turning-point of his life. The *saeva indignatio*, excited in him by this social conflict, turned to politics. That was the vent for his suppressed wrath. Had it not been for this exacerbating crisis he might have subsided into a family trustee for a family borough, or found employment for his energies elsewhere. It was at this time, I suppose, that

he was living much with his father, then Viceroy
of Ireland, and studying that Irish question which
afterwards had so great a fascination for him.
Even at this early period he evoked a domestic
storm by a speech about Ireland in " the quiet
rural locality of Woodstock," for which the
Viceroy had to apologise to the Chief Secretary
by declaring that his Benjamin must have been
mad or tipsy to make it.[1]   I do not doubt that
Randolph mischievously enjoyed the splash caused
by his outbreak.   On Foreign Policy he was
also at issue with his party.   But the General
Election of 1880 placed him in the more congenial
attitude of opposition.   It was then that he
sallied forth to attack the gigantic personality
of Mr. Gladstone, and, as if that were not employment enough, to take his own leaders in flank.
With these objects he formed, or co-operated
in forming, that small group of politicians,
popularly called the Fourth Party, which became
so famous and so effective.   Public attention
became instantly fixed on the attractive figure
of the intrepid young assailant.   He leaped
into renown.   He soon became the principal
platform speaker in the country.   It is no disparagement of others to assert that, in my
judgement at any rate, Randolph would at his
best have attracted a larger audience to a political
meeting than any one, not excepting Mr. Gladstone himself.   And in the House of Commons
it is not too much to say that his corner seat
below the gangway divided attention with the
centre seat on the Government bench where

[1] *Life*, i. 92.

XIII.

XIII.   throned the pale, eager form of the great Liberal
        leader.

        Then came the crisis, for which he had so
effectively worked. The quarry which he had
pursued with such ardour was hunted down at
last, and Mr. Gladstone's Government fell. As
the result was announced, Randolph, waving
his hat, almost gave the who-whoop of the
fox-hunter at the death. But he soon found
that he had only changed his battlefield, and
that he was at once locked in a fierce and silent
conflict with his own leaders. To the victors
fall the spoil, and the nominal victors were the
front Opposition bench. But the most gleaming
and popular personality in the party, the one to
whose tactics and vigour the victory was perhaps
in the main due, did not sit on the seat of the
chosen. What part was he to play in this division
of offices ? His was no docile character, ready
to receive passively whatever the gods might
allot, and to subside satisfied into any great
office of State. He was determined that the
leadership which he had so mercilessly criticised
should pass to more vigorous hands; and he
stipulated as one condition of his joining the
ministry that Sir Stafford Northcote should
leave the House of Commons. This demand, for
obvious reasons, placed the new Prime Minister
in a cruel position, and it was doubtful what
he could or would do. Sir Stafford Northcote,
indeed, had strong claims to the first post himself, and had, in default of it, already undertaken
the lead in the House of Commons with the
Chancellorship of the Exchequer; so that Ran-

dolph at one time believed that his conditions would be refused. It is the nature of tense spirits to be unduly elated and unduly depressed, and he came to me one night at the Turf Club in a mood very different from that in which he had shouted and waved his hat after the division. His talk was both striking and desponding. The main point was that he believed that Lord Salisbury would not concede his demands, and that he was almost disposed to leave the Tory party. As to this, I advised him to take counsel with an older man. There would have been no great change involved, for only Ireland and its issues, at that time not so prominent as in the succeeding year, stood between Randolph and the Liberal party; though then he scarcely realised the fact. But no such sacrifice was now needed. The Prime Minister yielded, and Sir Stafford Northcote was persuaded to retire to the House of Lords. This was an outward demonstration of Randolph's power, much more notable than his simultaneous appointment to the India Office. The two leaders, however, were wise to make the concession, for it would have been impossible to form a real government without his participation or approval; and though Sir Stafford was reluctant to leave the House of Commons, it is more than doubtful if he was then physically fit for the leadership.

I did not see Randolph again, except at dinners and the like, till the night in January 1885 when the Conservative Government was being turned out on the Address. I was listening to the debate in the gallery, whither he ascended

XIII.

to ask me to come to his room. I readily consented, as the debate was neither real nor interesting; for it dealt nominally with small tenures in England, while in the midst of all there loomed the stark form of the Irish question, which had come to deal death to the Tory Government and paralysis to the Liberal party. That was the issue on which every mind was silently fixed, while the audible talk was of the area necessary to support a cow. Of this talk with Randolph I recollect scarcely anything. But, as we passed along the lobby, he said, I remember, " Well, it is over, but it has not been bad fun." " Just what Fleury said of the Second Empire."

One incident in that lobby, however, impressed me more than our subsequent conversation. He offered me a cigarette as we were walking to his room, and I stipulated for a cigar. He had not got one, he said, but would soon get me one. At this moment there appeared in the passage a portly baronet of great wealth. " Here's a man who will have a good cigar," said Randolph. " Oh, ——, I want a cigar to give my friend here ; have you got your case ? " I never shall forget the precipitate veneration with which the baronet produced his case and offered his best and choicest. It was an object-lesson in Randolph's position.

During the short Liberal Government of 1886 he was predominant in his party ; unweariedly active in combining the strange and various elements of the Opposition, as this memoir sufficiently shows. And on the dissolution, he issued an address, which, his biographer truly says, as a specimen of political invective is not

likely soon to be outdone. It was justly censured for violence and extravagance. But coming from Randolph, whose seasoning was always
high, and issued at a moment of fierce and seeth-
ing political excitement, it was, I thought, not
ill-calculated for its purpose. At any rate, by
that or some other means, its purpose was
accomplished, and Mr. Gladstone's Government
was overthrown by a great majority.

Now we arrive at the culminating point of
Randolph's extraordinary career. Sir Michael
Hicks-Beach, who had been the Tory leader in
the House of Commons since Sir Stafford Northcote's acceptance of a peerage, insisted on ceding
the place to his younger colleague. Sir Michael's
own great ability, the confidence of his party, and
his past services, did not blind his penetration to
the fact that the popular personality of the party
was Randolph's, and he wisely decided that with
the power should go the name.

Randolph devoted himself with his usual
energy to his high task. Never was the House
of Commons led more acceptably than in that
short summer session. The secret of his success
lay apparently in personal example, discipline,
and courtesy ; but he was, besides, a favourite of
the House. I remember some one asking him
how long his leadership would last. " Oh, about
six months ! " " And then ? " " And then ?
Why, Westminster Abbey." I can hear him
saying it.

Nor were his triumphs parliamentary alone.
The officials of his new department were delighted
with him. He at once placed himself under their

tutelage so as to master those financial problems
which were new and strange to him, and delighted
every one with his powers of will and work.   In
the Cabinet, too, he was at first not less successful.
It is only necessary to quote one evidence of
this.   Northcote notes in his diary that Randolph
was " certainly the shrewdest member of the
Cabinet," [1] testimony which may well be un-
suspected, and is characteristically generous.
The young Chancellor of the Exchequer seemed
to tread on air ; he had only to fear the perils
that beset him of whom all men speak well.

Then, exuberant in his unbroken triumph,
he began to try his hand at " Tory Democracy,"
and delivered a famous speech at Dartford.   I
may, perhaps, be forgiven for remembering that
the day I read it I said to a friend, " Randolph
will be out or the Government broken up before
Christmas."   My friend gibed.   But the following
December, as I was dozing at midnight in a
railway carriage on the North-West of India,
he burst in with a newspaper.   " By Jove, you're
right after all."   " What about ? "   " Randolph
has resigned."

Before that event took place he had given a
public proof of that eccentricity of judgement
from which he was never wholly free, by going on
a foreign tour under an assumed name with his
friend, Mr. Trafford.   Randolph called himself,
I think, " Mr. Spencer."   By no conceivable
method could he have attracted more attention
to his incognito trip.   No face was then better
known.   He had been seen by tens of thousands

[1] Lang's *Sir S. Northcote*, ii. 215.

of his fellow-countrymen, his photograph was everywhere, he was in every caricature. When, then, the leader of the House of Commons went suddenly abroad, to Vienna and elsewhere, and was instantly recognised under this transparent disguise, English newspapers were perplexed, while the foreign press not unnaturally saw an international intrigue, which they endeavoured to emphasise by saddling his companion with the historic title of Strafford. Had Randolph gone in his own name he would have achieved his object of being undisturbed : as it was, his holiday consisted of a passage from one hornet's nest to another. But the incident illustrates a certain perversity of character, not unlike that popularly attributed to the ostrich. He was determined to be incognito, therefore he persuaded himself that he would be incognito.

v

His resignation was a striking catastrophe, and cannot be passed over in silence. It is largely to be explained by physical causes. Randolph's nervous system was always tense and highly strung : a condition which largely contributed to his oratorical success, but which was the principal cause of his political undoing. He would descend from the highest summit to a bottomless pit and up again, at the shortest notice ; that is the liability of the temperament of genius. Several passages from his biography, and, what is more, several of his acts, could be cited in support of this description. When he

XIII.   took office he worked unsparingly, which increased the strain on his nerves.   He had, moreover, a morbid suspicion of intrigue, not unusual among those who are themselves not averse to a little wire-pulling.   That suspicion would enhance the stress, for he would be watching others and tormenting himself.   Always impatient of opposition ; surrounded by people who told him, sincerely and justifiably, that he was the one indispensable person, the one man who counted and mattered ; convinced that he and they were in the right, he was irritated by the doubting and silent reluctance of his colleagues into an act of violence.   One exception must be made : Lord Salisbury's reluctance was neither doubting nor silent.   Northcote suspected that the resignation arose " from a little temper on both sides." [1] " Temper " does not probably describe Lord Salisbury's mood, though there may have been the irritability of the over-driven.

It is, however, to my mind more than doubtful if Randolph intended his resignation to be definite. But even if it were accepted he felt certain that he would be soon restored to office and to greater power on the shoulders of the party.   As it was, he lingered on at the Treasury, in a fever of agitation.   " I can't bear to leave this room," he writes thence to his mother, a week after his resignation, " where I can sit and think and hear everything quickly. *The matter is very critical, but by no means desperate.*" [2]   The sentence which I have italicised supports the view that he hoped to be retained.   It is strange, too, that he should

[1] Lang's *Sir S. Northcote*, ii. 279.   [2] *Life*, ii. 263.

have clung so closely to his official room, as if with a presentiment; for it is the spot least agreeable to a retiring minister.   I told him once, not long after the event, that after reading his letter to Lord Salisbury I had come to the conclusion that it was not intended as a resignation.   He answered that I was right, and that he only meant it as the beginning of a correspondence, but that Lord Salisbury clinched it at once.   Of course, he added, he intended eventually to send an ultimatum.   It is not necessary to take this as his deliberate view, for, offhand, he might readily express the mood of the moment; but I think it represents the truth, and is confirmed by his son. ". Lord Randolph Churchill had so little expected to fail in his conflict with the Cabinet that he had not clearly thought out how he would stand in that event." [1]   And again : " Of course," says Mr. Churchill, " he hoped the others would give way—would at any rate make some considerable concession which would leave him proportionately strengthened." [2]   The real fact is, I think, that, nervous, impulsive, overstrained, and impatient of opposition as he was, he discharged this menace of resignation at Lord Salisbury, as he had flung the same threat in the previous year, without calculation, as a warning rather than an act. The precipitate way of carrying it out, his inability to postpone the writing it out for a few hours until he had left the palace of the Sovereign, all show this.   By the bye, he certainly told me that he wrote it on arriving at Windsor, not after dinner, as is stated in the *Life.*   It is, however,

[1] *Life*, ii. 261.   [2] *Life*, ii. 243. ·

XIII. quite possible that he wrote one draft on arriving and the other late at night.

No one who knew him would have expected him to have acted otherwise, for the patient task of persuasion, or, to use a modern cant phrase, of " peaceful penetration," was wholly alien to his nature. That nature required a relief for its high-strung irritability in some sort of violence, and resignation was the only form that that violence could take. It cannot be seriously doubted that he expected to receive next day from Lord Salisbury a soothing letter like those of August 1885, and that at the next Cabinet his alarmed colleagues would make considerable concessions. But Lord Salisbury evidently felt that his stock of patience and of sedatives was exhausted. Had the Prime Minister been in the habit of personally seeing his colleagues, there might have been a blowing-off of steam, and the situation might for the moment have been saved. But that was not Lord Salisbury's way. Mr. Churchill seems to feel some surprise that Lord Salisbury's reply did not suggest an interview. It would have been much more surprising if it had, as it is doubtful if Lord Salisbury ever suggested an interview in his life. But on this occasion words were popularly attributed to the Prime Minister which indicated that though he must have felt some uneasiness at disconnecting himself with so popular a colleague, yet that a sensation of relief was predominant. It is probable that he was not a jealous man ; yet to his friends and surroundings, if not to himself, it must have been annoying to see the fierce light of public interest

turned entirely on Randolph, while the Prime
Minister, in reality a greater force, remained
unobtrusive in the shade. Lord Salisbury had
realised the more poignant fact that he himself
was a Tory, and that his young partner was a
Radical, constantly urging Radical measures.
The Prime Minister at every Cabinet meeting was
being pushed in directions that he detested.
" Salisbury," wrote Lord George Hamilton on
the 25th of November, " is getting to the position
where he will be pressed no more." [1] This from
the peacemaker of the Government was sufficiently ominous.

There were portents and warnings enough
on the path which Randolph had marked out
for himself, but he walked on heedless or blind.
Inevitable jealousy, sincere misgiving, accumulated resentment and distrust were all around
him ; not Daniel himself was more uncom-
fortably encompassed. He alone, elated, overstrained, and perhaps already afflicted, saw it
not ; or rather, while possibly observing signs
of conflict, never doubted that the victory would
be his. He had triumphed over the opposing
forces before, and felt sure of doing so again.
Yet all the time there was closing round him a
pressure of circumstance that was to drive him
from office. After each Cabinet, colleagues, we
may be sure, exchanged their impressions of
dismay, and asked each other, " How long ? "
or " What next ? "

Of the communications between ministers to
which Mr. Churchill alludes, nothing has been

[1] *Life*, ii. 228.

XIII. published, and the whole history of this dramatic transaction is, therefore, not in our possession. But their view is easily guessed. There had been frequent signals of alarm. " From the very outset," says Mr. Churchill, who, from the perusal of secret documents, probably knows more than it is discreet to disclose, " the new administration was uneasy. Discord stirred restlessly behind the curtains of Cabinet secrecy. . . . The autumn councils were not harmonious, whether upon foreign or domestic affairs." [1]

Foreign affairs were no doubt one difficulty, for Randolph distrusted Lord Salisbury's policy. " A wise foreign policy," he wrote to his chief at the time of his resignation, " will extricate England from Continental struggles and keep her outside of German, Russian, French, or Austrian disputes. I have for some time observed a tendency in the Government attitude to pursue a different line of action which I have not been able to modify or check." [2] Smith, strangely enough, was also a critic. " Our diplomacy is no doubt very weak," he writes on October 24, " but this does not entirely explain our powerlessness in Europe." [3]

Then there was the question of Local Government, there was the question of the closure, and there was an Allotment Bill. On all these points the orthodox ministers differed, no doubt, from Randolph. It was, moreover, rumoured that he was a difficult colleague, with much of the temper of the spoilt child ; and these stories were, I think, not unfounded.

[1] *Life*, ii. 219.   [2] *Life*, ii. 239.   [3] *Life*, ii. 26.

The stress came apparently to a climax in the XIII.
early part of December, when the budget was
produced. When he expounded this measure
to the Cabinet they remained silent, " but," he
said, " you should have seen their faces." [1] It
is strange that, after so ominous a warning, he
should have staked his all on a resignation with
any idea that it would not be cordially but
tremulously accepted. The significant silence
of the Cabinet was soon broken by not less
significant notes. Hamilton wrote for returns
of the incidence of taxation. Smith wanted a
printed memorandum. Salisbury had examined
the figures for three counties, as they would stand
under the new plan of Local Government, and
found them far from reassuring. It is probable,
then, that communications had been going on
between the members of the Cabinet for some
three weeks before the resignation ; and that
Lord Salisbury, though he sent round to his
colleagues copies (characteristically made in his
own handwriting) of Randolph's letter of resignation, was well aware of what their feelings would
be. Smith, four days before, had intimated his
intention of resigning if his estimates were cut
down. The Cabinet had then to choose between
Churchill and Smith. It cannot be doubted that
they had long made their choice. Smith at least
belonged to them, heart and soul. Rumour had
it that his earlier tendencies had been Liberal,
but all through his public life he had been a loyal
and consistent Tory. Randolph, on the other hand,
though brought up in the bosom of Toryism, and

[1] *Life*, ii. 212.

XIII.   a priceless ally in attack, in all positive policy
had shown signs of the most detestable heresy.
He seemed a political changeling. Smith they
could understand and trust ; with Smith they
could live comfortably ; Smith had about him no
angles and no surprises ; there was in Smith none
of that brilliancy which is the object of so much
instinctive distrust. Randolph, on the other hand,
was restless, overbearing, and, as regards policy,
capable of anything. Why should this confident
youth—for, politically speaking, he was only a stripling—tell the greybeards of the party that they were
out of date, and that the faith they had professed
all their lives was superannuated and futile ?

The choice of the ministers was made, we
may be sure, without hesitation, though not
without misgiving. That it was a deliberate
and personal choice, not based on a question of
public policy, is demonstrated by one simple
fact : " Lord Randolph Churchill procured by his
resignation almost every point of detail for which
he had struggled in the Cabinet." [1] Had the
Cabinet wished to keep him, it is obvious that
they would have conceded his demands before
and not after his resignation. If this view be
correct it would seem that it was his personality,
and not his policy, which had alienated his
colleagues. They did not feel confidence in him,
they were weary of his restless predominance,
they did not know whither he was going. Lord
Salisbury " had been," wrote Randolph, " for
weeks prepared for it, and possibly courted the
crash." [2] We may believe that Lord Salisbury

[1] *Life*, ii. 297.   [2] *Life*, ii. 262.

was not unprepared—though he had obviously made no preparation to replace his Chancellor of the Exchequer—but not that he courted the crash. Nevertheless, the crash was in all probability neither unexpected nor unwelcome to the main body of the Cabinet. On the other hand, his Radical friends congratulated him—(and the fact has its bearing on the nature of Tory Democracy)—not perhaps quite unselfishly, and not without the bitter herb of truth. " The party tie," as one reminded him, " is the strongest sentiment in this country—stronger than patriotism or even self-interest." [1]   " You ignore the power of the machine," wrote one who knew it well.[2]   The " machine " crushed him as easily as a parched pea. Had he chosen to fight for his hand and raise the standard of revolt, it would not have been so easy to suppress him. But he behaved with perfect loyalty and decorum.

He had made another mistake, he sincerely believed in the necessity for rigid economy ; so did Mr. Gladstone ; so did no one else. It is the great disappointment in connection with our new or renewed democratic bodies, parliamentaiy and municipal, that economy has no friends. So his resignation based on this issue fell flat and appealed to no one, except as regarded his own personality and power. So much for his political fall. He was never the same man again.

There was to be for him one more crisis—and only one. The facts of it are related with great impartiality in Mr. Churchill's book, and cannot be repeated here. It is enough to say that in

---

[1] *Life*, ii. 252.   [2] *Life*, ii. 254.

XIII.
—

1889 Mr. Bright's death had caused a vacancy in the representation of Birmingham, where Randolph, owing to a previous contest, had a strong hold, and where a powerful body of supporters urged him to stand. This candidature was strongly resisted by Mr. Chamberlain on the ground of a previous agreement between the Tories and the Liberal Unionists. Strangely enough, under these circumstances, Randolph left the decision as to whether he should stand or not to the two Liberal Unionist leaders and a member of the Government. The result, as Randolph must have known, was a foregone conclusion, and it was decided that he should not stand. The Randolph of 1884 would not have hesitated, or left the decision to a committee. But the Randolph of 1889 had no longer the nerve of his prime. He submitted, but with the shadow of death on his face. With a ghastly expression he faced the wrath of his devoted followers at what seemed to them a betrayal. There was no betrayal, there was only the failure of nerve power due to his malady. But it was in effect a second resignation and a final abdication. He had missed the last opportunity, which neither forgives nor returns.

VI

After this disaster he again went abroad ; this time with another common friend, Harry Tyrwhitt. I was in India, but we met, on our return journey, in Rome. He had just escaped from Sicily, then under rigid quarantine, to the mainland in an open boat, at the imminent risk of bullets : a thoroughly congenial adventure. In Rome we saw a great deal of each other, and had long talks. But as I have in the main forgotten these, my recollections of that time would be little superior in interest to those of Captain Sumph. I recollect, though, that his companion told me that Randolph would sit in silence for hours together, smoking cigarettes and pondering. But now he was in tearing spirits, perhaps at meeting old friends, and in his best vein ; full of audacious paradox, irony, and candour. He talked much of his resignation and his career, and declared that he would not live the last four years over again for a million a year. He had been successful enough, but he would not face them for all that. He reminded me, too, of our talk at the Turf Club. " Do you know, Lady ——, that but for Rosebery being not at home when I called I should have been a Liberal ? I went to his house to settle it all with him. But he had gone out ; and, as affairs could not wait, I remained where I was." Of course this was banter, he did not mean to be taken seriously. The fact was that he had gone to consult with some one—Lord Goschen, I think—and had come to tell me the result. But the determining factor was, it need scarcely be said, Lord Salisbury's concession. He declared that he had often mentioned that conversation, even to Lord Salisbury, who, he incidentally remarked, I remember, was " never happy out of that d——d laboratory at Hatfield."

I think that this was almost the last entirely

cheerful view that I had of Randolph. He was well in health, not devoid of hope, and he had shaken off the strain of his resignation. He was in many respects the Randolph of old times.

He returned to England soon afterwards, made a few parliamentary speeches—not very successful, I think, perhaps because of the difficulty of his ambiguous position—and went on the turf. This was a new passion with him ; inferior, indeed, in excitement, as Lord Palmerston once remarked, to politics, but new and absorbing. He embraced it with his usual ardour, won the Oaks (though he was in Norway at the time), and had his fair measure of success. He used to come to Durdans for the Epsom meetings until the end of his life, and was as gay and debonair as when he was an Oxford undergraduate. Racing remained a passion with him to the end. Almost every letter that I had from him in his last years of life was about that sport. Let not ambition mock these homely joys.

Then he went to South Africa. Already, I think, the cruel disease which was to paralyse and kill him had begun to affect him. There were soon symptoms of an irritability which, so far as I know, was rare with him. In old days he was often petulant, had something of the spoilt child about him ; but even his petulance was winning, and he was never really irritable, at least within my knowledge.

The beginning of the end was the end. The progress of the disease was slow at first, but its signs were obvious, and when it began his career was closed.

Why recall those last days, except to recall XIII. the pity of them?—his devoted mother hoping against hope for his future, his own feverish energy, the brilliant light fluttering out in the full glare of day. There was no curtain, no retirement; he died by inches in public.

The last time that I saw him I dined with him at his mother's house in Grosvenor Square; his brother-in-law, Lord Tweedmouth, was the only other guest. The next day he gave a farewell dinner to his friends, and the next he set out with his wife on a voyage round the world in a desperate hunt for health. I cannot even now make up my mind whether I wish that I had dined or stayed away. It was all pain, and yet one would not like to have missed his good-bye. I still cannot think of it without distress.

I saw him off at the station, and he wrote me one immensely long letter from Japan, containing great plans of travel, never to be realised. That, so far as I was concerned, was the end. The letter was written in September 1894. In January 1895 he died.

VII

It was a strange, fitful career, one of the most singular and interesting of that century, only less dramatic than that of Disraeli. He had all or almost all the qualities that go to make up success in politics. He was a born party leader, reminding one of Bolingbroke in the dashing days of Harry St. John. He was brilliant, courageous, resourceful, and unembarrassed by

XIII.   scruple ;   he had fascination, audacity, tact ;
——   great and solid ability welded with the priceless
gift of concentration ;   marvellous readiness in
debate, and an almost unrivalled skill and attraction on the platform ;   for he united in an eminent
degree both the parliamentary and the popular
gifts, a combination which is rarer than is usually
supposed.

He had also the vital mainspring of zest.   To
whatever he applied himself he gave for the
time his whole eager heart.   He was strenuous
at politics, but he was also at times devoted to
hunting, racing, and chess, and he took gas-
tronomy as seriously as Macaulay.   But whatever it might be, politics or pleasure, it possessed
him entirely ;   he did it with gusto, with every
nerve and every fibre.   He had, moreover, the
fascination of manner—an invaluable endowment
for a politician.   Thus, when he chose, which
was perhaps too rarely, he could deal successfully
with men.   He had also at his disposal the charm
of conversation, and this was as various as his
moods.   When he felt himself completely at ease,
in congenial society, it was wholly delightful.
He would then display his mastery of pleasant
irony and banter ;   for with those playthings he
was at his best.   Nor would he hesitate to air his
most intimate views of persons and characters ;
he did not shrink from admissions which were
candid to the verge of cynicism ;   he revelled
in paradox.   A stranger or a prig happening
upon him in such moods would be puzzled, and
perhaps scandalised ;   for his lighter and more intimate conversation was not to be taken literally.

He would hate this and that, embrace the most preposterous propositions, and defend any extravagance that might happen to enter his head; if he were opposed, he would carry it much farther. I remember once saying that a certain statesman had not shone at the Foreign Office; he at once declared that he deliberately regarded him as the greatest Foreign Secretary that had ever lived. This was not conviction, nor even opinion; it was only returning the ball over the net. When in this vein he produced table-talk which would have strained a Boswell to bursting; it was all gaiety, the delightful whim of the moment. He was, moreover, absolutely unaffected himself, and ruthlessly pricked the bubbles of affectation or cant in others. In graver discussion he had, when he chose, a subtle and engaging deference; his ideas were luminous and original. This deference must, however, not be taken to imply veneration, for from that bump his skull was singularly free. The only person who inspired him with anything like awe or respect was the great statesman, when he came to know him, against whom his bitterest philippics had been directed. Without veneration, if that be a charm, as to most of us it is when not excessive or misplaced, Randolph's conversation, whether light or serious, was all admirable of its kind. His son says truly that " he had a wonderful manner, courtly, frank, and merry, which he did not by any means always display." [1] The saving clause is not less true than the description; for at all periods of his life he would at times—

[1] *Life*, ii. 77.

XIII. suddenly as it were—shut himself up and become morose.

He had a faithful and warm heart ; from childhood he had been the best of sons ; and the whole soul of his mother was with him to the end. Nothing could exceed the pathos of her devotion to him in political adversity, or to his memory when he had passed away. While still a lad, he ruled his family with autocratic affection, and the affection was unstintedly returned.

His friendships were singularly staunch. There might be tiffs, but they would, as a rule, be passing. While they lasted, the horizon would be entirely black, and the human race engaged in a vast combination with the powers of evil against him. In these moods he sometimes tried his political friends severely, as both Gorst and Jennings could have testified ; for storms would arise in a clear sky, and the unexpected would happen. His political friends might almost have addressed him in the words of Martial's epigram :

> Difficilis, facilis, iucundus, acerbus es idem :
>   nec tecum possum vivere, nec sine te.

But if he seemed sometimes to enjoy a quarrel, he enjoyed a reconciliation still more ; indeed, at times I thought that he half enjoyed the quarrel for the sake of the prospective reconciliation. He had few if any permanent animosities, and these mainly under the pressure of his strenuous politics ; nor as a rule did he nourish them ; his biography affords many proofs of an irritable but placable nature. At all times of his life he attracted warm and lasting friendship, and out-side friendship he had the faculty of attract-ing devoted affection and service. His private secretary, Mr. Moore, was conspicuous even in that remarkable collection of ministerial assistants that the last half-century has witnessed : of men not unfrequently much more fit for high office than their temporary chiefs. Moore was Ran-dolph's right-hand man, and Randolph's resigna-tion literally broke Moore's heart, for he died within six weeks of the fatal announcement. The officials of the Treasury and India Office, who openly dreaded Randolph's advent, became almost instantly his loyal and zealous vassals. But this is not wonderful, for he gave himself no airs of superiority, was frank about any ignorance ("those d——d dots," [1] for example), grateful for help, and ready to show his gratitude.

Nor had he, what might have been expected in so ardent a nature, any jealousy of others ; none, at least, that I could discover. This is a merit of the rarest water—a real mark of superi-ority. The ambitious man who can watch with-out soreness the rise or success of a contemporary is much rarer than a black swan. But Randolph's was a generous nature in the largest and strictest sense of the word : generous and profuse both with money and praise. His lack of jealousy and his personal charm arose from the same quality —that there was no perfection or claim of per-fection about him. He was human, eminently human ; full of faults, as he himself well knew, but not base or unpardonable faults ; pugnacious,

[1] *Life,* i. 184.

XIII.   outrageous, fitful, petulant, but eminently lovable
———   and winning.

VIII

And here perhaps it is fitting to say something
of his speeches. No one reads old speeches any
more than old sermons. The industrious historian
is compelled to explore them for the purposes
of political history, but it is a dreary and reluctant
pilgrimage. The more brilliant and telling they
were at the time, the more dolorous the quest.
The lights are extinguished; the flowers are
faded; the voice seems cracked across the empty
space of years, it sounds like a message from a
remote telephone. One wonders if that can really
be the scene that fascinated and inspired. Was
this the passage we thought so thrilling, this the
epigram that seemed to tingle, this the peroration
that provoked such a storm of cheers? It all
seems as flat as decanted champagne. Of course,
in the case of speeches that are treatises, like those
of Burke, treatises clothed in a literary form and
carefully prepared for publication as pamphlets,
the remark does not apply. But then these were
not speeches at all, or at any rate not successful
speeches. Their triumph was literary and philosophical, not that of the arena and the moment.
Genuine political speeches that win the instant
laurels of debate soon lose their savour. All the
accompaniments have disappeared—the heat, the
audience, the interruptions, and the applause;
and what remains seems cold and flabby.

In turning over Randolph's republished
speeches, one is chiefly struck by their audacity

and their extravagance, as if he deemed that anything were good enough for the voracious enthusiasm of mass meetings. There is often the same profusion of diction as in Mr. Gladstone, but with how great a difference. Mr. Gladstone uses his words to guard carefully his every step of advance from possible attack on flank or in the rear ; Randolph dashes forward like Prince Rupert, without heeding liability or peril or the cold criticism of fact. Yet these dead speeches of his, though they now lack the vivid quality which made them, when delivered, so interesting and diverting, have a lingering charm of their own, if only from a delectable acidity which keeps them cool and fresh. And after looking through them again, it seems impossible to refrain from some citations of his brilliant, audacious banter ; so reckless in spirit, but so studied in form. Take his repartee to Mr. W. H. Smith on the question of equal treatment of Ireland in the Reform Bill of 1884 : " I have heard a great deal of the mud-cabin argument. For that we are indebted to the brilliant, ingenious, and fertile mind of the right honourable member for Westminster. I suppose that in the minds of the lords of suburban villas, of the owners of vineries and pineries, the mud cabin represents the climax of physical and social degradation. But the franchise in England has never been determined by Parliament with respect to the character of the dwellings. The difference between the cabin of the Irish peasant and the cottage of the English agricultural labourer is not so great as that which exists between the abode of the right honourable member for Westminster and the humble roof which shelters from the storm the individual who now has the honour to address this Committee. . . .

> " Non ebur neque aureum
>   mea renidet in domo lacunar,
> non trabes Hymettiae
>   premunt columnas ultima recisas
> Africa." [1]

I dare say that Mr. Smith laughed as much as any of the audience.   But there is in the comical comparison something of the old hostility of the patrician to the moneyed and mercantile classes : the same feeling which found expression in the sneer against " Marshall and Snelgrove."   I admit that this passage was not reprinted in the collected speeches, and should not, perhaps, be recalled ; the excuse must be that it is a gem, and an innocuous gem, of Randolph's humour.

But of course his principal shafts were reserved for the great chief of the opposite party.   And impudent (there is no other word) and personal as were these attacks, their humour and their very extravagance permit the most devoted admirer of Mr. Gladstone to chuckle for a moment. Take this for example from the most brilliant of his platform speeches, that at Blackpool in January 1884 : " For the purpose of religious devotion the advertisements grow larger.   The parish church at Hawarden is insufficient to contain the thronging multitudes of fly-catchers who flock to hear Mr. Gladstone read the lessons of the day ; and the humble parishioners (of

[1] *Life*, i. 345.

Hawarden) are banished to hospitable Noncon-
formist tabernacles in order that mankind may
be present at the Prime Minister's rendering of
Isaiah, Jeremiah, or the Book of Job."[1] Then
the famous tree-cutting scene : " For the purposes
of recreation he has selected the felling of trees,
and we may usefully remark that his amusements,
like his politics, are constantly destructive. The
forest laments in order that Mr. Gladstone may
perspire. . . . The working men were guided
through the ornamental grounds into the widespreading park, strewn with the wreckage and the
ruins of the Prime Minister's sport. All around
them, we may suppose, lay the rotting trunks of
once umbrageous trees ; all around them, tossed
by the winds, were boughs and bark and withered
shoots. . . . They come suddenly on the Prime
Minister and Master Herbert in scanty attire and
profuse perspiration, engaged in the destruction
of a gigantic oak, just giving its dying groan.
They are permitted to gaze and worship and
adore, and having conducted themselves with
exemplary propriety, are each of them presented
with a few chips as a memorial of that memorable
scene."[2] This leads to a somewhat strained
comparison of Mr. Gladstone's policy to chips.

Again : " Was it for this that Mr. Gladstone
pranced down into Midlothian, blocked up all
the railway stations in the North of England,
and placed the lives of countless thousands of
passengers and tourists in the utmost possible
peril ? "[3] And on the same Midlothian theme,
of which he seemed never to weary : " Well, the

[1] *Speeches*, i. 112.   [2] *Speeches*, i. 113.   [3] *Speeches*, i. 191.

journey to Midlothian has taken place, and there have been all the usual concomitants. The old stage properties have been brought out at every station : all the old scenery, all the old decorations, the old troupe, they have all been brought forward in a sadly tarnished and bedraggled condition, and the usual amount of seed has been sown by the wayside, and I imagine that the fowls of the air have devoured it." [1] A possibly bedraggled member of the old troupe may perhaps be allowed a tribute to the rollicking fun of the touch about the fowls.

Again : " We remember . . . when Mr. Gladstone flying with impetuous haste from one corner of the country to another, was hurled down by your southern division. Down through electoral space he fell, nor was his fall arrested till he had reached the distant borough of Greenwich. Down, too, at that time fell Lord Hartington, his colleague, whom an obscure group of villages in Wales received and nourished." [2]

It is needless to multiply examples of this style, of which the last is perhaps the most striking example. The Miltonic ring of " Down through electoral space he fell," ending with the farcical idea of Lord Hartington's being nourished by Welsh villages, is grotesque humour of no ordinary kind. If there be such a thing as good taste in political warfare, nothing could offend more glaringly against its canons than some of these quotations. All, again, is strikingly picturesque, but it is a picture wholly unlike the original. And so, as men can smile at caricatures

[1] *Speeches*, i. 334.   [2] *Speeches*, i. 98.

of themselves or those dear to them, the warmest admirers of Mr. Gladstone may be amused by these.

Randolph's humour may be fairly defined as burlesque conception, set off by an artificial pomp of style ; a sort of bombastic irony, such as we occasionally taste with relish in an after-dinner speech. Sometimes it is what one could imagine that Gibbon might have uttered had he gone on the stump. Sometimes its exuberance over-reaches itself, and it can scarcely have seemed other than a cynical experiment on the political digestion of his audience. Take, for example, this passage on the Whig party : " I can see the viscous slimy trail of that political reptile which calls itself the Whig Party gleaming and glisten-ing on every line of it. I see that most malignant monster endeavouring, as it did in 1832, to coil itself round the constituencies of England and to suppress the free action and to smother the natural voice of the English people." [1]

Poor old Whig Party ! Already moribund, if not dead ; never, at its best or worst, malignant or monstrous, though no doubt a little hungry, a little selfish, and a trifle narrow. It might possibly have been compared by a flatterer to a slow-worm ; but an analogy to a crushing, in-sidious, overpowering serpent was beyond the bounds of a jest. Not long afterwards he was to get to closer quarters, and compare the states-man who was then considered the representative Whig to a boa constrictor—with this difference : that the boa constrictor enjoyed his food, while

[1] *Speeches*, i. 194.

XIII.   the Whig loathed and sickened upon it. Later again, in a mood of grace, he was to expunge this passage from his collected speeches ; and, indeed, the care is notable with which he omitted from those volumes many passages which might cause personal annoyance, or which did not seem to stand the test of time and reflection.

Take, again, this description of Mr. Gladstone and the Liberal party : " The Prime Minister, his colleagues and his party—these children of revolution, these robbers of churches, these plunderers of classes, these destroyers of property, these friends of the lawless, these foes of the loyal." [1] It seems strange that this sort of thing did not overreach itself, but I think it went down very well.

There are, of course, many passages quite as wild ; notably those in which, under the guidance, apparently, of an eminent Arabist, he described the Khedive Tewfik in terms not inadequate to the greatest villain in history or fiction : " the conspirator against his father, the robber of his family, the banisher of his brother, the dealer in human flesh and blood, the betrayer of his allies, of his ministers, and of his country ; the man of magic and of sorcery," [2]—this was the condensation of charges set forth at length and leisure. Of course his popular audiences delighted in the pungent flavour and aroma of these personal attacks without troubling their heads as to accuracy or appropriateness.

But even at this period of irresponsible invective he could rise to higher and graver levels.

[1] *Speeches*, i. 46.   [2] *Speeches*, i. 79.

Note, for example, his solemn rebuke to those who would govern Ireland as a Crown Colony : " There are some foolish people who talk about disfranchising Ireland, and treating it as a Crown Colony. Do not listen to them. They are as bad in their way as the Radicals and Parnellites. The world would not tolerate such a spectacle ; the genius of nations would not suffer it." [1]

And in the same speech there is an analogy drawn between the contention of the Southern States in the American Civil War and the promotion of Irish Home Rule, which, however misleading it may be deemed, is a nervous and powerful specimen of political eloquence.[2]

Can there, again, be anything finer in its way than the description of British government in India ? " Our rule in India is, as it were, a sheet of oil spread out over a surface of, and keeping calm and quiet and unruffled by storms, an immense and profound ocean of humanity." [3] The diction is by no means perfect, but the idea is little less than sublime.

After his accession to office his oratorical style perceptibly and decorously changed ; it became more sober and more responsible. There were still excursions and alarms, notably a denunciation of Lord Ripon ; but this, though unmeasured and unjust, was not undignified in tone. There are also the utterances about Ulster : strong meat to be dealt out by a minister. Then in 1886, when he is out of office, there is his extravagant election address.

When he is in office again, he resumes a style

[1] *Speeches*, i. 93.   [2] *Speeches*, i. 91.   [3] *Speeches*, i. 212.

XIII. adequate to his responsibility. His speech at Dartford was indeed a remarkable declaration of broad and enlightened policy couched in adequate language. It stands as by far his greatest effort in his serious vein. Then came his separation from the ministry, and with that his speeches declined. He was now speaking not as the spokesman of a great party or as the daring leader of attack on a political stronghold, but as a lonely individual conscious of isolation and of an irreparable mistake, regarded with suspicion by his own side and some remnant of smarting animosity on the other.

Then again the shadows began to darken around him : it was obvious that he was stricken by some mysterious and disabling malady. In 1890, for example, he delivered a speech on the Parnell Commission, in which he employed a shocking and loathsome metaphor which, although it had been already used by Burke [1] in his undiscriminating greed for simile, would never have been handled by Randolph when in health. Then there was a long silence, in which his malady steadily increased. At last, in 1893, he reappeared to deliver a speech on the Home Rule Bill. He was a prey to a nervousness that he could neither repress nor disguise, but the House of Commons, which had always had a lurking tenderness for its once spoilt child, listened with pathetic attention to this " bald and bearded man with shaking hands, and a white face drawn with pain and deeply marked with the lines of care and illness, and with a voice whose tremulous

[1] *Posthumous Memoirs of Wraxall*, i. 72.

tones already betrayed the fatal difficulty of articulation," as his biographer describes him. Mr. Churchill goes on to say that " the quality of his speech showed no signs of intellectual failing." [1] Each must speak for himself. It may have been so, but I am sure the audience did not realise the fact. To them and to the orator it was one long pain—pain of watching and listening, pain of thick and almost unintelligible delivery, pain of memory and contrast, pain for the visible imminence of death. What the speech may have been none who heard it knew; for it was a waking nightmare. He went on making speeches; addressing audiences in the country with restless courage; and returned to London declaring that he had never held such meetings. This was the hallucination of disease. Great audiences came, indeed, to hear him once more, but they could no longer catch his half-articulated words, and soon went away in sorrow and astonishment. But this, happily, he did not realise.

He had, I think, modelled his oratory on Disraeli's : perhaps unconsciously, for in private life he did not abound in admiration for that remarkable man. This attitude arose, it may be, from a dislike to being supposed to have imitated Lord Beaconsfield ; and, indeed, at other times he may have taken a different view, for his conversational opinions varied from day to day, and were often the outcome of a passing whim. But when, for example, he described the Church of England as " an institution which elevates the life of the nation and consecrates the acts of the

[1] *Life*, i. 465.

XIII.

State," [1] he not merely said an eloquent thing, but said it in the words that Lord Beaconsfield would have used.

If, however, Disraeli was his model, he certainly in some respects exceeded the original. It is not too much to say that, with the exception of the famous philippics of 1846, Disraeli did not always hold his audience very closely, and that his speeches were better to read than to hear. Moreover, he did not test his powers on the platform, so that comparison is not very easy. For Randolph was, I suppose, at his best on the platform before a great audience. I infer this from the vast popularity that his platform speeches obtained for him, from their immense vogue, and the extraordinary anxiety to hear him. In liveliness, in vigour, in sureness of touch, in the power of holding an audience, he transcended, I suspect, not merely Disraeli, but every one in living memory except Mr. Gladstone, Mr. Bright, and Mr. Chamberlain. His secret would have been worth knowing, but I never had the good fortune to hear him on the platform. In these days when the front rows at a public meeting are bought by impartial spectators, who come to enjoy the principal speech as they would an Adelphi drama, it might have been possible for a political opponent to hear him. But then it was not so, and a political opponent at a meeting would not have been appreciated or welcome. My own surmise would be that the attraction of Randolph's speaking was due as much to the speaker as to the speech. The speech in itself

[1] *Speeches*, i. 138.

was always excellent of its kind, sometimes fantastic, often exaggerated, with passages of admirable humour, irony, and rhetorical power. But had these speeches been delivered by any middle-aged gentleman on the front bench, they would have been much less successful. It was Randolph's personality that was so winning : his audacity, his extravagance, his reckless party spirit ; his physical qualities, his slight form, his modulated but penetrating voice, even his perpetually twisted moustache ; and above all, perhaps, the fact that this stripling had come to stir the dry bones of party and to divert the jaded attention of the audience from actors, however eminent, of whom they were rather tired, to a fresh young character. He was, in a word, supremely interesting.

What makes his faculty the more surprising is that for a long time—indeed, I believe always —he wrote out his speeches before delivering them. When he had read the manuscript twice over he had learned it by heart. Armed with copious notes, without which, he once told me, he could not approach a platform, he was then ready for his audience. With great dramatic art of delivery he repeated the speech in a way that made it seem absolutely fresh and spontaneous. The manuscript was, I believe, sent to the press. Indeed, when he delivered his three speeches in Edinburgh—what he sportively called his trilogy—he left the manuscripts of all three speeches, with the dates on which they were to be delivered, in charge of a London editor. He consequently enjoyed another triple sequence—

XIII. of sleepless nights, in agony lest the wrong speech should be published on the wrong day. This painful experience made him determine to abandon the practice ; but I am not sure that he did.

In another point, I suspect, he resembled Mirabeau, whose speeches were also written, not always by himself—in the faculty, I mean, for utilising the brains of others.[1] I do not doubt that the Fourth Party and other friends often co-operated in the production of his more elaborate speeches. This does not in any way detract from their merits. The faculty of borrowing intellectually from others is a subtle one : it is an art in itself, that few can employ successfully. Sheridan would take the arm of a friend down to the House of Commons in friendly chat, and presently the friend would hear with admiring surprise his own ideas translated by Sheridan into a glowing and eloquent speech. The friend could not have done it, Sheridan could ; had it not been for Sheridan, the friend's ideas would have been altogether lost ; so that all parties gained by the process. It may then be taken for granted that Randolph's friends perceived with satisfaction their ideas appearing in Randolph's popular and ingenious language amid the rattling applause of his teeming audiences. And after all, no speeches are wholly original. No one can tell what unconscious forces of reading, conversation, and memory go to produce a great speech. An original speech—one in which all the arguments and illustrations were absolutely novel and

[1] *Life*, ii. 355 ; Gorst's *Fourth Party*, p. 245.

wholly beyond previous conception—would in all probability be a failure. Its originality would be fatal to it ; it would be regarded as an eccentric intellectual trick and nothing more. There are, of course, in most great speeches novel arguments and still more novel illustrations, but a speech of which all the arguments and illustrations are new has yet to be heard.

Randolph's method of preparation was, I think, to shut himself up absolutely for two days before the speech had to be delivered. During those forty-eight hours he was unapproachable, and then he issued forth with the speech red-hot. From his biography I infer that he sometimes took less time, but the former statement comes from himself.

What, then, is the last word to be said about his speeches ? Firstly, it is necessary, in reading them and in trying to appreciate their effect, to picture the dramatic delivery, the face and figure and youth of the orator. Secondly, it must be remembered that these speeches are not essays, not speeches to be read rather than heard, like Burke's and Disraeli's. Neither are they master-pieces of sustained and restrained oratory like those of Mr. Bright. Neither are they rolling rivers of majestic diction, the outlet of intellectual resources long - accumulated and constantly re-freshed, as in the case of Mr. Gladstone. But for the modern purposes of Parliament and the platform they were perhaps as available as any that have been mentioned. They did not as a rule raise the audience to a higher level, as was often the case with the others ; but they tickled

XIII.
the popular palate and gave it a constant wish for more. In this way he was able to bring home serious argument to the people, who took it enveloped in rhetorical jam. His earlier speeches, except those on Irish affairs, had scarcely the adequate weight of knowledge and experience, for his political education had only begun with his political career. So he had to pick up knowledge as he went along, enough for the purposes of attack, but not sufficient for the purposes of policy and office. This is apparent even in the carefully edited collection of his speeches. For example, he dallied for a moment with what was called Fair Trade, but dropped and repudiated it without compromise as soon as he had studied the question. When he became connected with a great department, he readily assimilated the facts presented to him by the officials, so readily that had his official career been prolonged it is not to be doubted that his speeches would have become the instructive and responsible utterances of a great statesman. As it is, we have little more than the Dartford deliverance to show what he might have done had he remained a minister, and lived.

So, oratorically speaking, he will live principally by the wit and humour and sarcasm of his youthful philippics. These will perhaps never be rivalled or, indeed, imitated. Their success consisted, I think, apart from their raciness and insolence, in the striking combination of the picturesque and the burlesque. People, as has been said, never read old speeches. But without reading or studying, there may be many for a

generation yet to come who will turn over the
pages of these startling discourses to pick out the
plums, and they will not be without their reward.

XIII.

IX

What, with such splendid qualities and his
illustrious name, might he not have accomplished?
Why, with all these dazzling attributes to his
credit, did he not achieve a complete success?
And then he was so young!

His career was not a complete success, and yet it
was far from a failure. While it lasted it eclipsed
the fame of almost all who were then engaged in
politics. Many, no doubt, severely censured his
methods and the violence of his attacks. A Whig
statesman, for example, ordinarily urbane, refused
after Randolph's letter about Lord Granville to
meet him in conference. And the antipathy was
almost as great as the enthusiasm which he excited.
Not a few good men thought him absolutely
wicked, and beyond the pale of political salvation. But, while he was a figure, he enlisted
public interest and public admiration as no one
did but Mr. Gladstone: his popularity, indeed,
was at one time almost unbounded. It was
made up of various elements, for on his head
rested the hopes and affections, as well as the
indignant censures, of many different sections of
the community. There was something of the
adoration with which famous pugilists were
regarded in the palmy days of the Ring: the
people loved to see the young David hurling his
stones—far from smooth though they were—at

XIII.

the giant whom they also loved. They delighted in the shrewd epigrams and the reckless but telling personalities of his speeches. To others he was welcome as seeming to diminish and impair the overpowering domination of Mr. Gladstone. But above all, the nation is always on the look-out for a man, a seer, a guide ; and such an one many thought they had discovered in this youthful combatant, or at least a leader with new ideas who would regild or rejuvenate the somewhat negative doctrines of orthodox Toryism. He had, at any rate, let some fresh air into the party system, so much, indeed, that it sometimes seemed a hurricane. Randolph appeared a very son of the morning. Nevertheless, because of this very splendour of promise, his achievement came in-finitely short of anticipation. He was in office but a few months, and then, like the son of the morning, he fell, not to rise again. Such a career, politically speaking, cannot be considered full or triumphant. Why was it not something more ?

The answer is twofold. In the first place it is to be found in the word " wayward," which is always associated with him in my mind. But it is also necessary to remark that we do not know when his fatal illness first began to affect him. I have been told that it was influencing him so far back as 1885 ; I cannot, of course, vouch for the fact, but I confess I think it probable. It is not that his intellect deteriorated, but that the malady would from time to time quicken certain tendencies into extreme violence. Take, for example, his attack on Mr. Gladstone as a second Reschid Pasha, and on Lord Granville, who had

answered this attack : caricatures wholly unworthy of him, neither wise, nor witty, nor
effective, produced within two days of each
other, and denoting a mind unbalanced and
almost unhinged.

His waywardness, however, is not altogether
to be attributed to disease. He was always so
from boyhood, but amiably and controllably so.
From the first moment that I can remember
him there was a tinge in him of the eccentric,
the petulant, and the unexpected. The stealthy
poison of his illness probably accentuated this
defect, in combination with the natural exhilara-
tion of prodigious triumph. Nothing, for example,
could be more extravagant than his first resignation in 1885, as told in his biography. He
might conceivably and even justly have protested against the communications carried on
by the Sovereign through Lord Salisbury with
India without his being a party to them, though
Lord Salisbury informed him of them. But his
resignation, and the terms of the correspondence
in which it was conveyed, are almost childish
when it is remembered that they came from a
young minister who had just achieved a great
position in his party and in the country by un-
sparing effort, who had forced himself into office
over the bodies of his leaders, but who now,
on a point scarcely, if at all, more substantial
than one of etiquette, suddenly discovered that
he " had always had great doubts as to whether
his being in the Government would be of any
advantage to the Government or to the party."
" All doubts," he adds, " on the point are now

XIII.

removed from my mind." And so he insists on his resignation. Then the fit wears off, and he consents to remain in office, appealing finally to the cool sagacity of Sir Michael Hicks-Beach. "Please forgive me," replies Sir Michael, "for saying that I think you looked at this matter rather too seriously last Friday. I think I should have been more inclined to laugh at the story of the telegram than to treat it as a proof of want of confidence on the part of the Queen and Prime Minister. If you had not been ill you would never have said of yourself in your letter to me that ' I have no longer any energy or ideas, and am no more good except to make disturbance.' "[1]

The delicacy and importance of the point involved are not to be underrated. There need be no discussion here of these. But it is abundantly clear that the issue could easily have been settled satisfactorily by explanation, as indeed it was. But no ! that was not Randolph's way at that time of semi-supremacy. The matter must be settled by a resignation, portentously offered and portentously withdrawn. It was burning the house down in order to roast the pig. The method in one so rational almost indicates the early shadows of the final malady, and it is to be noted that he admits that he was ill at the time.

I have already indicated more than once the second reason why his career was not a complete success—he was in the wrong party. He was, it is true, eminently patrician both by instinct and by birth. This he never concealed, nor could he have concealed it if he would. But his opinions,

[1] *Life*, i. 516.

his instincts, his aims, were all not merely Liberal,
but Radical. Nor was he in the least Imperialist.
This his son sets forth in terms : " Lord Randolph
Churchill was never what is nowadays called an
Imperialist." [1] This was no secret to his friends.
His sympathies were not with the growth and
development of empire, though he was proud of
his part in the annexation of Burmah ; his views
on foreign policy were not merely not those of
Lord Salisbury, but were in truth rather those
of Mr. Cobden and Mr. Bright. He might be
described without exaggeration as a thorough and
convinced Radical of the old type. He had
studied the Irish question on the spot, and always
maintained that Home Rule was impracticable.
But otherwise his views were those of advanced
Liberals.

This anomaly in a Tory leader must eventually
have complicated the party system, but when
the impetuosity of his nature is taken into
account it was sure to precipitate a crisis and
to make his position in the party impossible.
Had his character been different he might have
trained himself to the orthodox pace. Disraeli,
who had begun with views not wholly dissimilar,
had done so, with excellent results. But this
for Randolph's temperament was at that time
impossible. Moreover, he was intoxicated with
a success and popularity which Disraeli, as a
young or middle-aged man, had never achieved.
He thought then that he could take the party
with him. Here lay his fatal mistake. His
party was delighted to follow, so long as he gave

[1] *Life*, ii. 117.

XIII.

popularity to the name of Tory and to the policy
—say, of Lord Salisbury. But when he began to
launch a daring programme of his own, the party
shuddered ; when he began to insist, it rebelled.
Randolph stated this with unpleasant candour in
1888 : "Though honourable members do not in the
least object to my winning applause at great mass
meetings in the country, there seems to be a considerable difference of opinion when I attempt to
carry these opinions to a practical conclusion."[1]

Besides these individual and not unnatural
prejudices of his party, he had to combat
something more impalpable and more formidable — the party "machine." That he had
once captured but had now lost ; and that
organisation, however futile in other directions,
is now so developed that no individual, however gifted, can fight against it. Peel twice
and Disraeli once did, no doubt, when the
party "machine" was comparatively feeble,
pass measures against the will or conscience of
their party. But Peel fell as his Bill passed ;
and Disraeli was too wary to repeat his own experiment. It is more than doubtful if either Peel
or Disraeli ever attained the personal popularity
of Randolph in 1885. But that popularity was
not a sufficient base for a revolution in policy,
or for marching the Tory party over to Liberalism. Had Randolph returned to office he would,
I think, have learned his lesson and fallen into
line. Mr. Disraeli once boasted that he had
educated his party. But did not his party in
truth educate Mr. Disraeli ?

[1] *Speeches*, ii. 336.

x

Strange is the fate that has bound the Tory
party to leaders of uncongenial faith or suspicious
antecedents; but so it has been from the end
of the Liverpool dynasty till the epoch of Lord
Salisbury. The short Canning ministry, of whatever complexion Canning may be deemed, was
repudiated by the Tory party. The Duke of
Wellington, though undoubtedly a Tory himself,
was so dominated by his favourite doctrine that
the King's Government must be carried on at any
cost, and by his view of his relation as a paid
servant to the Crown, that he was willing to pass
any measure of any character that might be
considered necessary in the public interest, without reference to his own opinions. He emancipated Roman Catholics in the teeth of his former
professions; he was accessory to the repeal of
the Corn Laws, a repeal to which he was extremely
averse; he was ready to pass a Reform Bill which
he regarded as the ruin of the country. He
cannot, therefore, it would seem, be reckoned as
a party politician at all. Then comes Peel, who
will live by the two great Liberal measures that
he passed; who was, indeed, a staid and thought-
ful Liberal, the bulwark of the Liberal Government till he died, and who was excommunicated
by his party. Then there succeeds Derby, who
was a leading member of the Grey Government
and who harangued from the table of Brooks's
on behalf of the Reform Bill. He is followed by
Disraeli, the Radical candidate for Wycombe,
who, in an imagination of Oriental glow, blended

his Radical recollections with the professions required of a Tory, and so produced " Young England," or, as some think, Tory Democracy. What the old Tories, like the King of Hanover and his crony the Duke of Rutland, thought of the future leader may be read in the lamentations they poured forth over " the influence which Mr. Disraeli has acquired over several of the young British Senators." [1] They knew his past, they did not foresee his future. Then there is the figure of Randolph, a convinced Radical : him, too, the Tory party cast forth. There was for the party no absolute confidence, no unquestioning loyalty, from the time of Lord Liverpool's paralytic attack till it found itself in the comforting embrace of Lord Salisbury.

But let not the dwellers in glass-houses throw stones : the Liberal party has undergone much the same fate. Grey was a lifelong Liberal ; but he had shaken himself almost free from party ties before he became the Liberal Prime Minister. Melbourne was a languid and unconvinced Whig ; still, he cannot be counted as having ever been anything else, though he served for a time under Wellington. Russell was the golden exception, for he was a Whig from the cradle to the grave. But when we come to Palmerston we perceive one who was a minister during the entire period of the Liverpool administration, and who never shook off the traces of that connection. Then comes Gladstone, " the hope " of " stern and unbending Tories," who led the Liberal party with so much renown, but who was proud to own

[1] *Lives of the Lords Strangford*, p. 224.

to the Conservative temperament to the end of XIII. his life.

At first sight it must appear remarkable that parties and leaders should be so ill-mated, but on reflection there seems no reason for surprise. When it is considered how hereditary is the transmission of politics in this country, it seems rather wonderful that, after reading, travel, and thought, the family dogmas are not more often questioned. Men are netted early into political clubs ; or fall, when callow, under the influence of some statesman ; or stand as youths for some constituency before they have considered the problems of life. Many never consider them at all ; but those who do must often find themselves in disagreement with the politics which they have prematurely professed. Some, too, must find that, while they remain staunch to what seem the fundamental tenets, the party itself, under erratic guidance, or lured by the prospect of momentary advantage, is wandering far from its fold ; and so, while they themselves remain orthodox, they are isolated by the unorthodoxy of their friends. Add to which the politician sees the seamy side or comfortless interior of his own party alone ; he is not admitted to the drawbacks of the opposite faction ; so that the one in some respects seems more alluring than the other. If all these things be considered, it will seem marvellous that there are not more political conversions or perversions than there are.

XI

XIII.   Let us go a little more into detail. Had
——   Randolph's party no reason to shudder? What
is Toryism and what is Tory Democracy? The
Toryism associated with the names of Eldon and
Sidmouth has long been dead. The Toryism
of Lord Derby died under him in 1867 like an
overtaxed horse; and it then became recognised
by the most stern and unbending partisans that
the old Tory *non possumus* was impracticable.
Since then Toryism has become more flexible;
it has, indeed, under the occasional pressure of
men or of public opinion been a singularly
adaptable creed. This is not said by way of
reproach, for politics are the sport of circumstance, and principle the slave of opportunity.
The Tory creed, so far as it implies maintenance
of historical continuity and calculated, practical,
well-meditated reform without unnecessary risk
to precious institutions, is a respectable and
healthy faith. But there have been startling
variations. Disraeli had long thrown out hints
about Lord Bolingbroke, Lord Shelburne, and
a Venetian constitution. What it all meant no
one quite knew; and the world at large, especially the Tories, treated it with unseemly and
unjust ridicule. No one who lived and mixed
with politicians before 1874, or who has read the
memoirs of that time, can forget the despair and
distrust with which Disraeli inspired his followers.
Might not salvation be found by shelving or dis-
carding him? by such a combination, for example,
as making the Duke of Somerset Prime Minister,

and relegating Disraeli to the serene duties of Chancellor of the Duchy, or even to complete repose ? [1] This was the project of Cairns, Disraeli's closest political ally, who nevertheless seems at that time to have had an imperfect conception of the character and aims of his friend. To such straits was the party driven. Anything, they declared, but Disraeli ; under him victory was impossible. What a mere adventurer he was ! What a fantastic alien ! What nonsense he wrote ! But what if the nonsense should mean a majority ? That, of course, would be a different thing. This majority came in 1874 ; and as at the sound of the sackbut, psaltery, and dulcimer, the whole party fell down and worshipped. It seemed now clear that the gospel of Toryism was to be found in some spirited novels. As it turned out, the Toryism of 1874 had no trace of " Young Englandism," and not the least savour of the popular sympathies of *Sybil*. Still less was it even remotely tainted with the Radical " education " of 1867. That was well enough for a season of dexterous impotence : power involved or required more, as, for example, a spirited foreign policy. But, to the last, sages who had studied the romances of the young Hebrew would wag their heads in corners and predict that the edifice would be crowned by something with regard to Palestine which was to be found, if anywhere, in *Tancred*.

Then came Mr. Gladstone and the travels of political triumph associated with Midlothian, and all faded into mist. Disraeli died ; and the

[1] Lang's *Life of Lord Iddesleigh*, i. 246.

XIII.　Tadpoles and the Tapers were left wondering
what Toryism was next to be. The prophet had
vanished and had left not a shred of his mantle
behind. With Lord Salisbury, a real Tory, who
was something of a cynic and a pessimist as well,
the policy assumed a new, or perhaps resumed an
old, shape. It defended the Church and property,
or property and the Church ; and was, if absolutely necessary, prepared to make some little
advance under severe pressure. There was to be
nothing spontaneous ; the watchword was to
be " Needs must when the devil drives." The
pressure came with more or less severity, firstly
from Randolph Churchill, and secondly from
Mr. Chamberlain.

Lord Randolph Churchill was half aristocrat
and half Bohemian : the aristocratic part was in
his blood ; his Bohemianism came from the fact
that he was, inexplicably enough, if his home and
early associations be considered, born and bred
a rebel, as much as any Bohemian a rebel against
the accepted and conventional standards of life.
He loved as much as any Bohemian to shock and
even outrage the commonplace. He respected
as little as any Bohemian the ties of circumstance
and tradition. It was this Bohemianism that
found its vent and field in the Fourth Party ; it
was this which seems to have enlisted the secret
sympathy of Lord Beaconsfield. " I fully appreciate your feelings," said Lord Beaconsfield in
1880 to Sir Henry Wolff, " and those of your
friends ; but you must stick to Northcote, he
represents the respectability of the party. I
wholly sympathise with you all, because I never

was respectable myself.   In my time the respectability of the party was represented by ——, a horrid man ; but I had to do as well as I could ; you must do the same."[1]   None the less was Randolph an aristocrat, and he would display from time to time strange vestiges of the traditions in which he was reared.   The aristocratic part of his nature made him dislike the opulent middle class ; his Bohemian instinct turned him to Radicalism ; the only subject that he had really studied was the Irish question, as to which his conclusions were those of neither party, but which kept him in the Tory ranks.   As to his respectable leaders in the Commons, they made him gnash his teeth, both as an aristocrat and as a Bohemian.

His advent, indeed, seemed for a time to paralyse the Tory chiefs, as his popularity was unbounded, casting their figures completely into the shade.   Moreover, while his wit, his irony, and his invective delighted his audiences, scarcely less did these enjoy his hints of a popular policy which should strike at the root of the matter and eviscerate the obsolete formulas of authoritative Liberalism.   Intoxicated, not unnaturally, with his position, he treated his colleagues as negligible quantities, gave the rein to his advanced views on Ireland and domestic questions, and went " full steam ahead," forgetting, or not perceiving, or not caring, that he had left the party and its organisation a long way behind him.   So that when, to clear the air and make his position apparent, he staked his all on a petulant resig-

[1] *Life*, i. 157.

nation, petulant in method if not in spirit, he found himself almost alone. The Tory priests and pharisees shunned him, and there was scarce a political Samaritan in sight.

In the historic biography of Lord George Bentinck, to which reference has already been made, there is a dramatic passage which Randolph might well have considered : " When Prince Metternich was informed at Dresden, with great ostentation, that the Emperor had arrived— ' Yes, but without his army,' was the reply." Disraeli goes on to describe the division which, in 1846, wrecked Sir Robert Peel's Government, and the announcement of the hostile majority whispered to the minister. " Sir Robert did not reply, or even turn his head. · He looked very grave, and extended his chin, as was his habit when he was annoyed, and cared not to speak. He began to comprehend his position, and that the Emperor was without his army." Randolph in 1886 had arrived ; he was a conspicuous and brilliant figure ; but he had no parliamentary army behind him, and his supporters in the country were silenced by the action of the party in the House of Commons, and of the party Caucus.

Were the Tories to be blamed for this desertion of their young paladin ? This cannot, I think, be seriously contended. They had long been out of breath in trying to follow him, and when he was stripped of the glamour of office and leadership, they saw him as he was, not a Tory but a Radical, indifferent about the Church and heedless of property. Had he remained in office long

enough to produce his famous budget, the scales
would have fallen even more completely from their
eyes, for they would have seen that he was prepared to tax the very cartridges with which they
killed or missed their game.

This, then, was Tory Democracy; it was the
wolf of Radicalism in the sheepskin of Toryism.
When Randolph, after his resignation, became
more and more emancipated from Tory tradition,
and more hopeless of reunion with his party, he
scarcely cared to conceal the fact. In November
1885 he had sent to Lord Salisbury a proposed
sketch of policy, which included local government
on a purely popular basis, with a large devolu-
tion of powers, the enfranchisement of future
leaseholds (whatever that may mean), similarity
of treatment between England and Ireland in
respect of local government, and concession to
the Roman Catholic hierarchy on educational
questions. At Dartford, when leader of the
House of Commons, he set forth a programme
of large legislation on land, local government,
temperance, elementary education, and rating;
and though the language was vague, it was none
the less alarming to the patriarchs and pontiffs of
Toryism. Finally he set forth to the Cabinet and
prepared for immediate production a democratic
budget, containing graduated death duties and
local option as regards the drink traffic.

This, as we have seen, was the final ground of
his resignation. That event is noteworthy in connection with Tory Democracy, because, though it
put that phrase out of fashion, and deprived it
of all prospect of ministerial countenance, it also

XIII. removed all drag or control from its unofficial
development.

So three years afterwards he was making
speeches in the Midlands, urging drastic temperance reform, Irish local government, and Irish
land purchase, in terms so elastic that his audience
" gasped," and a Tory member, who had besought
him to come and speak, now besought him to
stay away.[1]

All this, indeed, was well enough ; but it was
not Toryism or anything like Toryism. Mr.
Chamberlain at once sounded a note of menace
and alarm, with that trumpet which has given
forth so many notes of menace or alarm. Lord
Randolph Churchill, he said, had " borrowed
from the cast-off policy of all the extreme men of
all the different sections. He took his Socialism
from Mr. Burns and Mr. Hyndman ; he took his
local option from Sir Wilfrid Lawson ; he took
his Egyptian policy from Mr. Illingworth ; he
took his metropolitan reform from Mr. Stuart ;
and he took his Irish policy from Mr. John Morley.
Is this Toryism ? " he asked.

There could be no doubt as to the reply. And,
indeed, Tory Democracy, in the person of Randolph, had by no means reached the limits of its
tether. " In these later years," says his son,
" Lord Randolph Churchill was drawn increasingly towards a Collectivist view of domestic
politics . . . and he favoured or accepted doctrines and tendencies before which Liberals recoiled,
and even the most stalwart Radicals paused embarrassed." [2] When Tory Democracy is stated in

[1] *Life*, ii. 402.   [2] *Life*, ii. 428.

terms as Tory Collectivism, there is no further need to expatiate on the anomaly involved.

And so Randolph Churchill moved onward, on broadening lines it may be said, but farther and farther from Toryism. In his letter from Mafeking of November 1891, we have seen that he considered the end of Tory Democracy to have come with the accession of Mr. Balfour to the leadership. " So Arthur Balfour is really leader, and Tory Democracy, the genuine article, is at an end." [1] It is not easy to trace the subtle connection between the leadership of Mr. Balfour and the disappearance of the genuine article. But in the following year Randolph again emphasised his policy in a striking letter to Mr. Arnold White, gave his blessing to the Labour party and their aims, so far as he understood them, and urged in vague but eloquent terms their assimilation by the Tory party. " It is our business," he wrote, " as Tory politicians to uphold the constitution. If under the constitution, as it now exists and as we wish to see it preserved, the Labour interest finds that it can obtain its objects and secure its own advantage, then that interest will be reconciled to the constitution, will find faith in it, and will maintain it." [2] If not—so much the worse for the constitution and the Tory party. His " ifs," it will be seen, were capacious.

In the same year he urged on Mr. Balfour the Miners' Eight Hours Bill, trusted that " Gorst might have a little labour fling," and declared that he himself would abandon dear delights tc

[1] *Life*, ii. 452. [2] *Life*, ii. 459.

XIII. vote for the measure, adding, half seriously, "I do
not think that I would do this for the Monarchy,
the Church, the House of Lords, or the Union." [1]

All this might be Democracy, but it certainly
was not Tory. In fine, Tory Democracy was a
good catch-word for reconciling Toryism and
Democracy, if that were possible. But Toryism
means something which Democracy cannot recognise, and Democracy means something which
Toryism cannot supply. Toryism could not of
its own free will be reconciled, for then it would
have ceased to be Toryism, and party divisions
would have become a greater illusion than, in the
opinion of some, they are already. In the womb
of the future there may no doubt be embryos of
this description, but then it is clear that the
opposing faction will have also to change its
character. All that is beyond our compass to-
day. What is certain is that Tory Democracy
was an imposture, an honest and unconscious
imposture no doubt, but none the less an imposture. It was in reality a useful denomination or resource for any one who found himself
with Radical opinions inside the Tory party, and
who did not wish to leave it. And so the Fourth
Party, half at least of which was in this position,
and which was wholly a band of rebels, found
itself in sole possession of the sacred mystery.

XII

The history of the Fourth Party has been
written by Mr. Harold Gorst with the unwinking

[1] *Life*, ii. 461.

gravity of an augur, and with a natural desire   XIII.
to point out that it was not entirely composed of
Randolph.

As a matter of fact, it consisted of Sir H.
Wolff, who supplied diplomacy and experience ;
Sir John Gorst, who represented organisation,
law, and experience ; and Randolph, who furnished the audacity, the voice, and the magnetism ; all three brimful of ideas, and endowed
with abilities of no common order.   Mr. Balfour
was the outrigger of this frail but daring craft ;
he was of it for a time, but not in it.

It was, indeed, originally an escapade, carried
on with high spirits and with the tongue often
in the cheek.   As it prospered, it became formidable and therefore serious ; yet it embodied
nothing but a negative.   Its aim was to oppose,
hinder, thwart, and wreck the work of the Government in every possible way.   This object, which
from the parliamentary point of view is regarded
as legitimate, and even laudable, was carried on
with zeal and ingenuity.

Nothing was sacred for them any more than
for the traditional French sapper.   Randolph,
for instance, had he not been absent, would have
taken pride in marring the effect, so potent and
beneficial both at home and abroad, of the
unanimous vote of credit on April 27, 1885.   In a
vehement letter to Lord Salisbury he indignantly
censured the silent acquiescence of the Opposition on this occasion.   " The effect in the House
of Commons," he writes, " has been deplorable." [1]
Lord Salisbury shared his regret.   " I hope the

[1] *Life*, ii. 382.

XIII.   papers will attribute the collapse to our patriotism ; at least, that is the only hope with which
one can console oneself," [1] wrote the experienced
statesman ;   and   the   desired   consolation   was
happily forthcoming.   Had any object but injury
to the Government been in view, neither could
have ignored the European importance of the
vote ; as it was, neither seemed able to perceive the interests of Britain when the interests
of the Ministry were involved.   This confusion
also complicated the attitude of the Fourth
Party towards the Reform Bill of 1884.   " Tory
Democracy," we are told by Mr. Churchill,
" wanted to pass the Bill, yet wanted to destroy
the Government " : [2] a strange rendering of the
old cry, " Measures, not men."   " We want the
measures without their authors " was apparently
the view of this political group.   Again, the
Fourth Party convinced itself that the hapless
Khedive Tewfik, who was so sorely bestead, was
a scoundrel of the deepest dye.   As to Mr.
Bradlaugh, he was the punchball round which
the giddy factions played.   Any issue, indeed,
was welcome to and utilised by the little party.
All was fish that came into their net.   As a parliamentary exhibition it was superb.   It amused
the House, it interested the nation, it harassed the
Government.   But this last was its sole object, for
it had no positive policy, except an occasional
mystic allusion to Tory Democracy.

  And so we are told that if we can find the
elusive secret of Tory Democracy it will be in the
custody of the Fourth Party.   Sir John Gorst

          [1] *Life*, ii. 383.   [2] *Life*, i. 327.

evidently believes in it, but he does not disguise
his doubts as to any authoritative connection
between his political views and those of official
and orthodox Toryism. " From that epoch "
(1886), he mournfully remarks in a prefatory note
to his son's history of the Fourth Party, " Tory
Democracy, which was the ideal on which Mr.
Disraeli's domestic policy was based, has been
by the party leaders discredited and abandoned.
The few members of the party who still cling to
the principles of Mr. Disraeli are suspected of
being Radicals and Socialists."[1]

Why is it, may be asked in passing, that this
suspicion never rested on Mr. Disraeli during
his leadership of the party ?   It appears to stig-
matise those who believe that they have adopted
his principles and ideals, but never to touch
himself.

The reason is twofold.   In the first place, it
has to be demonstrated that Mr. Disraeli ever
became seriously responsible for any form of
Tory Democracy.   He may have blown bubbles;
he certainly wrote political romances.   But a
romance is not a programme, and novels can
never be manifestoes.   Strange were the recesses
of that interesting and complicated character ;
but it may be permitted to surmise that no one
was so much amused at the solemnity with which
the fanciful rodomontade of *Coningsby* was treated
as Disraeli himself.   In the second place, whatever may have been his views on Tory or " Young
English " Democracy, he was not prepared to be
a martyr to them.   He never carried them into

[1] Gorst's *Fourth Party*, p. v.

2 A

XIII. practical effect, for the obvious reason that he
would have shattered his party had he done so.
From 1874 to 1880 he enjoyed supreme authority,
but without lifting a finger for Tory Democracy.
It is by his acts, not his words, that a minister
who enjoys real power is judged, and by this test
Disraeli's affection for Tory Democracy, if he ever
felt any, must be held to have been extinguished
by his majority, while those who suffer for clinging
to what they deem his principles must be held to
be gratuitous martyrs.   But this is no disparagement to the memory of that extraordinary man.
A statesman, however much he may be animated
by the ideal, has to deal with the real, with
facts and circumstances as they are.   A much
less astute politician than he would realise, on
attaining power, that the reconciliation of " the
two nations," as they are called on the title-page
of *Sybil*, could not be achieved by the leader of a
Conservative party as then constituted, or likely
to be constituted.

We must, therefore, seek for something more
definite in Tory Democracy than the policy of
Mr. Disraeli.   Randolph was fortunate enough to
find it in one of his epigrams.   " Some of Lord
Beaconsfield's phrases," he says, in his article
on " Elijah's Mantle," " will bear any amount
of microscopic examination.   Speaking in Manchester in 1871, by the alteration of a letter in
a quotation from the Vulgate, he revealed the
policy which ought to guide Tory leaders at the
present time : *Sanitas sanitatum, omnia sanitas.*
Such was the quotation in which a careful mind
will discover a scheme of sound progress and

reform, of dimensions so large and widespreading that many volumes would not suffice to explain its details." Happy the statesman whose epigrams are interpreted in so liberal a spirit by a careful mind. That *Sanitas sanitatum* was by no means an original phrase, but had been employed some two centuries before Disraeli uttered it, would not impair its merit were it really such a fruitful germ of policy as Randolph seemed to imagine. The many volumes required were, however, never written ; and so, even if Tory Democracy be embodied in this naked formula, we are not carried much farther.

We are, therefore, still left face to face with the question as to whether Tory Democracy was in any sense a boon or a legacy of Disraeli's ? Has Disraeli, indeed, any responsibility for it ? What were the principles to which Sir John Gorst alludes which have entailed ostracism on those who cherish them ? They are, at any rate, not those of " Young England " ; whatever else it was, Tory Democracy was not identical with, and bore no resemblance to, the doctrines of " Young England " as preached in *Coningsby*. " Young England " was something feudal and ecclesiastical, though benignantly popular. It endeavoured to saddle the narrower Toryism on the Whigs, while reserving the realm of imagination for itself. " A high Tory," said a leading son of " Young England," " . . . meant a high Whig of the Eldonite school." [1] This was a complication, for if Eldon were not a Tory, where was Toryism to be found ? " Young England,"

[1] *Angela Pisani*, by George Smythe, Viscount Strangford, iii. 210.

XIII.   at any rate, itself perceived that it was something
——   which Eldon could neither have blessed nor
understood, and prudently anticipated criticism
by dubbing him a Whig. The positive doctrines
were, for the nineteenth century, scarcely less
original ; the aristocracy was to assert its ancient
rights, and exert a patriarchal influence ; the
Established Church, paramount and supreme,
was to train and inspire the nation ; the large
bounty of the monasteries was, in some vague
but Anglican way, to be revived ; while a grateful
peasantry received copious ale and beef, as
formerly, at some ecclesiastical gate, and enjoyed
on the festivals of the Church the diversions set
forth in the *Book of Sports*. This, at least, was
the impression produced by the writings of the
new school. But there was nothing of this in
Tory Democracy ; that was rather Radical and
rather Socialist, without any peculiar tenderness
for the Church or the aristocracy. The fortuitous
discovery of *Sanitas sanitatum* does not bridge
the gulf between " Young England " and the
later creed. " Young England " was a poetical
ideal of Toryism ; Tory Democracy had nothing
Tory but the name.

There was, however, this point of resemblance
between the two groups, that in both cases the
leaders were carried far away from the original
idea. Just as Randolph found himself on the
verge of Collectivism, so George Smythe, the
original of Coningsby and the embodiment of
Young England, travelled nearly as far from his
political base and involved himself in much the
same contradictions. He had been won to the

new departure " by the mediaeval halo cast over XIII. politics as well as religion." [1] Like his friend, John Duke of Rutland, who has just left us amid manifestations of universal esteem and regret, " he dreamed of an almsgiving Church protecting and cultivating the affections of a dependent peasantry." [2] And how did he end ? By claiming " the sanction of Tory principle for free trade, secular education for the masses, extension of the franchise, the abolition of all religious disabilities, concessions to Dissenters, and the disendowment of all Church establishments, considering that the less the minister of heaven has to do with the affairs of the earth the better." [3] No wonder the old King of Hanover, the last of the antediluvians, on reading this speech wrote that it was, " though beautiful in language, diabolical in substance. I am glad if you can see conservative principles, or any principles, but such as are dictated by the accursed apostate and traitor Peel." And he ends by speaking of " the address, so well given and well coloured, but still you see the figure of Satan behind it." That, in lurid form, is the real feeling of real Tories (if there be any left) towards these new departures. What is the use of opposing Liberalism, they seem to say, if doctrines such as these are proposed by Tories ?

The truth is that there are and always have been men who believe that so long as they call themselves Tories they may blamelessly and harmlessly preach what doctrines they please : just as in some religious circles a man who believes

---

[1] *Angela Pisani* (Prefatory Memoir), vol. i. p. xiv.
[2] *Ibid.* p. xv.   [3] *Lives of the Lords Strangford*, p. 243.

xiii. himself to be numbered with the elect holds that his sanctity justifies his acts, and that he may do pretty much what he pleases. This is the explanation of pious but fraudulent men of business, who are sometimes inaccurately denounced as hypocrites. But the acts of the unregenerate are, in the judgement of the elect, to be differently appraised and weighed in different scales. A Liberal measure from Liberals is something to be thwarted and denounced : a Radical measure from Tories has a halo about it.

But is there not a more general explanation ? Is it not true that men often pursue their own thoughts, heedless of the party bond, and that they wake from their absorption to find that they have strayed far from the party camp ? And when they realise this, when they find that they are no longer orthodox in the party sense, they are apt to ask themselves if it be necessary, or even possible, to join any other section ; their own faith has disappeared, can they embrace a new one ? In any other they find much to repel, enough at any rate to make the exchange not worth making. So they remain content with the old label, careless if it be challenged, and become a sort of political freethinkers. Does not the same thing happen in religion ? Those who ponder for themselves the grave problems of life and eternity not unfrequently become dissatisfied with their own Church without being attracted by any other, so they remain nominally what they were, or pass silently into agnosticism. The analogy is not remote, for the ideal political party in point of belief, aspiration, and devotion should be little less than a political Church.

But to return to Tory Democracy, the best specimen of a Tory democratic speech that occurs to me is one that Randolph delivered at Birmingham in April 1884 ; it was almost his first expression of the idea.   It began with a benediction of the Caucus, which was then an institution most repugnant to his party.   It went on with a defence of the House of Lords, " that bulwark of popular liberty and civil order " which " should be preserved solely on the ground of its utility to the people," and of the Established Church ; and it concluded with urging social as against organic reform.[1]   But as regards social reform, since both parties profess the same aims, it must be in their methods that they differ ; so that the mere allusion to the object does not elucidate the position. The mixture, however, of high Toryism of the old school with the approval of the Caucus, and the democratic ending, seem a good illustration both of the features and of the difficulties of Tory Democracy.

In later years Randolph gave a definition which is both candid and probable.   " What is Tory Democracy ? " he asked.   " Tory Democracy is a democracy which supports the Tory party." That seems simple enough.   He goes on to say that this support must be given not from caprice or disgust, but from conviction of the excellence of Tory principles.   " But Tory Democracy involves, also, another idea of equal importance. It involves the idea of a government who, in all

[1] *Speeches*, i. 131-140.

branches of their policy and in all features of their administration, are animated by lofty and by *liberal ideas.* That is Tory Democracy." [1] It is a strange, vague, wordy passage until the outburst of frankness at the end. Tory Democracy involves a government imbued with liberal ideas. It is no doubt true that he used the adjective as an epithet and not in the party sense. Here the capital letter assumes importance. The biographer gives it, the editor of the speeches withholds it. I have no doubt myself that it should be " liberal " and not " Liberal." But as it is a question of ideas, the spirit of the passage confirms the contention that Tory Democracy was simply Liberalism under another name. Nor, indeed, did Randolph in confidential intercourse make any secret of the fact. " The work is practically done," he wrote to Lord Justice FitzGibbon in December 1886, before ever his successor had been appointed ; " the Tory party will be turned into a Liberal party." [2] Did he really believe this ? The conversion, at any rate, never took place. But the sentence sufficiently reveals the inner purpose of Tory Democracy. It was employed to enable Liberals by conviction to remain Tories by profession.

Randolph was much too acute not to know this. His difficulty must have lain, not in that consciousness, but in the obvious fact that every one else was fully aware of it. He had to a large extent convinced others of the tenets of Toryism ; what he could not convince was himself. It is, of course, both easy and true to say that social

---

[1] *Life*, ii. 330. [2] *Life*, ii. 264.

questions are not the property of the Liberal
party ; that they are not the sacred game of the
Liberal preserve. It is also true, I think, that
Liberals, when they have had the power to deal
effectively with them, have not always used it.
But neither does this make those problems the
property of the Tory party, for they are not mere
flotsam and jetsam. No party in power can afford
to ignore them, for they are permanent, inevitable,
and sometimes menacing. They present themselves to all statesmen ; and, as has just been said,
the difference between the two parties is rather
one of method than of aim. If Toryism means
anything, it means a cautious and limited spirit
in dealing with such questions. If Liberalism,
on the other hand, means anything, it means that
it has to deal with them in a large spirit, unfettered
by class, or interest, or privilege. If there be no
such difference, the parties are practically one
except in name. That there is such a difference,
and must from the very constitution of the two
parties be such a difference, is proved by the
attitude of the real and staunch Tories to Disraeli
in 1867, and by their repudiation of Randolph
in 1886, when both approached domestic questions, not in a cautious and limited, but in a large
and liberal spirit.

XIII

Randolph was indeed the fruit and blossom
of our parliamentary system. No more complete
and extreme product of that historical arrangement has ever been seen. That system requires

XIII. for its working two sets of protagonists. One does the administrative and legislative work of the country and defends what is done. The other is anxious to do the administrative and legislative work of the country and, in the meantime, condemns what is done. To the one side all is light, all is white ; to the other all is shade, all is black : there is no twilight, and no grey. The outcome of this sometimes illogical but continuous conflict is the government and guidance of the British Empire. In the same way, justice, pure justice, is the result of the contest between two sets of advocates on two different sides. The only difference is that the politicians professedly speak from conviction, while the lawyers professedly speak from their briefs. In effect, however, the result is much the same. The advocates of the Government happen to find everything done by the Government right, and the advocates of the Opposition happen to find everything done by the Government wrong. It is a strange and perpetual but not fortuitous coincidence. That state of things was not invented by Randolph, it is of immemorial tradition. He took things as they were, and plunged into the fray with the keen enjoyment of an undergraduate on the fifth of November, giving and receiving hard knocks with almost equal pleasure. He fought his fight in the recognised way, according to the working of our constitution. He attacked savagely when out ; he did his work and defended it as well as he knew when he was in.

What was considered blameworthy in him by onlookers as well as by the party opposed to him was the violence of his diatribes. Was this censure justified ? Extreme as these were, they were certainly milder than those directed by Fox against North, or those of the Opposition leaders against Walpole. On reading Randolph's speeches in cold blood, and looking back on the circumstances through the mitigating lens of time, and the juster proportion afforded by a score of years, it would seem that his real offence lay not so much in the method as in the object of attack. . He was denouncing not a minister of ordinary virtues and vices, but an austere and lofty statesman whose character and ability, while no doubt exciting great antagonism, at that time evoked, apart from politics, something like general veneration. Gladstone was neither a North nor a Walpole. His was a figure of supreme moral dignity ; to his followers he was little less than sublime ; to his opponents he was an object of respect ; to the people at large, to the silent judgement of those who deal little in party politics, he was a national asset. Directed against him, Randolph's attacks were considered as attempts to hold up to ridicule and contempt a statesman who should have been secure from that particular form of assault by a stripling who might have been his grandson. There was, therefore, something repellent to the taste of serious people in his pugnacity ; but then this pugnacity, it must be remembered, for the very same reason, tickled the imagination of multitudes who do not discriminate, but love a fight as a fight without heeding the cause, and delight in seeing an audacious light-weight sparring up to a recognised champion.

XIII.

Northcote also understood this consecrated warfare of parties, and played the game well, though under stricter and more limited rules than his young critic. He was too old and too sagacious to move on headlong and careless, as Randolph lightly did. He could not, and would not, always oppose; he was conscious that the interests of the country might conflict with the tenets of party, and was aware that opposition should have a sense of proportion. Where he failed was in manner. His voice, his diction, his delivery, were all inadequate. With real ability, great knowledge, genial kindness, and a sympathetic nature—all the qualities, indeed, which evoke regard and esteem—he had not the spice of devil which is necessary to rouse an Opposition to zeal and elation. He went through protracted campaigns in the provinces, delivering lengthy speeches accurately reported, from which the reader and the listener, however edified, carried away no phrase or passage that struck a spark. It was all excellent and irreproachable, but destitute of the tart phrase which bequeaths a memory, still more of the fang which leaves a wound. Let exception here be made, however, of his exquisite adaptation of the ballad of " Sir Patrick Spens," one of the happiest rhetorical allusions to be found in the whole range of English oratory. But when Northcote warmed there was, or seemed to be, a note of apology in his voice; there was also what is known as the academic twang, an inflection which cannot be defined, but which is not agreeable to the House of Commons. He lay, moreover, under unjust suspicion from having been Gladstone's private secretary ; for he was held not to have sufficiently shaken off the awe with which he had regarded his former chief. This was neither fair nor true. He stoutly and victoriously maintained his first budget against the criticisms of the great financier who had preceded him in office, and ever afterwards combated him with spirit ; the misfortune was that it was in a tone which, physically considered, seemed almost deprecatory. In truth, his gentle yet chivalrous nature was not aggressive, and thus he furnished another example of the axiom that the party man who is willing to go half - lengths will be distanced by the party man who readily goes all. So it was for a while with him. Around him there gathered abundantly affection, loyalty, and gratitude, all just and deserved. But they availed him nothing ; it was Randolph who, without these precious attributes, won. And by a strange fate they vanished together, for Randolph's resignation was simultaneous with Northcote's tragic but happy death ; it was, in a way, the indirect and innocent cause of it.

But to return from this contrast to Randolph and his methods. While he battled on party lines he was a party idol. It was not till he began to go counter to party ideas that every one fell foul of him. Then he remained a party man in form, but in substance and spirit he was far away. That he should have allowed his principles to conflict with his party is a proof of high sincerity, for no man was ever in a sense more a

XIII. party man—more devoted, that is to say, to the name and tradition of party.

This at least is certain, that he had the true political instinct for a constitutional country; he was a born parliamentarian. He could feel with singular judgement the pulse of both Parliament and people, when he allowed himself time to do so or while he remained cool. When he lost that touch, at the time of his fall, he was absorbed in his own work and intoxicated with a popularity which would have turned almost any head. To many of us it also appears that he had the instinct of a statesman, as apart from a partisan, and that had he kept his health and controlled his froward fits he would have sobered down into a great minister. That surmise, for it cannot be more, rests on his serious and responsible speeches, which must be strictly distinguished from his Opposition raids.

What is his place in history? Only History can say. That Muse has a sieve of her own; much that was reputed corn is found to be chaff, and unexpected treasures of grain are found in it. Private members of Parliament, like Francis Horner, survive the highest officers of State. Men like Newcastle wield the power of the country for half a century, and are only remembered as objects of scorn. Intellectual princes like Fox and Canning enjoy their political supremacy but for a few months, while to the honest mediocrity of Liverpool after a long tenure of high office there comes a fifteen years' tenure of the Prime Ministership; it all seems a chance, though there is nothing perhaps less accidental. The nearest

parallel to Randolph may possibly be found in
Charles Townshend—like him a young politician ;
like him, for a space, the darling of the House of
Commons ; like him Chancellor of the Exchequer
for a tenure to be counted by months—Randolph
five and Townshend twelve ; both sparkling,
wayward, and incalculable.   Both luminaries
were, for their hour, to employ Burke's famous
sentence, lords of the ascendant.   Both had to
acknowledge one mightier figure—Townshend in
Chatham, and Randolph in Gladstone.   Both
ended young.   Townshend died Chancellor of the
Exchequer at forty-two ; Randolph's official
life terminated at thirty-seven.

It is scarcely worth while to pursue the analogy,
for such resemblances are seldom more than
vague and general.   In the main point it con-
spicuously fails.   Randolph had the makings of a
statesman, Townshend had not.   To live politically from day to day, to allow vanity to be tickled
or temper irritated into any course however
perilous or even ruinous, to be as fitful as a
summer's breeze : that was Townshend.

Randolph in the blind heat of Opposition
might be all this, but when invested with power
he took grave and large views.   Nothing, for
instance, could have tempted him to the incredible
fatuity of being taunted on the spur of the moment
into a pledge to tax the Colonies, a few months
after he had repealed the Act for that purpose.
Everything we read of Charles Townshend tends
to the conviction that he was a poor creature
with a brilliant brain.   Randolph had a brilliant
brain, but no critic will ever call him a poor

creature. Townshend left a sinister memory in the loss of the American Colonies. Randolph, on the contrary, was the instrument of adding Burmah to the Empire.

But putting Townshend aside, is it possible to conjecture Randolph's historical position? In one sense he cannot fill a large page, for he left behind him no great measure. Nor did he found a school or inaugurate a policy ; for Tory Democracy is seldom mentioned in these days, save in the mournful accents of some bereaved devotee. But he will long be cited as a political prodigy, he will encourage those who wish to play a great figure in youth, he will be studied for the methods of his extraordinary success. Such studies and encouragements may well be fallacious, for imitations do not answer ; but they will keep his name alive. And who knows but that in the reorganisation of a new Conservative party the phrase Tory Democracy may once more be heard, and utilised with all the enthusiasm which its capacious denomination is calculated to inspire.

Of parliamentary reputation Randolph is sure. Short careers in Parliament by no means imply oblivion. The name of Hamilton survives almost tediously by a single speech. Charles Townshend lives by another. Archbishop Magee, though he delivered others that were notable, maintains his renown by his famous oration on the disestablishment of the Irish Church. Hawkins was long remembered for one striking effort on the Reform Bill. The single session of 1866 was at once the occasion and the term of Lowe's oratorical splendour.

Randolph's real parliamentary life lasted six years—from 1880 till his resignation. His son indeed says that his speeches from 1887 to 1890 " were the best in manner and command he ever made." [1] What this exactly means I do not know, but it does not affect the view here taken of his career. Whatever else these speeches may have been, they cannot be called successful, whereas the speeches from 1880 to 1886 were an almost unbroken triumph. After his resignation he lost his self-confidence. Grattan once observed that no one had heard Fox to advantage who had not heard him before the Coalition ; or Pitt, who had not heard him before his resignation in 1801 ; for though they both afterwards spoke with surprising ability, " each felt that he had done something which required defence : the talent remained, the mouth still spoke great things, but the swell of soul was no more." This subtle and extravagant distinction—for, after all, the oratorical masterpieces of both Pitt and Fox were delivered in two May evenings in 1803, twenty years after the Coalition and two years after the resignation—was, in a sense, true of Randolph. After his resignation he spoke without confidence or authority or satisfaction to himself. He told his friends that the reason he spoke in the country was that he could no longer speak in the House of Commons. There he had no followers and few friends, and was treated with unkindness and mistrust. There is a sad instance of this given by Mr. Churchill, when he asked for a glass of water in the middle

—— XIII.

[1] *Life*, ii. 380.

XIII. of a speech and could find none to fetch it.[1]
Again, there is the painful and public separation
from Jennings, almost his last parliamentary
associate and confidant, with the pathetic notes
which are printed in the biography.[2] In any
case, his definite career may be fairly limited to
six years. During that time he gained signal
victories in Parliament, in the country, in the
councils of his party. During that period he
captured the Caucus, and overthrew his leaders,
and gained the ear and attention of the nation.
But, somehow, all these victories were fruitless
and barren. After his victory in the Conservative
Union, he, in the opinion of Mr. Gorst and others,
suddenly surrendered to the defeated faction.
When he had overthrown his leader, he could
occupy but not retain the place. The ear and
the attention of the nation seem to have availed
him but little when he needed them most. " He
was a Chancellor of the Exchequer without a
budget, a leader of the House of Commons but
for a single session, a victor without the spoils," [3]
says his son.

   All this is true, but it is not the whole truth.
The fairy godmother had perhaps denied him
one necessary gift, but she had given him all, or
almost all, the others. Many have risen to the
highest place with far less of endowment. And
even with his unfulfilled promise he must be
remembered as one of the most meteoric of
parliamentary figures, as the shooting - star of
politics, and as one who, when in office, strove
for a broad and enlightened policy to which

---

[1] *Life*, ii. 415.   [2] *Life*, ii. 420.   [3] *Life*, ii. x.

he pledged his faith and his career. He will be pathetically memorable, too, for the dark cloud which gradually enveloped him, and in which he passed away. He was the chief mourner at his own protracted funeral, a public pageant of gloomy years. Will he not be remembered as much for the anguish as for the fleeting triumphs of his life ? It is a black moment when the heralds proclaim the passing of the dead, and the great officers break their staves. But it is a sadder still when it is the victim's own voice that announces his decadence, when it is the victim's own hands that break the staff in public. I wonder if generations to come will understand the pity of it, will comprehend the full tragedy of Randolph's marred life.

There is, of course, as has been said, a different view from all this, a view that must constantly be kept in mind in considering Randolph's position. To many excellent persons, both Tory and Liberal, Randolph was little less than an incarnation of evil, a reckless and insolent icono- clast ; a conspirator against the fathers of his own political creed, while outraging and insulting the venerable chiefs of the other. He was, in their judgement, unscrupulous, violent, unprin- cipled ; an intriguing schemer, a ruthless plotter ; one who, to serve the personal ambition which was his sole motive, would stick at nothing. His son has wisely not shrunk from setting down some of the abuse of which he was the object,[1] and it all now seems trivial enough. But much of all this obloquy only proved that Randolph's shafts

[1] *Life*, i. 275.

XIII. had produced wounds that rankled. There were at least grains of truth in the lampoons, but only with regard to his course as an unregenerate free-lance, before he had assumed responsibility and office, and entered on the graver, larger life of administration and policy.

This may, of course, be a wholly mistaken estimate of Randolph's character. Misgivings may well beset the pen that traces it, for it is written by one who feels for him all the affection of a long friendship, but who was always his political opponent. I see, as all the public saw, many faults ; but I remember what the public could not know, the generous, lovable nature of the man. I cannot forget the pathos of the story ; I mourn, as all must mourn, to whatever party they belong, that he had not time to retrieve himself, not time to display his highest nature ; I grieve, as all must grieve, that that daring and gifted spirit should have been extinguished at an age when its work should only have just begun.

END OF VOL. I